BLOODY SCOTLAND

Also by Malcolm Archibald:

POWERSTONE
WHALES FOR THE WIZARD
THE DARKEST WALK
A SINK OF ATROCITY
GLASGOW: THE REAL MEAN CITY
WHISKY WARS, RIOTS AND MURDER
FISHERMEN, RANDIES AND FRAUDSTERS

BLOODY SCOTLAND

Malcolm Archibald

BLACK & WHITE PUBLISHING

First published 2014
by Black & White Publishing Ltd
29 Ocean Drive, Edinburgh EH6 6JL

1 3 5 7 9 10 8 6 4 2   14 15 16 17

ISBN   978 1 84502 789 6

The publisher has made every reasonable effort to contact copyright holders of images in the
picture section. Any errors are inadvertent and anyone who, for any reason, has not been
contacted is invited to write to the publisher so that a full acknowledgment can be made in
subsequent editions of this work.

A CIP catalogue record for this book is available from the British Library.

Typeset by RefineCatch Limited, Bungay, Suffolk
Printed and bound by Gutenberg Press Ltd, Malta

FOR CATHY

Contents

'There is hardly a crime committed or a riot perpetrated but what may be referred to the intemperate use of ardent spirits and that mostly in the night time.'

— Dundee Police Commission, 1834

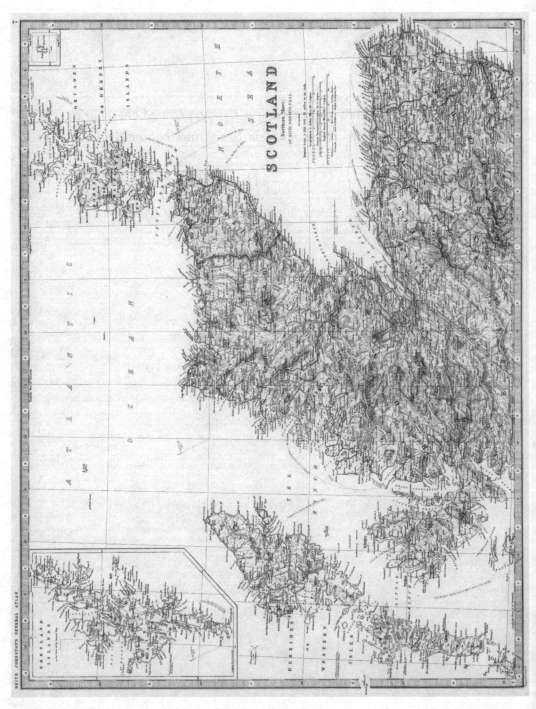

Alexander Keith Johnstone's 1873 map of Scotland (published in two parts)
© National Library of Scotland

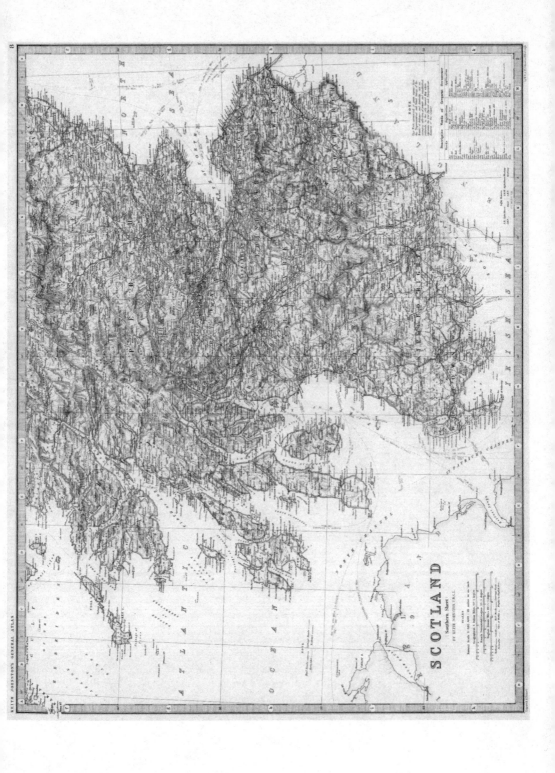

KEITH JOHNSTON'S GENERAL ATLAS

SCOTLAND
Southern Sheet
BY KEITH JOHNSTON, F.R.S.E.

Acknowledgements

I would like to thank the following people and institutions for their help in creating this book: the staff at Inverness Library; the Highland Archive Centre in Inverness; the North Highland Archives in Wick; the A.K Bell Library in Perth; the National Archives of Scotland; the Police Museum in Glasgow; the Local History Department, Central Library, Dundee; Iain Flett and the staff of Dundee City Archives; Rhona Rodgers and Fiona Sinclair of Dundee Museum and most of all my wife, Cathy.

Author's Note

Bloody Scotland continues my series of nineteenth-century true crime books that began with *A Sink of Atrocity* and continued with *Glasgow: The Real Mean City; Whisky Wars, Riots and Murder* and *Fishermen, Randies and Fraudsters.* It is not in any sense an academic book, although the information is as factual as possible and the events are as accurate as can be ascertained, given the weaknesses and discrepancies of evidence given by diverse people in the tense atmosphere of a court of law.

In the main, *Bloody Scotland* tries to avoid those crimes that have already been well documented, but tells of others that history has hidden. For example, the mass murders of Burke and Hare are not included, as they have been extensively written about elsewhere, while I have delved deeper into the Madeleine Smith poisoning case featured in *Glasgow: The Real Mean City*, the Ardlamont case introduced in *Whisky Wars* and the Dunecht mystery included in *Fishermen, Randies and Fraudsters.* Many of the murders, robberies and events were perpetrated in locations outwith the major Scottish population centres, hence their absence from more mainstream histories.

Although *Bloody Scotland* is full of horrors, it only scratches the surface of what is a massive subject. The selection process was long and painful, and for every crime included, 100 have been considered and discarded. This book is a sequence of snapshots of life in the underworld of nineteenth-century Scotland. It is intended to entertain as well as to unveil the reality of the seething cauldron of unrest, dishonesty and downright evil that sheltered behind the *Brigadoon* facade that many believe was the face of nineteenth-century Scotland.

The presentation method is thematic rather than chronological or geographical. There are chapters on different types of crime, such as assault and robbery, and on aspects of life that were peculiar to the period and attracted criminal behaviour, such as the railway navigators and body-snatching. However, where a story was sufficiently complex or considered to be interesting on its own, it has been granted a stand-alone chapter, such as the siege of John Street in Dundee.

While some people may view Scotland as a romantic land of bens and glens, or a nation where nothing much happened, this book may be a revelation. For the people who survived day by day with the constant threat of highway robbery, rioting navvies, brutal murders and clever thieves, life was often hard. If *Bloody Scotland* tears down only a corner of the curtain erected by false history, it has achieved its purpose.

Malcolm Archibald, Moray, 2014

Introduction

Scotland is a small country at the north-western periphery of Europe. She has a ninety-six-mile land boundary with England, but otherwise is surrounded by thousands of square miles of ocean. This near isolation has helped create a nation like no other. The coastal people lived by the sea and on the sea, while the Borderers in the deep south of the country had to endure centuries of invasion and spoliation by English armies and bands of reivers. For the best part of a thousand years the Scottish nation stood in independence, repelling all attempts at foreign conquest with a grinding determination that formed a character noted for stubborn pride and taciturnity. Throughout the Middle Ages, every town and city lived with the constant possibility of destruction by an enemy, be that an English army from the south or an eruption of the Gaelic clans of the north and west. It may have been the constant preoccupation with imminent conflict that formed a people who lived with the spear to hand and a readiness to decide quarrels by quick violence.

Internal demographics and geography helped create a nation split into three distinct sections: the Southern Uplands, where the riding surnames of the Borders acted as a barrier to invasion from the south; the central Lowlands, from where urban Scots traded with Europe and created cities; and the Highlands, with their ancient Gaelic culture and links with Ireland. When the northern isles of Orkney and Shetland became part of Scotland in the fifteenth century, the nation was complete.

All these areas had their own unique history, as well as sharing that of Scotland as a whole, and they created their own historic crime. The Borderers were renowned for reiving and family feuds; they brought the word 'blackmail' into the language. The cities could be powder kegs – with Daniel Defoe the novelist believing that if the Edinburgh mob had discovered that he was an English spy they would have torn him to pieces – while the Highlands were known for clan warfare and cattle theft. With such a bright history, it is not surprising that by the nineteenth century Scottish crime should be widespread, diverse and endlessly fascinating.

That century was a time of immense change that left no part of Scotland unaltered. The notorious Highland Clearances wiped out scores of communities, destroyed clachans that had endured for centuries and drove the indigenous peoples from glens they had inhabited since the memory of man. They were also instrumental in introducing new farming practices into the Highlands, a process that created its own resentments. The transport revolution altered the countryside of the Highlands and Lowlands, as railways thrust from town to town. While pickpockets haunted the stations, travellers shared the carriages with professional gamblers and the occasional sexual predator. Criminals also escaped by rail, but the formation of the railway police helped bring the balance back in favour of law and order.

Road transport also altered throughout the century, with the massive improvement of road surfacing and an increase in travel. Throughout the century thieves and robbers escaped in gigs and stagecoaches, but highway robbery was much more common in the early decades, when roads were poor and speeds slower. Sea transport altered dramatically, with steam replacing sail power. As ships increased in size, the bulk of sea transport shifted to the larger ports. However, there was crime at sea throughout the century, from brutal murder to smuggling, illegal fishing and even piracy. Jack ashore could be troublesome at times, and the dock areas of Scottish cities and towns supported their quota of seedy, raucous pubs, low lodging houses and brothels that were often a front for pickpockets, muggers and other crime.

Perhaps even more fundamental in altering the style of life in Scotland was industrialisation and the associated urbanisation. Industry brought jobs to towns and cities, while the mechanisation of farming made tens of thousands redundant; they were forced to seek the industrial jobs. The consequent shift of population created pressure on city housing stocks, with the result that living conditions could be shocking. Many town centres degenerated into slums as landlords divided and subdivided property to maximise their profit. Slum living was seen as synonymous with prostitution, drunkenness and general crime. Areas such as these were often thought to be the breeding ground for a specific criminal class of people who lived amongst the general population and who had to be eradicated by transportation.

When new housing was built, it was often shoddy and ill designed, so people crammed into substandard tenements that were concentrated around the workplaces, be they mill or factory or shipyard. For many in the nineteenth century, life was a dull round of work and retreat into cheerless, single-room dwellings that lacked even basic sanitation. It was no wonder that men and women sought sanctuary in the many public houses and much crime was blamed on drink.

Alcohol was the besetting sin of the masses, and drunken brawls disfigured town centres on Saturday evenings. Worse was the constant round of wife-beating as men returned home from the pub to take out their frustration on their women. Sometimes it was the wife who went too far, or who nursed her resentment to a point where she took revenge on her man with the blade of a knife, the iron rod of a handy poker or the more calculated addition of poison to his porridge. Domestic bliss was not universal in the days of Victorian values.

Fuelling the Industrial Revolution was coal. Scotland had known coal-mining since the early Middle Ages, when the monks of Newbattle in Midlothian had exploited the ground they owned. In the nineteenth century there were scores of mines across the Central Belt and over the Forth in Fife. The miners lived in small communities based around whichever pit they worked; some of these villages vanished when the coal was worked out; others have remained to become part of the landscape. In the early decades of the century colliers were nearly despised for their ignorance; the rest of society shunned them. Perhaps there was a reason for that, as they were one of only two groups of people in the country who had been serfs until as late as 1799. The other group were the salters. As the century rolled on, the mining communities grew in number and importance; coal was vital to the economy. Their living and working conditions improved, so that model communities such as Newtongrange in Midlothian were built, but the job remained hard and dangerous. Collier crime was usually brutal, violent and ugly.

Another factor that altered society throughout the century was emigration and immigration. Hundreds of thousands of Scots emigrated to the colonies and to the United States. Hundreds of thousands of Irish immigrated to Scotland to find work. The industrial west and Dundee were the main recipients of the Irish, and the impact was not always immediately beneficial. At the beginning of the nineteenth century, Scotland was mainly a Presbyterian country, but many of the Irish were Roman Catholic and, at a time of religious upheaval, the influx of this faith created problems. The incomers were not always welcomed and the animosity was returned with interest.

Religious squabbles, sometimes drink-fuelled, augmented the burdens of poverty and poor living conditions in many Scottish urban centres.

Added to Irish immigration was internal migration, both permanent and temporary. With the Clearances and the pull of employment, thousands of countrymen from both Highlands and Lowlands moved to the cities. Some slotted in without problems but others needed more help and local societies were formed to assist them to become accepted as part of the social scene. Other migration was seasonal, as Highlander and Hebridean men travelled to the east coast for fishing, while their womenfolk worked as gutters and packers in the fishing ports. They followed the shoals of herring around the counrty, adding their language and colour to the local communities. Sometimes the cultural clash between the Gaelic-speaking Highlanders and the Scots-speaking Lowlanders led to confrontation and riot.

The fishermen were not a quiet breed of men, whichever culture they clung to. The fishing industry expanded through the century so the Scottish coasts were ringed by fishing villages old and new, each with a distinctive culture but eternally linked by the bond with the sea. It was a hard life; perhaps the hardest of lives, with death a constant companion as the open boats braved the treacherous North Sea or the perils of the Minch and the Atlantic. Such a life did not breed men who shrank from trouble, and the fishing villages, so quiet today, were often the scene of riot and disorder.

Arguably even more troublesome were the Railway Navigators, the infamous 'navvies' who built the railways. It was in the nature of the job that they laboured in gangs of scores and hundreds, and operated in tough conditions. They were a clannish breed who tended to settle any disputes within their own mobile communities, but when they descended on small villages miles from proper authority they could create their own type of havoc and unleash the hounds of crime. Mayhem, assault and murder often followed in the wake of the railway navvy.

The Industrial Revolution may have benefited the nation financially, but for the people who crammed into the burgeoning towns, life was hard, work unrelenting and the new discipline of the time-clock and factory whistle unwelcome. Long hours under hard taskmasters, particularly in the early decades, led to unrest. The rise of urban living gave birth to new political ideologies and a realisation that the current system was less than ideal. The old chaotic politics of the eighteenth century was challenged by people who the upper classes termed 'radicals'. These radicals sought a fairer balance of power, and the century was marked by the slow and painful march to democracy, as a growing middle class and a more educated working class sought more rights and more power. There was also trouble as workers formed unions, initially termed 'combinations', that challenged the factory and mine owners over wages and working conditions. Sometimes these combinations faced the owners in bloody stand-offs; at others they faced incoming workers who accepted lower wages as an alternative to hunger and pauperism.

The upper classes did not relinquish political and financial control gracefully. Every little step had to be fought for and martyrs were made along the way. The Republican Rising of 1820 saw the last beheading in Scotland, and the Chartist troubles of the late 1830s and 1848 witnessed riots in towns and cities across the country. The authorities did all they could to place a lid on the simmering resentment of people who had nothing and lived in hovels while the political elite owned everything and built themselves palaces. The road toward political reform may have been paved with good intentions but the cement that bonded the slabs was carved from trouble and mixed with blood.

Yet at the same time as class awareness grew, there was still interest in the lives of those who were perceived as 'social betters'. The comings and goings of the aristocracy were recorded in newspapers much as the lives of sports personalities or film stars are today. Ordinary people watched in awe as the glittering cavalcades of the landed elite waltzed through the century, with their dramas very much centre stage in the theatre of life. The humble workers counted their pennies and planned for better days while the unfortunates for whom work was only a pipe-dream clamoured for crumbs from the tables of the rich, or took to petty theft and sordid assault. Despite the changes, there was also great continuity for many people in Scotland. Work on the land was as much part of life as mining or fishing, and the age-old system of feeing fairs, of ploughing and harvesting and of raising cattle and sheep continued day after day, year after year. Hard men and women, slaves of plough and soil, the crofters and farmers had their share of drunkards and brawlers who endured a life that was anything but a rural idyll. The bothy system throughout the Lowlands saw young men crammed together in often vastly unsuitable habitations. They worked long hours in a hard job and tensions or personality clashes could cause friction and even murder.

The seasonal markets were a magnet for card sharps and fortune tellers, travellers and wanderers, fair men and foul who preyed on the farm servants with no sympathy for the hours of backbreaking toil they had endured to earn the terribly few pennies they had to spend. Seasonal fairs were always a focus for trouble and the police watched them with care.

Further out on the fringes of the farms, in the policies of the landed rich, in the hills and heather moors and gaunt granite ridges, game-keepers kept lonely vigil over deer and fish and pheasant. Opposing them were poachers; some were of the casual variety who sought only a rabbit for the family or a fish for the pot, but there were also professionals and dangerous gangs who came from the city armed and looking for trouble. Keeping the lord's game secure was a constant battle in which the keeper was often outnumbered and ill supported, but one in which he often sought to equalise the odds by the use of spring traps and an unrelenting attitude to life. There was little romance in the sharp bang of a shotgun, and no pity in the toothed jaws of a man trap.

In the early decades of the century, the ghoulish grave-robbers were detested by all save the medical profession. These men dug up fresh corpses and sold them to anatomical schools for big money. The lecturers required a constant supply of corpses for teaching purposes, but the relatives of the deceased objected to the desecration of their loved ones' remains, which led to some ugly scenes if they caught the 'resurrection men'.

Last in this listing of Scottish crime were the illicit whisky distillers; the men and women who made their own peat reek amongst the glens and moors from the shifting shores of Solway to Scapa and beyond. Theirs could be a community effort or a lonely vigil amidst the haunted mists of the west, while the Excisemen came hunting with all the power of authority backed by musket and sword. The illicit distillers carried their produce from one end of the country to the other, across sea and loch, river and moor, hill and field. They could be the man next door or the wild denizen of the furthermost clachan. They were ubiquitous, wild, bad and often dangerous to know; they were part of the fabric of Scottish society.

The nineteenth century, then, was very much an age of movement – physical, social and political – as men and women stirred restlessly against the bonds of parochial control and tradition. Tension became part of life as people challenged established, static authority to seek new freedoms. Beneath the shortbread tin veneer of tartan conformity, and hidden by the products of muscle, skill and engineering genius, Scotland was a seething mass of troubles. Invariably such an array of tensions created a plethora of crime.

The growth of industrial towns alarmed many people in authority, who viewed these places as out-of-control hotbeds of vice and crime. There was a new scientific interest in crime and the causes of crime, and theories of crime prevention and cure abounded. The new police forces patrolled their beats, while judges tried to cleanse the land of crime by sending those who came before them to Australia, or break their minds with solitary confinement or the silent system in stark stone prisons. Overall, Scottish crime in the nineteenth century was as varied and fascinating as crime could ever be; but it was also sordid, ugly and cruel.

1
Resurrection Men

Some crimes are universal, but others are specific to place or time. Body-snatching was one such. It flourished in the eighteenth and early nineteenth centuries and died out completely with the passing of the Anatomy Act of 1832. Until that time, body-snatching was big business, with relatively large profits to be made for a few hours' gruesome and mildly dangerous work. Indeed, it could be so lucrative that some criminals specialised in digging up the bodies of the dead. One such was a London ex-prizefighter named Ben Crouch. He was the son of a hospital caretaker and worked in London for four or five years from 1809 onward. He sold his grisly goods to St Bartholomew's Hospital and maintained a monopoly by informing the police of any rivals, by tearing up graveyards he did not use, so the corpses were exposed and no good for anatomy, or simply by terrorising the hospital staff so they would only buy corpses from him.

Scotland may also have had professional body-snatchers, but most were small-time operators after a quick buck. The process of digging up corpses by so-called resurrection men was a major worry throughout Europe, but the crimes of Burke and Hare have pushed Scotland to prominence as a centre of the trade. Perhaps that is fair, as early nineteenth-century Edinburgh boasted one of the finest anatomical hospitals in the world. However, Burke and Hare were more mass murderers than resurrection men. Their story is too well known to be repeated, especially as there were so many other body-snatchers on the prowl in Scotland. Indeed in 1821 the Reverend William Fleming of West Calder reported that, 'Few burial grounds in Scotland have escaped the ravaging hands of resurrection men.'

The idea that trainee doctors should study human anatomy was incorporated into the very fabric of Scottish surgery. The 1505 charter of the Royal College of Surgeons insisted that such knowledge was essential. The theory was sound but the practice creaked with difficulties. Where could a trainee surgeon obtain human bodies? The authorities tried their best by sentencing convicted murders to be hanged to death and their bodies given to the local anatomist, but there simply were not enough Scottish murderers to go round. The professors of anatomy must have prayed for an extensive crime spree, but in the meantime made do with the corpses of dead orphans and unbaptised children, as well as whatever the gravediggers unearthed from the shadows of the tombstones in the night-shrouded churchyards.

Defending the dead

In an age when many people believed that the bodies of the dead rose from their graves to meet their Maker, there was genuine horror at the prospect of their deceased relatives being dissected. As well as being downright indecent, mutilating a corpse jeopardised life in the hereafter, so people took great precautions to defend their recently departed family members. Graves were dug deep, with layers of branches in the soil to hamper the hurried spades of resurrection men. Huge stone slabs known as mort-stones were placed on top of new graves to discourage digging. Only when the body was too decomposed to be worth unearthing was the mort-stone moved to guard another recent guest. Corpses could also be chained to the coffin, and in Dundee one grieving father even booby-trapped his child's coffin with an explosive device. There were also mort safes – iron grilles in which the coffin lay – or mort houses, with mighty stone walls and locked heavy doors, though stone walls do not security make as long as locks can be picked ... Once again, the dead were kept behind these closed doors until they were too decomposed to be useful.

How long would it be until the bodies were safe from the resurrection men? That question is not so easy to answer. In a case in the High Court in June 1823 Dr Barclay, who had taught anatomy for twenty-five years, said that bodies decomposed at different rates. He stated that some were unrecognisable after just forty-eight hours but others could last much longer. He quoted a case where a lascar (a seaman from the East Indies) was still recognisable after two weeks. After three weeks, Barclay declared, a corpse was not fit for dissection and dissectors had to mark bodies so they knew one from the other. So the grave watchers could be on guard for some considerable time after a corpse was buried.

The grave-robbers had their own techniques to circumvent at least some of the security measures. They knew the mort-stones indicated a new grave so they dug into the soil at the head, knocked open the end of the coffin and hauled out the corpse. Stealing a dead body was not considered a crime, but stealing clothes most certainly was, so the grave-robbers frequently stripped the dead of their coverings, and with them the last of their dignity, so they carried away a naked pale body.

Despite all the passive defences, a watching committee proved to be the most effective preventative method. Many communities set up these groups of dedicated men, with a number of volunteers taking shifts to guard graveyards throughout the hours of darkness. Most had small stone buildings – watchtowers – built at one part of the graveyard so the men on duty could watch over their silent neighbours, while refreshing themselves with whisky, perhaps telling ghost stories and wishing the long hours of the night would tick away more quickly. Some of these watchtowers had loopholes so the sentinels could fire at any grave-robbers – if they could see them in the bitter dark of a winter's night.

Even with the watchers, the lure of quick money enticed the more unscrupulous of men to leave their houses at the dead of night, heft their spades, huddle closer into their long cloaks, pull their bicorn hats hard down on their heads and venture forth to meet the dead. Sometimes the night did not go entirely as planned.

Raid on Prestonkirk

It was always better to dig out a fresh corpse, so the resurrection men would have known that Catherine Mack of West Fenton in Haddingtonshire (now East Lothian) had died, and they were probably watching when she was buried in Prestonkirk churchyard in East Linton on Saturday, 3 January 1819. The family was too poor to afford the expense of a mort house or even a mort safe, so they trusted in the Lord and in luck to protect the body of their loved one. Sometimes more was needed.

Jane Frizzel was married to the gravedigger at Prestonkirk and knew every inch of the churchyard. She knew the graves and she had known many of the people they contained; she also knew the people who lived in the area, so when she saw two strangers walking through the churchyard she was immediately suspicious. When she saw them stop above the still fresh grave of Catherine Mack, she guessed they were up to mischief but she did not know how to stop them.

About eleven o' clock on the night of 6 January 1819, three silent men slipped into Prestonkirk churchyard to disinter the body. Their names were George McLaren, John Kerr and George Campbell. They came equipped with spades to dig up the body of Catherine Mack, ropes to raise her to the surface and an iron crow-bar to open the coffin. They also carried a selection of sheets, some in which to wrap the physical remains of Catherine Mack. They did not enter together: Kerr and McLaren rose from behind the bushes that screened one boundary of the churchyard. They moved slowly and in a half crouch, dodging from gravestone to gravestone as they approached the manse and checked the door. Only when they were sure that it was locked did they move to the interior of the churchyard.

The third man, George Campbell, then climbed over the stone wall of the yard and headed straight for the grave of Catherine Mack. The other two were already there. They spread one of the sheets on the ground and began to dig, piling the loose earth on top of the sheet.

The three men worked in the dark of the evening, with the soft slither of spades in earth, the occasional click as they encountered a stone and a gasp or two of effort the only sounds in the winter-quiet churchyard. After about quarter of an hour, one looked up as something alerted him. He murmured a warning and all three stopped digging and began to run.

It was then that the hidden watchers made their presence known. Although Jane Frizzel had not told him about the suspected grave-robbers, somebody who signed himself 'Justice' had sent an anonymous letter to John Gibb the postmaster, saying that some men from Edinburgh would try and dig up a corpse from the churchyard. Gibb notified the Prestonkirk constable, Ralph Plain, who immediately got a magistrate's warrant to arrest anybody he caught digging up graves. He did not know how many there might be, but he knew it was best not to work alone; grave-robbers could be a desperate breed. He gathered a small band of helpers: his own son, John Gibb and his son, also called John, and a man named Robert Hamilton. Plain told them what might happen and asked them to find a weapon.

Plain's posse had arrived in the graveyard before dark, and the constable positioned them around the tombstones, facing Catherine Mack's grave. Two of the watchers, including Plain, carried muskets and the other two hefted stout cudgels in case of trouble. They had already been in position for some three hours before the resurrection men made their appearance.

As soon as the grave-robbers began to move away from Catherine Mack's grave, Plain stood up, snapped open the cover of his lantern so the light highlighted his quarry, pointed his musket and called for them to stop. One man immediately stood still but the others made a mad dash for the wall. Plain's men followed them like a pack of hounds after a brace of foxes. There was a stumbling stramash among the gravestones as the light from Plain's lantern bounced sinister shadows from the ancient stones, but the watchers caught the resurrection men as they tried to scale the boundary wall. Plain took his prisoners to a secure location and sent his assistants to search the churchyard. They found the shovels, crowbar, rope and sheets.

When Plain quizzed the prisoners, they admitted that they had intended to dig up Catherine Mack's body but added it was the first time they had done anything of the sort and promised never to do anything of the sort again, sir, if you let us go free? Ignoring their promise, Plain brought them before the local magistrate and then escorted them to Haddington jail. Further questioning brought some interesting revelations: George Campbell was the personal servant of an Edinburgh surgeon named Robert Allan, who would certainly have liked to get his hands on a fresh cadaver. George McLaren was another Edinburgh man; he worked for Dr John Smith. Kerr was only a labourer and probably just the hired help.

When the case was heard at the High Court in June 1819, the grave-robbers said that a man named Lawrie had sent them to dig up the body; it was expected that the letter sent to John Gibb, signed 'Justice', was also by the same man, which suggests that Lawrie, whoever he was, set them up. All three were sentenced to one year in jail, with the warning that they would have been transported if they had been successful in carrying away the body.

Robbing Lady Yester's graves

The judge was not mouthing empty threats. In January 1803 a man named Archibald Begg appeared before the High Court in Edinburgh. He was found guilty of robbing dead bodies and was banished from Scotland for fourteen years, with the stipulation that if he returned he was to be whipped through Edinburgh.

In September 1807 a sharp-eyed neighbour saw a ladder against the wall of Lady Yester's churchyard in Infirmary Street in Edinburgh and notified the nearest policeman. The officer sprang his rattle, which summoned a number of people willing to help. Acting together they grabbed one lame, grey-haired old man who was trying to descend the ladder, and another in nearby College Wynd. They also found the body of a woman that the pair had been trying to steal. The woman was returned to the earth from where she had come and the two men were sent for trial.

The men were Robert Phillip and lame Archibald Begg, the latter returned from exile. He was a professional grave-robber. The judge ordered that Begg should be whipped as the original sentence required, and a huge crowd encouraged the executioner to lay on with a will. In the intervals when the cart trundled through the streets, the crowd hissed, booed and threw dead cats, rotten vegetables and other rubbish at Begg, with a few bold boys braving the guard to rush forward and knock him to the ground. The city guard were hard pressed to keep the mob at bay.

Law was innocent

Begg's case was not unique. The resurrection men were anything but popular with the general population. Another example of the crowd's ire occurred on 19 April 1823 when the Linlithgow police caught a man named John Law trying to pass a forged bank note. As they carted him off to the police station a number of men attacked, not to rescue the prisoner, as was not unusual in such situations, but to get at Law. They believed that he had tried to steal the body of a recently deceased child to sell it to the anatomists. In this case he was innocent.

As the mob attacked the police, Law was momentarily grateful to them, but that feeling did not last as they began to punch and kick him so that he was quite badly injured. Two men, David Morison and Alexander Wardlaw, were arrested and charged with mobbing and rioting.

At the same High Court sitting on 2 June 1823, Thomas Stevenson, also known as Thomas Hodge, was charged with 'violating the sepulchres of the dead at Larbert' in Stirlingshire. It was the second time that Stevenson had been charged with this crime, but he pleaded not guilty. The case came to trial, which is far better for the historian, as it means there are many more details recorded.

In old rural Scotland it was hard to commit a crime and remain unseen, as everybody knew their neighbours and anything unusual was seen and commented on. In this case a farm servant named John Forrest, who lived a few miles outside Linlithgow, had been on his way home from the local mill. Forrest saw a man lift three very large objects from a dung heap and place them in a gig. The size of the objects, and the fact they had been hidden in a midden, made Forrest suspicious, so he took note of the man's appearance. He was dressed in a tartan cloak and a glazed hat. Forrest ran to fetch his master, Adam Scott, farmer at Gilston, and both returned to the midden.

By the time they got there the gig had gone, but Scott spurred his horse along the road toward Linlithgow. Faces turned as they heard him clatter over the cobbles, but he caught the gig in the centre of the town, rode alongside and grabbed the reins. The driver had no option but to stop. He glanced nervously backward, where he had fastened the apron over the body of the vehicle. As Scott shouted his suspicions that he had been grave-robbing, a crowd gathered and demanded he show them what he had in the gig. The man refused, saying it was none of their business and anyway, where was their warrant? Scott hurried to get a magistrate to sign a warrant as the crowd took matters into their own hands.

James Douglas was one of that crowd and helped to pull down the apron of the gig; there was instant pandemonium as the contents were revealed. There were three dead bodies inside: a man, a woman and a child, each tied with a rope around the ankles and the neck. That was enough: the crowd bayed for blood. The man in the tartan cloak jumped off the gig and tried to run, but a burly man named David Brown grabbed him by the front of his cloak and held him tight. The mob immediately surrounded the prisoner and tried to tear him to pieces; boots and fists flew as the man in the tartan cloak cowered and yelled under the onslaught. There might have been murder had a brave man named Liston not pushed through the crowd and rescued the prisoner, but even so the tartan cloak was stained with the blood that flowed from the body-snatcher's face and head. In the meantime, James Douglas helped carry the bodies to the town house.

Although the resurrection man was reeling, battered and bruised, the mob was not yet satisfied. They released the horse from the gig, hauled the carriage to the market cross and set it alight as they danced around, shouting and cheering.

It did not take long to identify one of the bodies as Janet Moir, who had been buried in Larbert graveyard on 17 January 1823. The case against the man in the tartan cloak was already proved to everybody's satisfaction, but the legal process had to be followed through. When the case reached the High Court, Thomas Stevenson, the alleged resurrectionist, gave his side of the story. He said he had been a weaver and a seaman but now worked as a porter. He had been innocently walking along the road to Linlithgow when a gentleman on a gig had offered him a lift. Of course he had said yes to save his weary legs, and had been surprised when the driver asked him to dismount for a few moments while he performed a private message. He had done so, but when he rejoined the gig, something had been put inside. He did not know what it was and did not like to ask. As they neared Linlithgow the anonymous and kindly gentleman had handed him the reins and asked him to drive through the town from west to east, and he would meet him on the far side.

The jury swept aside this defence as a fairy story and found Stevenson guilty. His defence asked for a lenient sentence as he had already been held in jail and because the mob had treated him so roughly. Lord Pitmilly did not agree and sent him to Australia for seven years.

There were many other instances, but most have been forgotten, swept away by time and the memories of Burke and Hare.

2

Robbing the Stirling Mail

The early nineteenth century was the golden age of coach travel. Before the steam trains pounded and rattled their way through the country-side, horse-drawn coaches were the queens of passenger transport. While the stagecoaches carried more passengers, the mail coaches had their own legend and lore. With guards blowing long brass horns to announce their arrival, they followed strict timetables, changed horses at regular stops and carried a limited number of passengers at higher rates than the ordinary stagecoaches.

They could also be the target of robbery, due to the low bulk and sometimes high value of the Royal Mail packages they carried. Every mail coach carried letters and packages, but when they also carried gold or notes for the bank, they became a very tempting target indeed. Men on the criminal side of the law would be tempted by such a haul, but could be put off by the burly guard who sat by the driver with his blunderbuss or brace of heavy pistols. However, the coaches were not immune and such a robbery occurred on 18 December 1824, when the mail coach between Stirling and Edinburgh was targeted.

This was no conventional highway robbery, with a masked man riding up to the driver to present a pistol and the expected demand to 'stand and deliver'; instead the robbery was carefully planned and carried out without any violence or threat.

William Home, coach guard

The thief or thieves were well aware that the coach carried more than mail. When it was at Stirling, John Boyd, the teller of the Bank of Scotland, gave three parcels of bank notes to William Home, the guard of the coach. Home was a stocky, responsible man who took his duties seriously. He had been guard of the Stirling coach for eight years; as the owners of the coach refused to take responsibility for the bank's money, Home accepted the burden on his own head. He signed for the notes and stowed them safely in a locked box under his own footstool. With his large boots positioned on top of the box for the entire journey, Home was certain the bank notes were safe. John Nicholson, who worked in the bank in Stirling, was not so sure. He eyed the passengers who sat inside the coach and told Home he thought some of them looked a bit suspect.

At quarter past three the guard blew a long, throbbing blast on his horn and the mail coach left Stirling for Edinburgh. There were seven passengers: three men and a woman inside and two men and one woman outside. Every coach carried passengers. The more expensive seats were in the relative comfort of the coach's interior. Outside on the roof, a number of hardy souls paying lesser amounts braved the stern Scottish weather in their hats and greatcoats and scarves.

The coach had a number of stops on its route. The first was at Falkirk, where one of the inside passengers left and another man took his place. Home opened the mailbox to put in another packet, checked the contents, locked the box again and settled down for the second stage of the journey. The next stop was Linlithgow, where Home accepted another packet. Mail coaches had a sword case, where any firearms taken from the passengers were held for the duration of the journey. Home put the Linlithgow packet in this case. The coach pulled away; the driver whipped up the horses and they rolled on toward Edinburgh.

Winchburgh was the next stop, but here Home made a mistake that was going to cost him dear. He opened the box, but this time he forgot to lock it again. The coach rolled on, with the horses' hooves a rhythmic drumbeat and the passengers swaying together as they rounded the bends of the road. They reached Kirkliston at 6.40 p.m., with the night so dark that the yellow glow of the coach lamps was the only light amidst stygian gloom. The coach was a rumbling island isolated in its own little world. They rolled to a halt, with the driver sawing the reins so the horses stopped.

Home slipped off his seat and entered the post office to pick up the mail. He was not gone above a couple of minutes, but then he helped change the leaders – the front horses. The coach's schedule allowed a five-minute halt, and that is all it took before the coach was on its way once more with seemingly nothing amiss.

The mysterious gig

However, all was not well in the mail coach. When the coach had set off from Stirling, one bold man had purchased an outside seat and had sat in the cold as they had jolted and sped along. Soon after, a gig had pulled up behind the coach and followed in its wake. Such a procedure was normal, as the gig would rely on the horn of the mail to clear a fast passage to Edinburgh, so the guard would not have been overly suspicious of the vehicle following him. A couple of miles past Linlithgow the gig had overtaken the coach. It had remained just in front of them with only its nearside lamp working and the occupant whipping the single dark horse as it negotiated the curves of the dark road.

When the coach had made its routine stop at Kirkliston, nobody was surprised when the gig also stopped and the driver and passenger eased cramped limbs and wandered into the public house for a much needed refreshment: whisky to combat the bitter chill of the journey. As the driver and guard of the coach entered the post office, the man who had joined at Stirling slipped from his outside seat, took three parcels from the foot box, said he was not going any further and disappeared into the night.

When the driver and guard returned minutes later, they did not notice the theft and drove away toward Edinburgh, while the gig that had been accompanying them apparently took the road to Queensferry. The mail had been robbed and at that stage nobody knew anything about it.

The robbery was not discovered until the mail coach stopped at Corstorphine, then well outside Edinburgh, and Home put another bag in the mail box. He saw that the bank notes were missing and nearly panicked. Feeling sick, but not sure what to do, Home drove to the post office in Frederick Street in Edinburgh and stammered out his version of the theft to the representatives from three banks who were waiting for their money. By that time he was very agitated at the loss and a bit confused. The parcels contained banknotes, to the value of around £13,000. One parcel was for the Bank of Scotland, one for the Leith Bank and the third for the Commercial Bank of Scotland. The respective banks were naturally upset and the Leith Bank sent John Jack, their porter, to escort Home back over the coach route. They spent most time in Kirkliston, where Home had worked out that the robbery had taken place. Despite their best efforts and persistent questioning, they found nothing of any importance. Home was sacked from his job as guard, and questioned by the police as a possible suspect. He must have felt as if his whole life had fallen apart; it was the first time he had lost anything in his time as a guard of the coach. 'I am a ruined man,' he said.

Three suspicious men

The police made their own inquiries and learned that three men had been seen acting in a suspicious manner. One was particularly distinctive; he had a false nose made of 'pasteboard or parchment'. The police were also very interested in the gig that had accompanied the mail coach for so long, only to disappear at the same time as the bank notes. In this case, the police inquiries bore some results.

Thomas Boyd and John Leitch were both Kirkliston locals; they were walking along the Queensferry Road on the evening of the robbery. Only a few moments after the mail coach had passed they found a light-coloured coat on the ground. As they lifted it, two men ran past them, each carrying a square parcel. Further on, Boyd and Leitch found two cloaks; when they searched the pockets they found a small parcel and a white neck cloth. It was a busy road that night, for a third man appeared panting out of the gloom, claiming the cloaks were his and demanding they hand them over. When they shrugged and handed the cloaks to him, he gave them a shilling 'for their trouble.'

Boyd and Leitch returned the same way on the Sunday morning and found a horse and a broken gig lying in the ditch by the road, about three-quarters of a mile from Kirkliston and half a mile from the gates of Dundas Castle.

The police put two and two together. They believed that the thief had grabbed the packets and run. He had an arranged meeting with the gig further down the road, but a few miles later the gig was damaged and all three men left it. They hired a post-chaise for Edinburgh and paid the post boy three shillings.

That theory was not entirely correct. One mystery was cleared up when a commercial traveller named Colin Laing told them he had driven the gig with the single lantern. He had kept company with the mail coach for security, as it was a dark road and he was carrying valuable goods.

The police also found a witness to the actual robbery. Mrs Dobbie lived in Kirkliston and was at the door of the post office watching the bustle. She saw a man dismount from the rear of the coach, cross the road and run to the westward. A second man came out of the stable, stared at her and joined the man who had descended from the coach. Mrs Dobbie heard them whispering in the dark but told the police that she could not identify either of them.

The police inquiries had gone in circles. They had found out a possible sequence of events, but had neither a name nor a concrete suspect. Other police forces were also on the case. In Newcastle the police were busy, as three suspicious men had arrived on the Edinburgh mail coach in late December. The Edinburgh police had informed them that they were searching for three men; perhaps this was them? The Newcastle police learned a few names and took steps to round the suspects up. One name they heard was Robert Murray.

Returned convict

Thomas Forsyth, head constable at Newcastle, travelled to Thirsk in Yorkshire with Sergeant Stewart of the Edinburgh police and a Mr Edwards of the Bank of Scotland, to arrest Robert Murray. The suspect was in bed at the inn when they hammered at the door. He opened up, bleary-eyed and suspicious, and the police thundered in. At first Murray claimed his name was Graham, but at length he admitted who he was. When he was searched, the police found a number of bank notes, but none of them had been stolen from the Stirling Mail. Murray mentioned Bristol in an oblique fashion, and the police brought him back to Edinburgh and held him in the Calton Jail. He refused to help the police with their inquiries except to say that one of his travelling companions was named William Darling.

Murray was an interesting character. As was common among criminals of the period, he had a false name. When he was a young boy, he was named Heron; he had broken the law and was transported to Australia for life. However, he managed to ingratiate himself with Governor Hunter, who brought him back to Britain and recommended him for a position with a bookseller in Bond Street in London. In 1813 he attended a royal fete and was caught stealing a nobleman's golden snuff box. That was the end of Murray's freedom.

He was sent to the prison hulks – the old, disabled ships moored off shore, in which prisoners were contained before being transported to Australia. However, Murray was resilient and escaped to infest the country again. He was later arrested on suspicion of being involved in the robbery of a mail coach in England. He was tried on that charge and found not guilty, but was convicted for being 'at large without lawful cause' and was again transported for life. This remarkable man escaped from Botany Bay a second time and returned to Britain.

If anybody asked about his frequent absences from the country, Murray claimed that he had been in the navy of the Honourable East India Company and had served in the East before coming back to Scotland.

The police painstakingly investigated his movements, sifting through scores of witnesses and asking a thousand questions. They discovered that Murray had stayed at a lodging house on Rose Street in Edinburgh's New Town for weeks. On the Saturday of the robbery he had hired a gig from a man named Smith, but he claimed he had lost the road in the dark and when he had dismounted to ask directions, the horse had bolted and he'd lost the gig. That was the vehicle Boyd and Leitch had found broken in the ditch. When Murray returned it to Smith, he paid for the damage without any hesitation.

The police widened their net, as they followed the trail of the gig. They spoke to a man named John Crocket at Queensferry, who said that on 18 December two men in a gig had asked about stabling for their horse. One of the men was Murray. Crocket directed them to Halliday's Inn. The police spoke to other witnesses in the area who remembered Murray being there on the night of the robbery. They followed a trail of hired gigs and post-chaises through Edinburgh to Musselburgh and Haddington. Murray, once known as Heron, had changed his name again. He used the name Graham on this occasion: every time.

The police were very interested in two more men who had travelled to York by the same coach as Murray, paid for a shared room in the same hotel and refused the porter's requests to carry their luggage. A Newcastle officer named Forsyth pursued the two men as far as London, where the trail ran cold. The men vanished into the stews and urban jungles of the metropolis. The police returned to Murray, frustrated but not surprised.

Murray was hauled before the High Court in Edinburgh. The prosecution did their best, but the defence stonewalled them at every turn. Murray did not deny that he had been in the locality of the robbery, but without decisive proof the jury refused to convict him. The verdict was: not proven. The robbery was never officially solved. However, Murray's story did not end there. No sooner had the jury found the case not proven, than Mr Lavender of the Manchester Police arrested him on a charge of being a convict at large and once again he was in custody. No doubt he spent the remainder of his life alternating between prison and crime.

3

Policing Old Edinburgh

In the sixteenth century Edinburgh was a rollicking, rowdy capital, with the people jammed between the royal castle and the palace, and the cathedral of St Giles about midway between. Lords and ladies mingled shoulder to shoulder with the good neighbours in a form of society that was not democratic but certainly lacked the extremes of class consciousness that became common later. In 1603 King James VI accepted the English throne of his deceased cousin Elizabeth and Edinburgh became a capital without a king. The nobles followed in James's royal footsteps and some of the colour and wealth drained from the city.

Expanding city

The seventeenth century saw some major developments, with more lands, or tenements, being built. There was religious trouble of course, and the occasional riot, but nothing Edinburgh could not handle. Then in 1707 came the hammer blow of full union with England, and the Scottish parliament joined the king in travelling the near 400 miles to London. With neither court nor government remaining, Edinburgh altered. The city was perhaps frustrated but vibrant, home to tens of thousands of people and still the capital of the country and headquarters of the Church and Court of Session. It was dynamic, with new tenements replacing old, but the overall pattern of the city remained the same.

Later in the eighteenth century, the Scottish Enlightenment spread literature and philosophy from its Edinburgh base and a desire grew for an improved capital city, one worthy of the brains and talent that was crammed within the constricting walls.

Although peaceful by the standards of other European cities, Edinburgh could still explode into violence on occasion. As well as the famous Porteous Riot of 1736, when the mob hanged the Captain of the City Guard, there were bread riots. For instance, in 1784, when the distilleries used great amounts of barley at a time of a bread shortage in Edinburgh, a mob marched to the Haig distillery at Canonmills. The workers defended themselves with muskets, Sheriff Cockburn read the Riot Act and the mob withdrew, leaving their casualties behind them. A second attempt, on the home of the vocal Baron Cockburn was forestalled when the 9th Foot marched from the Castle and charged with the bayonet. Two of the rioters were later whipped through Edinburgh and transported for fourteen years. Such was the way of the world.

This was Auld Reekie, named after the thick reek of smoke that pumped from innumerable chimneys to lie heavy in the unlit closes and wynds and roll between the tall lands so that only the caddies – the city guides who knew everything and everybody – could find their way around. There was no municipal lighting until the nineteenth century, when whale oil was used for a limited number of street lamps. Only after the oil lamps were converted to gas on the High Street in March 1820 were the streets even moderately well lit, and in those years, untold horrors lurked in the dark closes of old Edinburgh. A pamphlet written by a man calling himself 'Citizen' describes the old part of Edinburgh as: 'Cowgate, Canongate, High Street, Lower Pleasance, Market Street ... the social condition of the masses is not merely wretched but revolting.'

Edinburgh was a city of character and of characters, where the old stones wept at hidden horrors and the smile of the morning concealed the scowl of the night-time sin. Even before the New Town was built, there was a duality about Edinburgh where drinking clubs met in oyster bars or laigh houses and a drunkard's shout could be heard from the Bible classes of the Elders of the Kirk. This was the city where Nicol Muschat of Boghall murdered his wife in Holyrood Park. This was the city where Deacon Brodie worked as a carpenter during the day and robbed his customers at night, the city where Captain Macrae shot Sir George Ramsay on Musselburgh Links in a duel over Macrae striking an insolent servant. This was the city where Lord Grange paid a bevy of Highlanders to kidnap his wife and spirit her away to St Kilda for seven years of isolation. This was the city of General Joe Smith, or Bowed Joseph, the Cowgate cobbler who led the mob in savage democracy when the magistrates acted against the public interest.

One of his best moments was the burning in effigy of John Wilkes, the sneering, cynical English nationalist whose writings so severely damaged relations within the still raw union.

Divided city

After 1767, change came at an alarming rate. The first New Town was projected, planned and eventually built in a regulated, formal and hierarchical style quite unlike the shoulder-rubbing neighbourliness of the Old Town. The sandstone streets of terraced houses made no allowance for geography, but carved their way east and west between two geometrical squares, ornamented by formal gardens. Centred on

George Street and flanked by Princes Street and Queen Street, they were named in deference to the Hanoverian dynasty and became the cornerstone of a new Edinburgh. The movement of the wealthy and the respectable from the crowded, congenial Old Town to the draughty, cold, but modern New was slow and haphazard, but inevitable.

The Old Town gradually subsided into the less desirable section of the dual city, as those citizens with money or pretensions of quality crossed the valley or slithered down the Earthen Mound toward the New. Edinburgh gained a new name, Athens of the North, a new reputation for classical architecture and a new pretentiousness. Edinburgh gained a reputation as a place of dignity and restraint, or as a place of 'fur coats and no knickers', where pretentiousness and snobbery invoked gentle mockery from those not fortunate enough to live in the capital. It was this Edinburgh – with its ancient core, its neoclassical streets and its outer suburbs of tenements and industry – that slogged through the decades of the nineteenth century. Such a city needed a proper body of men to guard it.

Town Guard

There are two possible dates for the foundation of the Edinburgh Town Guard: 1513 or 1679. In 1513, Scotland was in disarray after the defeat of Flodden, and the burghers of Edinburgh daily expected to see an English army appear in the Lothian plain. The citizens of Edinburgh built a wall around the city to guard against possible English attack. Named the 'Flodden Wall', parts can still be seen in various places in the Old Town. A watching force was created, with one man in four on nightly or daily watch. That body lasted until 1648, when the town council reduced the numbers to a body of sixty men under a captain. At first the force followed the old system and was recruited from every fourth burgher in the city, but it became obvious that a more professional force was required to police Edinburgh.

In 1679 a Guard of forty men was raised and in 1682 this figure was raised to 108, but lowered to seventy-five after 1750. Many were recruited from the Highlands. The Guard dressed in red uniforms, the same colour as the Royal Army, and carried a musket during the day or the ferocious Lochaber axe at night. That was a pole weapon with an axe blade at one side and a downward curving hook at the other. In 1789 the men on night duty were supplied with rattles to use if they needed to summon help.

If the people of Edinburgh needed help, they would call, 'The Guard! The Guard!' – and the Guard would come running. According to the Edinburgh-born writer Walter Scott, and the portraits of Edinburgh caricaturist John Kay, toward the end of the eighteenth century one of the corporals of the Guard was John (or Iain) Dhu, a ferocious-looking man who appeared to be quite an expert with his axe. When the King's Birthday riots of 1792 were at their height and the mob was tossing dead cats and stones at the Guard, he was said to have killed a rioter with a single swing of his axe.

A lieutenant led each of the three companies of the Guard, who maintained order, stopped riots, defended the authorities and guarded the tolbooth. They also sounded their drums at eight each night, marching through the main streets of the town. By the early nineteenth century they were becoming an anomaly. They were anachronistic in the new century of professional police and when they were finally disbanded in 1817 their time was long past.

For much of their existence, the Town Guard were based in a guard house opposite the Tron Kirk on the High Street. It was long and low and ugly. Outside stood a wooden horse, astride which in the seventeenth century might be perched a drunk, with his position made all the more uncomfortable by the muskets that were tied to his feet and a cup balanced on his head. This punishment was quite common in armies of the eighteenth century, and shows, if anything, the quasi-military character of the Town Guard. In the western end of the guard house was the captain's room; there was a burghers' room for special prisoners, a common hall in the centre and at the east an apartment for the tron-men or city sweeps. Under the captain's room was the black hole in which unruly prisoners and coal were stored.

Even after the formation of the police in 1805, there was one last flick of the Guard's tail when in 1814 they fought a pitched battle with the garrison from the castle and, old as they probably were, the Highlanders of the Guard won. Three years later the Guard was finally disbanded. Taking their place was the uniformed police and things would never be the same again.

Founding the police

Although there is a general conception that Robert Peel's Metropolitan Police Force, founded in 1829, was the first in Great Britain, the truth is greatly different. Glasgow had a force in 1779, and had been continually policed since 1800. The Police Act for Edinburgh came into operation in 1805, with John Tait as Judge of the Police Court. Similar bodies were established in Paisley in 1806, in Aberdeen in 1818 and Dundee was policed by a force of uniformed men from 1824. The Scottish concept of police also differed from that in England, with an idea of 'the Public Good' as important as law enforcement to the Scots. In his book *An Institute of the Law of Scotland* (published posthumously in 1773), John Erskine of Carnock wrote that the 'laws of police are calculated for providing all the members of the community with a sufficient quantity of the necessaries of life at reasonable rates, and for the prevention of dearth'. Scottish policing was proactive, rather than reactive.

The first General Police Act in 1833 followed in the wake of Peel's Metropolitan Police, allowing any Royal Burgh, Burgh of Barony or Burgh of Regality to form a police force. But Edinburgh was one of the forerunners in the police business, and the force had to learn the rules of professional policing the hard way, by trial and error. The early police were not liked. They were regarded as an arm of respectable authority to keep the working classes in their place. Perhaps for that reason there were frequent attacks on them. The early police were also notorious for being inefficient and frequently drunk.

Possibly the best indicator of the various duties of the new police was the daily police court. The Edinburgh Police Court began operation in 1805. In its first year alone there were 2,876 diverse cases. There were simple offences such as butcher's dogs loose in the markets and carters drinking at toll bars, to coal men using inaccurate weights, people selling obscene prints, wynds and closes being obstructed by dung heaps, dangerous riding, crimes against public morality such a profanity on the Lord's Day and disorderly houses. Added to that were swindling and the reset of stolen goods. There were also the more serious thefts, assaults and duels, housebreaking and riot. The police had experienced a busy year, but that was to be the norm in nineteenth-century Edinburgh.

As well as the uniformed police, Scottish cities had watchmen who protected the streets during the hours of darkness. These men were not always respected. They were known as 'Charlies' and often spent most of their shift secured in their small shelters, emerging only to shout the time. They were armed with a long staff, carried a lantern and wore a long brown cloak or greatcoat, sometimes supplemented by a broad blue bonnet. It was customary to deride them, yet they did a necessary job in attempting to keep the streets safe and frequently cleaned up the swarming drunks or helped stop burglaries and assaults.

In the 1830s, the Edinburgh watchmen earned twelve shillings a week, but a penny-halfpenny was deducted to pay for having their lanterns cleaned. They worked between twelve and fourteen hours a night, and had daytime court appearances if they had been involved in an arrest. They were also on call during the daylight hours for events such as fires, riots, elections and executions.

In July 1836 they petitioned for a rise of four shillings a week, but would have accepted half that. Months later the city authorities gave a blunt refusal and over 100 watchmen held a very well organised meeting in Advocate's Close, where they decided to take strike action. When they told the superintendent of police, he replied that anybody going on strike would be sacked.

On 15 October there was great consternation when only thirty-six of the 160 watchmen arrived for the night shift. The superintendent called in the day men, sergeants and the criminal officers to take their place and even he and his underlings had to mount their horses to patrol the outer parts of the city.

Sometimes the police had other duties apart from chasing thieves or preventing assaults. On Monday, 6 October 1823 a variety of terrible sounds arose from the vaults under the South Bridge. These spaces had been built up, and the enclosed area used for a variety of purposes. The people of Blair Street complained to the police, and three constables opened the outer door and peered into the gloomy interior.

Badger baiting

They pushed in, stooping under the low roof, and realised that the vault was crowded with men and animals. The men were from the lowest dregs of society, in the terminology of the day, the refuse of the 'flash mob' gathering in response to an advertisement. The vault had been renamed Badger Hall and the men and their dogs were there to indulge in badger baiting. The fancy had trapped the badger in a six-foot-long box, with a dog-sized hole at one end. They had paid one shilling apiece for the privilege of stuffing their dog into this arena, with the victorious dog earning its owner a guinea, but there were also side bets among the fancy.

The police tried to clear the vault, but they were vastly outnumbered by the inhabitants and driven back, with one constable bleeding badly from a dog bite. They rustled up reinforcements but by the time they returned to Badger Hall the fancy had left and there were no arrests. It was all in a day's work for the men who guarded Scotland's capital city.

4

Of Banks and Bankers

In the nineteenth century, every city and many sizeable towns in Scotland had their own private bank. Naturally the owners and managers of these establishments made them as secure as possible, but there were always predators on the prowl and intelligent, unscrupulous men watching and waiting for an opportunity to strike ...

Greenock Bank Robbery

As far back as the twelfth century, Greenock was a fishing port, but it was trade with North America that saw the burgh rise in importance and prosperity. From the seventeenth century Greenock's shipping and shipbuilding industry blossomed, and many in the town became wealthy. By the 1820s the Greenock Bank stored much of this wealth and was obviously a tempting target for enterprising rascals from around the country. The owners of the bank did all they could to defend the money for which they were responsible, with a number of secure locks and the addition of a messenger who lived on the premises.

The outer bank doors had two locks, one above the other, as well as four bolts. Locks could be picked, but bolts were hard to draw from outside. Augmenting the outer doors were two more within the building, but they had no locks. The windows had wooden shutters with brass bolts outside and iron bolts within.

The Greenock Bank did not occupy a separate building but was part of another. In this case it was in two rooms on one wing on the ground floor of the Exchange Building or Assembly Rooms. This building was near the centre of the town and nearly directly opposite the Tontine Hotel. To enter the bank, customers had to enter the hall of the Exchange Building and go through the door opposite the coffee shop. At that time the coffee shop was the commercial and social hub of the town, with business deals being struck and national and international events discussed over the newspapers the shop carried. It was open nearly every day of the year and was frequently busy. It was unfortunate for the bank that the coffee shop was open seven days a week, for that meant the outer door of the Assembly Rooms was left open. The first line of defence of the bank was very much a paper tiger.

On Sunday, 9 March 1828 the bank was robbed.

The robbery had been planned well in advance. Although the facts were never fully proved, the sequence of events seems to have been something like this. In June 1827 a man named Henry Saunders travelled from London to Greenock. He was a married man with a very respectable wife of independent financial means, but she possibly did not know the nature of her husband's work. It was probably just as well that she did not come to Greenock, for Saunders was a professional criminal and the Greenock Bank was his target.

When Saunders examined the bank to see how best it could be robbed, he called himself Richard Eldin, which was just one of his aliases. Some people in Scotland called him Henry the Butcher, which perhaps argues for a man of violence. The story of nicknames could explain so much about nineteenth-century criminals about which history is reticent. Under whatever name he chose, Saunders was one of these characters whom the police knew to be on the wrong side of the law but could never quite pin down. For example, when a bank in Ledbury in deepest England had been recently robbed, Saunders had been pulled in for questioning but was released due to lack of evidence.

But now he was in Greenock. Saunders lodged with a woman named Catherine Wilson and gained a reputation as a respectable and quiet man. During the day he visited the coffee shop, observed the to-ing and fro-ing in the bank, and took copious notes. As soon as he had worked out the best method of attack he returned temporarily to London.

In November he was back in Greenock, once again lodging with Catherine Wilson, but this time he brought a friend with him, a small, apparently timid man with a bad squint, who called himself Mr Gray. The two rose early each morning, claiming they were going swimming in the sea, although why anybody would want to venture into the Firth of Clyde at six on a November morning nobody saw fit to ask. In reality Saunders and the mysterious Gray were probably measuring the locks of the bank. There were various methods of doing this, with a favourite one being to press wax inside the lock to make an impression of the mechanism. The people of Greenock were only mildly curious about their visitors; Englishmen were not unusual in a busy port and these two were presumed to be merchants.

On his earlier visits, Saunders had presumably discovered that the bank was at its most vulnerable between half past five and six in the morning. The bank messenger, Robert Love, slept in the bank every night, with his head pressed against the safe. However, every morning at half past five he left the bank unattended and walked to his home in Mansion House Lane, as well as checking that the morning mail gig to Largs left on schedule. He was not obsessive; merely keeping tabs on his second job as contractor for the mail. He would be back in the bank by six o'clock, so if Saunders and Gray hoped to rob the bank they had only a thirty-minute window in which to operate. They did their sums, decided that the time constraints were too narrow and continued to watch. Plan A was a non-runner; they needed a Plan B.

If the weekdays were out, then Saunders and Gray might try the Sabbath. That was Love's day off; the bank was unattended but as the door faced the coffee house, the attendant and customers would be able to see anything untoward.

It is possible that Saunders entered the bank on a number of occasions during the half-hour when Love was absent, making wax impressions of both the safe and the locked drawers inside the bank. He also almost certainly met his friend Mr Gray in a lodging house in Hamilton Street.

In early December 1827 Saunders and Gray left Greenock for a while, but returned again, once more staying with Catherine Wilson. She heard the rasp of a file on metal from their room from time to time, but assumed they were wrights or smiths busy at their work. On 7 January 1828 the two Londoners left their accommodation and moved from inn to inn; they also continued to watch the movements of the men who worked in the bank, and those of its regular customers. On Sunday, 2 March 1828, the two men spent most of the day in the coffee room, watching the bank door opposite to time Love's movements.

On the evening of Saturday, 8 March they were at the George Inn, and two other men joined them. The newcomers had hired separate gigs from the same stable, run by a Glasgow man named McFarlane, so possibly they did not want it known that they were together. They braved the wild weather as they took the road to Greenock, parked the gigs in streets on either side of the bank and left them there, as the good people of the town huddled in their houses to shelter from the storm.

Next morning Love followed his normal routine, leaving the bank unattended. Mr Gray walked in to the coffee shop and asked to view the papers; he claimed to be interested in a shipwreck in the Gulf of

Mexico. As he was keeping the people in the coffee shop occupied, Saunders walked straight through the hall and used the false key he had filed to open the front door of the bank. He was an expert thief, so the double lock was not a problem to him.

Saunders has left the building

Once inside he had no difficulty in opening both the unguarded safe and the money chest. He extracted all the notes and coins he could. He raked in over £28,000 of the Greenock Bank's own notes and over £4,000 of other banks' which, together with the gold and silver, amounted to an astounding £34,116, eight shillings and sixpence. Before he left, Saunders thrust a ring into the lock of the safe, so that the banker would have considerable difficulty in opening it on the Monday morning. With the doors all neatly locked behind him, Saunders left the building.

Stuffing the money into two carpet bags, Saunders hid them under his greatcoat and left the bank. He gave a signal to Gray and immediately stalked to one of the gigs, where the driver waited patiently. Gray made his excuses and also fled the Assembly Building. He ran to the second gig, whose driver whipped up and rolled out of Greenock at great speed.

The four men and two gigs raced in different directions, but sharp-eyed men at Govan noticed Saunders' smart black gig with yellow spars racing through the village. Saunders hired another gig from John McIntyre of Gorbals and drove to Hamilton, carrying two heavy cases. From Hamilton, he and Gray drove another hired gig to Crawford near Lanark and then to Carlisle and Preston. They arrived in Liverpool on the evening of 10 March, from where they booked two outside seats on the London mail coach.

In the meantime, Saunders' silent and nameless partners reached Edinburgh, where they visited four different banks to cash the notes for coin. The tellers at the Royal Bank, William Forbes' Bank and the British Linen Bank were very helpful and happily handed over £4,800, but the Bank of Scotland's tellers proved stubborn and refused to cooperate. The robbers called it a day, hired another post-chaise and left Scotland for the south with their spoil.

The robbery was not discovered until Love and two bank officials, McLeod and Alexander Thomson, arrived for work on the Monday morning. As he did every working day, Thomson handed the keys to Love and asked him to open the outer doors of the safe. There was no problem with the first but the second door seemed jammed. Saunders' ring had done its work. The lid of the money chest had been left open and the interior was bare. At first Thomson blamed Love, saying he had not locked the chest, which was an accusation Love hotly denied. When Thomson found a discarded skeleton key, he realised that professionals had been involved, and that was confirmed when he found the ring Saunders had placed inside the door lock.

Inquiries begin

The long round of inquiries began. Bank officials and the police found out that three suspicious men had been seen near the Exchange Buildings early on the Sunday morning and one had been in the coffee room around eight. The thief had obviously left the skeleton key behind, but the bank needed to call a locksmith to open the jammed door. Once the bank authorities discovered the extent of the robbery, they offered a reward of 200 guineas. News of the robbery was spread around the country and the banks in Edinburgh admitted that a 'little ruddy faced man with an English accent' had exchanged notes there. The police worked out that four men were involved, and learned that they had stayed in Glasgow; two in Blythe's Court and the other pair in Whitelaw's Inn in the Gallowgate, from where they travelled to Airdrie and had then taken a chaise to Edinburgh.

The descriptions continued: the man with a squint was tall and thin and another was dark-complexioned and had the marks of smallpox. The name Henry had been heard. Some of the information was conflicting: the police were told that two men had left for the south on Monday evening, and one on the Tuesday morning. Armed with these new details, the bank circulated advertisements in the local and national press. They upped their original reward to £100 for the apprehension of the thief and a whopping £600 for the recovery of the money; they spread the descriptions of the men being sought.

According to the advertisements, one was stout (meaning burly) with a sallow complexion marred with the pits of smallpox. He had an English accent and large dark eyes, but his curly hair was reckoned to be a wig – that might have been Saunders. The second man was tall and thin, with a squint in his left eye – probably Mr Gray – while the third and fourth were both described as being around five foot seven, wearing dark-coloured clothes and having 'a shabby-genteel appearance.' The advertisements also mentioned a fifth man of 'florid complexion' who also spoke with an English accent. He was stout and had his hat rammed down on his head.

The bank sent one of their officials after the men who had exchanged the money in Edinburgh. He traced them from Edinburgh to Haddington, Dunbar and Berwick and through England as far as Doncaster, but there the trail died. The men had dismissed their post-chaise driver and had vanished. The police suspected that they had left their own coach or gig in Doncaster and had re-claimed it for the journey south.

The nameless gentleman sent by the bank continued on to London and immediately approached the chief magistrate at Bow Street for help. His magistrate's name was Sir Richard Birnie and he still retained the Banff accent he had carried south with him from Scotland. The bank official also informed the authorities at the Bank of England. Birnie sent two of the famous Bow Street Runners, Bishop and George Leadbetter, to scour London for the robbers.

Contacting the robbers

In the middle of May, a constable named Waddington arrested Saunders in London and locked him up securely in St Martin's Watch-house. At this point the case took a number of twists and turns. A number of the bank owners and managers held a meeting and apparently decided not to pursue the matter any further. They claimed that they had already lost too much money to risk legal expenses in prosecuting a man who may not be the guilty party. However, the apparently tranquil acceptance of loss hid some frantic behind-the-scenes moves, as officials from the bank somehow contacted a lawyer who represented the thieves.

By the middle of June, about half the money was recovered. The method adopted for handing the notes back was simple. The bank officials and the thieves' lawyer agreed a spot to hand over the cash, then the official rolled up in a hackney coach. A porter approached the coach and handed over a box with £20,000 in it. In return the bank dropped all actions against the thieves; presumably that was the real reason why Saunders was allowed to walk free.

Whatever the bank had decided, the Lord Advocate did not agree and he pursued Saunders with every legal means at his disposal. Not aware that the most senior legal figure in Scotland was on his trail, Saunders continued as if he was as innocent as a new-born baby. Toward the end of June he caught a stagecoach from Paddington to London. While he was en route, he saw a couple of police officers standing by the road and cheekily asked the driver to stop. He took the officers to an inn and was happily taunting them with his freedom over a bottle of wine when one of the officers, Constable William Edwards, announced that he was back under arrest. There is no record of Saunders' response but presumably he was not impressed. Before the day was done, Saunders was securely handcuffed to an officer and on the coach to Glasgow.

The fashionable criminal

That autumn, crowds gathered to see this minor criminal celebrity when he appeared before Lord Meadowbank in the Glasgow Circuit Court. The newspapers described him as a handsome man of about five foot ten, slightly balding and in his late thirties. Fashionably and smartly dressed in a brown surtout with a black waistcoat and trousers, Saunders looked very much at ease as he looked over the sea of Glaswegian faces.

Although the prosecution had summoned a large number of witnesses, very few actually appeared in court, which probably weakened the case. The prosecution tried their best but the evidence was contradictory; when they stood in the dock, many of the witnesses decided that they could not positively identify Saunders. At the end of the trial, the jury found Saunders not proven. He walked free, as dapper and fresh as ever.

There were rumours that Saunders spent £700 on his defence, which was a huge amount of money. His defence witnesses were well chosen and his lawyer had brought them up especially from London for the occasion. Some people murmured darkly about London thieves being able to buy their way to freedom and there were tales about bribed witnesses.

In August some of the missing Greenock bank notes turned up in London. Richard Birnie informed the directors of the bank and Mr Alexander travelled down to London. He found out that the notes had been found at the looking-glass factory of a man named Parkinson, hired some Runners and raided the Soho address. Alexander and the Runners arrested Parkinson and Ann, his wife, bundled them inside a closed coach and drove them to Bow Street. When Parkinson was asked from where he had obtained a Greenock pound note, he said that a few weeks previously a Scotsman named Grant had bought a number of mirrors and paid with the Greenock notes. Both Parkinsons were charged with using stolen notes.

Repercussions from the robbery continued as the police refused to halt their investigations. They pursued another Londoner named William Wyse, a notorious character who constantly balanced on the precarious tightrope between wealth and the gallows. He was suspected of being the man who exchanged the stolen Greenock bank notes in Edinburgh. Wyse knew the Old Bailey well, having been previously convicted of receiving stolen banknotes, but that time he escaped on a technicality. The police had him in their sights and a warrant was issued for his arrest, but once again he seems to have escaped, as his name does not appear in any trial in Scotland.

Henry Saunders seemed to like Scotland for in December that year he was spotted in Perth, along with a band of known London robbers. With a reputation such as his, the banks all across Scotland were warned to be on their guard but there was no final showdown, no spectacular theft and no arrest. With that chance sighting, his career in Scotland faded away and he was lost to history. Nobody was ever brought to justice for the robbery of the Greenock Bank.

The murder of William Begbie

Edinburgh's Old Town was just made for crime. It centres around the long spine of the Royal Mile that descends from the castle to Holyrood Palace, and extends on either side in a maze of buildings separated by tiny alleys knows as closes and wynds. On a winter day the height of the tenements can block out the sun, while in the dark of an evening or the shrouding black of night, every sinister sound could presage a predatory assailant.

By the nineteenth century the area was in the throes of degeneration, as the elite slowly drained from the Old Town to the New. In 1806 this process had started but the Old Town still had places of major importance. One such was the headquarters of the British Linen Company Bank in Tweeddale Court, just above the Canongate.

In the late afternoon of 13 November 1806 William Begbie, a messenger of the British Linen Company, was carrying over £4,000 worth of bank notes from the Leith branch of the British Linen Company to Tweeddale Court. Begbie was married with four children; he was a steady, responsible man. He was also fairly tall and he carried the money in a yellow bag, which made him a distinctive figure as he walked up the quiet loneliness of Leith Walk.

Dogged by Mackoull

A score or so of yards behind him, another man followed Begbie, jinking from side to side, dodging from shadow to shadow and occasionally crossing the road in case Begbie should turn around and see him. In the parlance of the time, he was 'dogging' the messenger. Nobody has ever positively ascertained the identity of the dogger, but the evidence of the day suggests it was a slippery Londoner named James Mackoull. He was a skilled pickpocket and thief, well known to the authorities and often hunted, but he was adept at avoiding conviction.

In the early months of 1806 Mackoull was living in New Street, off the Canongate, but he was more often found in the Ship Tavern in Leith. In common with many criminals of the era, Mackoull travelled under a number of aliases, including James Moffat. While in the Ship he pretended to be a German merchant forced out of Hamburg by Bonaparte's invasion. It did not take the people of Leith long to break his cover: he spoke little German and lacked the knowledge of a merchant. Mackoull seemed to laugh off the discovery of his lie and continued the routine he had adopted.

When Mackoull was not planning or carrying out robberies, he took regular walks down by the policies of Bellevue between Edinburgh and the coast. At that time the city had not expanded so far and this northern area was semi-rural, with fields and orchards separated by stone walls. Mackoull made his money in Leith by gambling with his colleagues and possibly by picking the odd pocket or two. On that November afternoon he was smartly dressed in a long black coat that he pulled tightly around him to keep out the wicked Edinburgh wind.

It is not known whether Begbie realised he was being followed, but if so he made no move to avoid his dogger. He took the most direct route home, up Leith Walk and Leith Street, across Princes Street, past the noisy Theatre Royal and Shakespeare Square and up the North Bridge with the great dark below sucking coldly at him. He entered the Royal Mile and into the fifteen-yard-long Tweeddale Court, and there, in the noisome dim of the late afternoon, he was stabbed. Presumably the man who was following him was the murderer.

Murder

There was no witness to the stabbing, but only a few moments later, a passing seaman saw a man in a long cloak running out of the close, and some children saw a man flee down Leith Wynd. Naturally nobody thought anything of it until a young girl found Begbie's body at around five in the evening. There was a knife sticking in his heart, with the hilt wrapped in a wad of blood-stained paper. The paper ensured that Begbie's blood did not spatter onto the murderer's clothes

Murders were not unknown in Edinburgh, but they were not common. Inquiries began immediately. The Edinburgh authorities searched the houses of ill repute for the known thieves and any other suspects, while mounted men were sent to patrol the roads around the city for anybody who even looked suspicious. The bank offered a reward of 500 guineas for any information leading to the capture of the murderer or the recovery of the stolen money. A handbill appeared on the walls of the capital:

Hue and Cry
ATROCIOUS MURDER AND ROBBERY
Reward of
FIVE HUNDRED GUINEAS

At five o clock this evening William Begbie, Porter to the British Linen Company at Leith, was Stabbed and Murdered in Tweeddale's Close, leading to the British Linen Company's Office in Edinburgh, and Robbed of a Sealed Parcel in a Yellow Canvas Bag containing the following particulars, viz –

£1300 of Sir William Forbes & Co notes in notes of £20 each

£1000 in notes of Leith Banking Company, of £20 each

£1400 in notes of different Banks, of £20, £10 and £5

240 Guinea Notes of different Banks

440 Twenty Shilling Notes of different Banks

As the weapon with which the Murder was committed was found upon the spot, it is requested that any person who may have recently sold a Common Bread Knife with a wooden handle, stained of a red colour, will immediately give intimation as undermentioned.

Whoever will, within three months from this date, give such information to the Managers of the British Linen Company of Edinburgh, the Sheriff of the county of Edinburgh or judge of Police, as shall be the means of discovering the person or persons who committed the foresaid Murder and Robbery, shall receive a reward of

FIVE HUNDRED GUINEAS

To be paid upon conviction of the offender or offenders and farther, in case any one of the associates shall make the discovery, his Majesty's pardon will also be applied for in his favour.

NB – it is intreated that Bankers, Merchants and others will take notice of all notes of the above descriptions which may happen to be presented to them, especially if by persons of suspicious appearance.

William Begbie was seen walking up Leith Walk between four and five o clock in company with a man – This person and any other that saw him will please to call as above and give information.

Edinburgh Nov 13 1806

Every exertion has been made and is still making, to discover the perpetrator of the above murder but hitherto without effect.

Although a number of people were arrested, there was not enough evidence to convict anybody. The authorities came to suspect Mackoull, but he was not immediately pursued. On the very day that Begbie's body was discovered, he left his lodgings in New Street and disappeared. Instead the authorities suspected a man named Robert Johnstone. A King's Messenger named George Williamson hunted him from town to town until March 1807, when he arrested him in Berwick-upon-Tweed. However, after Johnstone was closely questioned he was released. His alibi was sound.

Recovering the money

About the same time, Mackoull must have thought the dust had settled. He returned to Edinburgh and resumed his walks to Bellevue, but if he had hoped to profit from the robbery he was disappointed. He may have been in the area when some of the money stolen from Begbie was recovered in the Bellevue area. A tradesman was walking and saw an interesting packet stuffed into a boundary wall. He investigated and found that it was a large bundle of bank notes. There was £3,000 in the bundle, enough to make a man rich for life but in a show of incredible honesty, the finder handed it over to the sheriff's office. The bank rewarded the finder with £200, which was four years' wages for a skilled man and definitely not to be sneezed at. However, there was still a large amount of money left unaccounted for.

Mackoull may have known what had happened to it. He was a man who always had a story to hand. He claimed that when he had left Edinburgh he had travelled to Dublin, where he won £10,000 at the gambling table. Perhaps that is correct; more likely it was a complete fabrication. After the discovery of the Begbie loot, he left Edinburgh to live in Glasgow. Mackoull was never arrested for the Begbie murder but was tried and convicted for the later robbery of the Paisley Bank in Glasgow and sentenced to death. He died in jail after being reprieved from execution.

The murder of Begbie was never satisfactorily solved. Other high-profile cases of the period proved every bit as difficult to crack.

Robbing the Aberdeen bank

The Aberdeen bank robbery was another case that baffled the police of the day. It was a theft that should never have taken place, as the bank's precautions were extensive for the time. The Aberdeen Banking Company's banking house had two iron safes that were kept in a small passageway patrolled by a large dog. There were two tellers, each of whom had the keys to only one safe, and the keys were kept in separate locked desks. Whenever the bank was unoccupied, the safes were protected by a locked wooden screen which was on a powerful spring. The safe's doors could not be opened or the screen removed without triggering an alarm bell. The alarm was situated in the room where Alexander Morrice, the manager of the bank, slept, so even when he was not on duty at the bank, he would be immediately alerted if anybody was tampering with the safes.

Morrice was also the treasurer; he lived in the same building as the bank, in the apartments next door. As a further precaution, he employed two servant girls in the house, who had standing orders that they must never both be out of the house at the same time, so the bank building was never unoccupied: if the alarm sounded, there should have always been somebody to hear it.

Nevertheless, the thieves of the nineteenth century were very professional and studied the bank to ascertain any security weaknesses. They found inevitable flaws in the system and exploited them to the full.

On Sunday, 6 May 1838 a group of boys found a bunch of keys lying in the street, right beside a small bag with 'Aberdeen Bank' written on it. Being naturally curious, they picked up both and handed them to their father. The father sent keys and bag on to the police, but they merely treated the find as lost property, put them on a shelf and forgot all about the matter.

On Monday, 7 May the tellers returned to the Aberdeen Bank and discovered the place had been robbed.

Sunday robbery

The thief had known exactly what he was doing. He had entered the bank, broken open one of the teller's desks, taken out the key and opened the smaller of the two safes, to which that key belonged. He had touched nothing else in the building and left everything in the condition in which he had found it. He had even relocked the screen, so the alarm was silent when the treasurer returned from church. The thief had also carried the keys of the screen with him, so the teller had to break the lock to get into his own safe. As so often in the period, the thief had chosen a Sunday; Morrice would be at the church. That should have left two people in the building, but one of the two servants had also been at church, while the other, either by providence or calculation, had decided to go out that day. The dog was either drugged or befriended and all the contents of the safe – gold and bank notes, amounting to an estimated £16,200 – had vanished. The thief also stole a number of blank bank bills that Morrice had already carelessly signed.

Naturally suspicion fell on the servant girl who had disobeyed her instructions that the house should never be left unattended. When the police questioned her, she initially said that she fell asleep and heard nothing, but eventually she admitted that she had gone out between eleven in the morning and one in the afternoon, which pinpointed the exact time of the robbery. It is possible that she was asked, persuaded or bribed to leave the house, but the police did not charge her.

The police searched the bank and found a crowbar, skeleton keys and steel files lying around, but these had not been used. As the front door was bolted from inside and there was no sign of a forced entry, the police's initial impression was that the thief or thieves had hidden in the bank the previous evening and emerged as soon as it was safe. Their other theories were that they had entered the building by forcing the door of the manager's house, or that the servant had left a door open for them or even let them in.

The police asked the usual questions and came up with two suspects who had been seen in the area. One man was short and described as having 'much the appearance of a Jew'. He had dark hair and dark whiskers and wore a blue cap and a blue cloak with a velvet collar. The second man was only described as 'tall'. The police were aware that a notorious gang of London thieves had been infesting Glasgow. They had been so well watched that they achieved nothing in that city and the police believed they had become frustrated, had argued and split up, with two moving to Aberdeen for easier pickings.

The police and the bank officials thought that the robbers had caught the three o'clock mail coach for Perth and Edinburgh on the

Sunday, so two bank officers followed the same route on the Monday. There was speculation that the robbers had parcelled up the stolen money disguised as a packet of Finnan haddies – a specific type of fish delicacy – and sent them on to Glasgow. But speculation and theories do not solve crimes.

The bank issued advertisements giving the type and numbers of the stolen notes and altered their bank bills so the name 'Alexander Morrice' was no longer used, thus making the bills worthless. They also offered a reward of up to £500 for information leading to the arrest of the thieves.

The police were naturally suspicious of the known London thieves who had been in Glasgow and set their officers on an immediate search. They also recruited a Bow Street Runner named Henry Goddard, who would know the Londoners by name, face and practice. Goddard travelled up to Aberdeen to help. However, it was not until October that an officer, William Forrester, arrested a man named William Walsh, who was a well-known thief. Walsh was around thirty-eight, five foot seven in height and nondescript but appeared respectable, the sort of man who would not stand out in a crowd. Forrester had been in Liverpool on a completely different case and had seen Walsh get off the Birmingham to Liverpool train.

There was no real evidence, but Walsh was remanded in custody to allow the police to make further inquiries. A number of lodging-house keepers from the Aberdeen area claimed to recognise Walsh as having stayed with them early in the year but their statements were not enough to hold him. Walsh was released and the case was never satisfactorily solved.

Another case that attracted much attention centred on the Commercial Bank of Scotland in the 1850s. What could connect a case of fraud carried out by an ex-provost, and a nasty abortion and suicide? The answer is obvious: a young bank clerk named William Reid.

William Reid and the Falkirk bank case

William Reid was a respectable man from a good family. He lived with his widowed mother in Smallburn Cottage, by Polmont near Falkirk, but spent some time with his brother-in-law, the Provost of Falkirk. In the 1850s he came to public attention when he fell foul of the law.

There were a number of interesting factors in the case, including the high status of the main culprit in the fraud, and the position of William Reid. He had no need to work, as the death of his father had left him relatively wealthy, but either he chose, or his mother advised him, to accept a job as a teller in the Commercial Bank in Falkirk.

The trouble began when Jean Malcolm, wife of Donald, a hay dealer of Callander Road, Falkirk, paid £600 into the Falkirk branch of the Commercial Bank. She handed the money to William Reid, who passed it to Thomas Gentles, the accountant, but that was the last seen or heard of it. Reid had worked for the bank since 1842 and was thought of as a young man of impeachable character and honesty.

Reid and Gentles were accused of embezzling the money, with or without the aid of Henry Salmon, the agent or manager of the bank. An audit found an array of discrepancies, as monies amounting to nearly £3,000 paid over the counter had not reached the Malcolms' account. Other accounts had also been short-changed: Alexander Learmonth, a Falkirk flesher (butcher) was short of nearly £1,400 and Robert Robertson of Gourock was missing £680. Henry Salmon was also accused of tearing counterfoils of receipts from their books for all the named accounts. What was worse, Salmon had been seen as one of the pillars of Falkirk society. He had even been Provost, and was a Justice of the Peace; he seemed to have enough money in his position as bank agent to buy a small estate and he spoke of mining for minerals under his land. The police made inquiries and the story unfolded stage by stage.

Donald Malcolm had been a very prosperous businessman but he had become ill. His wife Jean had taken over the business and run it successfully for some years. As she was a personal friend of Salmon and trusted him implicitly, Jean Malcolm paid the company's £600 into her account in Salmon's office. She also asked Salmon to open an account in her name. Salmon obliged on that occasion. Other transactions were paid to Reid or Gentles so all three were involved.

Alexander Learmonth usually paid his money to Reid, but on one occasion when he paid it to Gentles, the accountant thought that the balance in the book did not tally with his records. Learmonth had known both Reid and Gentles for years and trusted both. Robert Robertson also paid his money to Salmon in person, but had less personal knowledge of the teller and accountant. Again all three were involved, but in Robertson's case, Salmon was the principal recipient of the money.

The day-to-day work of the branch was fairly routine, with the manager and both suspected members of the staff heavily involved. Salmon kept the keys for the bank safe, in which all the money was held. There was an office boy who got the keys from Salmon every morning and opened up the bank, before leaving the keys on Salmon's desk. Gentles used to remove the money from the safe, while Reid placed it in the cash drawers for the day's transactions, with all the notes securely held in a tin box. Reid took in each customer's money and passed it over to Gentles to put in the safe. Gentles marked the amount into two cash books, known as the scroll and clean cash book. He signed the books and Reid countersigned the customer's book with his initials.

Mackenzie's suspicions

When Reid eventually left the bank, a man named Mackenzie succeeded to his position. Mackenzie must have been a meticulous and confident man, for he not only found various discrepancies in the system, he also reported them. Mackenzie discovered that Salmon had been withdrawing money and not signing for it; he found that many sums of money had not been entered into the books, and that cheques issued in Salmon's name had been entered as bank notes. It was obvious that Gentles knew all about it. He would instruct Mackenzie: 'That does not go in the book.'

On one occasion Mackenzie retaliated by saying: 'There it is in the books and you may tell Salmon it won't come out again.'

After Mackenzie's report, the head office ordered an audit. Overall the teller and the accountant had helped Salmon embezzle thousands of pounds that belonged to various customers. The bank employees had embezzled a huge amount of Mrs Malcolm's monies simply by not entering the sums paid into the books. The same system had been employed for Learmonth, except when one deposit of £460 was entered, Salmon erased the initial figure '4' so the entry read '£60.' Other entries had been clumsily torn from the books. Surprisingly, neither Reid nor Gentles gained a penny from the embezzlements, but all the money went to Salmon, who worked for the bank from 1820 until May 1857.

In that time, Salmon embezzled an estimated and amazing £26,000. He had nurtured and trained Reid and Gentles in his own system when they were very young boys, so all they knew of banking came from him. They were brainwashed, but Gentles at least was very aware that he was breaking the law. At the time that Reid had aided Salmon in his large-scale thefts, he earned a mere £10 a year himself. When an inspector came to audit the branch, Gentles approached him and said quite openly: 'You will probably have to wind up this branch before you leave Falkirk.'

It was a strange succession of crimes that benefited only one man: Salmon. The other two took daily risks and broke the law on numerous occasions but did not gain anything for their actions. When he was found out, Salmon did not face the court but committed suicide, either through shame or to escape the public humiliation and a long spell in jail.

Reid and Gentles were charged with breach of trust and embezzlement. Both were found guilty by a majority but recommended to the mercy of the court. They were sentenced to eighteen months in Perth Penitentiary. When they heard where they were bound, both men were very dejected and close to tears. In December that year, Gentles was pardoned, and thanks to a large amount of public sympathy and a petition, Reid was also released shortly afterward. In view of later events, it may have been better for him had his sentence been longer.

Perhaps it was the spell in prison that affected Reid, or maybe he had always had a tendency to misfortune, but not long after his release he lurched into an even more serious sequence of events that was to cost two people their lives.

Train of disaster

Even after his twelve years or so working in the bank and his spell in Perth Prison, William Reid was still a young man, with a young man's natural interest in women, but either women of his own circle avoided him, or he wanted a simple sexual relationship with no complicated attachments. He took a fancy to twenty-one-year-old Margaret Taylor, his mother's domestic servant at her house, Small Burn Cottage in Polmont. It is not certain how Margaret reacted to her master's advances but nature took its near-inevitable course and the girl became pregnant. Unsure what to do, the couple decided on an abortion, which was illegal and highly dangerous.

They called on a young doctor named Thomas Girwood, who was known to perform such operations, and on the morning of Sunday, 5 September 1858 he used drugs and instruments on Margaret. However, Girwood failed to extract the foetus and Margaret weakened during the day. Reid asked a Dr Myrtle if he could come and look at Margaret, but did not mention the abortion.

At the same time as Taylor was suffering, her widowed mother, Janet Taylor, had a terrible nightmare that her daughter was in pain, and hurried to her home. When she entered, she found that her dream had been very accurate; her daughter was in bed, very pale, and there was a 'bad smell' in the room. Dr Myrtle said 'your daughter has suffered much', but at that point he was still ignorant of the truth of events.

Margaret asked her mother to come closer and whispered to her that she had miscarried. Naturally shocked, Janet asked: 'Who is it to?'

'To the master: Mr Reid,' Margaret said.

'Oh Maggie, Maggie: I thought I had taught you better things,' Janet replied.

'Oh Mother, Mother, if you but knew how I've been tried by him.'

Margaret was in a lot of pain and asked her mother how long it would be until she was better. Janet said it should not be long as she was in such great pain. After one of the bouts Margaret confessed that there had been an abortion.

'What would he think if he saw what I was suffering?' Margaret said, and then added. 'He took an instrument and opened the neck of the womb.' Then she mentioned Dr Girwood.

When the pain grew worse, Janet begged Dr Myrtle to return. He examined her and removed the foetus.

'I am fast sinking, Mother,' Margaret said.

'Oh yes, we'll have to part, Maggie,' her mother said. There are no words to describe what she must have been feeling at that moment.

Dr Myrtle left to find old Dr James Girwood, the father of the man who performed the failed operation, but Margaret died, on 6 September 1858, before James Girwood arrived. Janet Taylor was naturally distraught.

Long before Margaret had died, Reid had fled to his mother's house, changed his clothes and caught the 9.30 train to Glasgow, where he booked a room in the North British Imperial Hotel. Rather than use his own name, he called himself Hardy, which was his mother's maiden name. He may have intended fleeing to Liverpool, where he had an uncle, or even to America, but he certainly had no intention of staying to help the young woman he had made pregnant and had left in such pain.

Once the police realised how Margaret had died, and that Reid had fled, Superintendent William Shaw and Sergeant Crawford left Falkirk for Polmont. They called at Small Burn Cottage, learned that Reid had run to Glasgow and rather than wait for the next passenger train, they flagged down a goods train and travelled at speed but in less comfort across country.

When they reached Glasgow, Crawford remained to scour the city while Shaw caught the next train south in case Reid had continued his journey. He checked with every station master between Glasgow and Carlisle, and inquired to see if Reid had left the train, but when he found no trace he retraced his steps.

By fate or skill, Crawford and Shaw met Reid in the streets of Glasgow and immediately arrested him. Reid was locked in Stirling jail until his trial. In the meantime, as soon as the younger Dr Girwood realised he had killed the girl, he staggered into McNaughton's pub in Falkirk's High Street. He asked for paper and ink and wrote a letter, which he asked not to be sent until eleven the next morning. As he sat in the pub he ordered four ounces of laudanum from a local chemist and hired a coach.

McNaughton accompanied Girwood toward Linlithgow, but on the journey Girwood apparently fell asleep. When McNaughton failed to wake him, he realised something was wrong, and dashed to fetch his father, Dr James Girwood. But it was too late. Girwood had committed suicide with the laudanum. He had reason to be ashamed; a post-mortem found that Margaret had died from internal injuries caused by the abortion.

Reid appeared before the High Court on 10 November charged with murdering Margaret Taylor by 'procuring her, being pregnant, to abort'. Reid pleaded not guilty and the jury agreed, as far as the charge of murder was concerned. However, he was found guilty of procuring abortion and sentenced to seven years' penal servitude.

There were worse criminal acts than robbing a bank, and bankers could be predators as well as victims.

5

Pirates of the Hebrides

As so often in the Hebrides, there was a wild wind blowing on Monday, 23 August 1821. Kenneth McIver, the sixty-two-year-old tacksman of Tolstay Farm near the Butt of Lewis, was working his land when he saw the men hurrying toward him. He stopped and came to meet them.

The men were his tenants and they had an interesting story to tell. The previous day they had been walking near the coast when they saw a disabled vessel about a mile offshore. They launched a small fishing boat and approached to see if they could help, but saw nobody on board. The vessel was a schooner; she was on her beam ends, copper-bottomed and waterlogged, with her topmasts gone. The Lewismen fastened their boat on to her, hoping they could tow her to a sheltered bay, where she might be salvaged and searched for possible survivors.

Unfortunately, a sudden squall rose and parted the lines. The wind drove the wreck toward Tolstay Head, where she ran aground in a small cove. On the Monday morning the Lewismen had gone on board but the schooner was empty of life. Her name was *Jane*, she was of around 100 tons, and when she beached, much of her cargo had spilled out into the surrounding sea.

There were hogsheads of oil, bundles of paper, boxes of beeswax and other commodities bobbing in the choppy waters of the Minch. As soon as the Lewismen had ascertained there was nothing they could do to help, they told Kenneth McIver, who contacted Roderick McIver, the Surveyor of Customs. Roderick McIver immediately sent four of his men in the customs cutter to investigate the mysterious shipwreck.

Shipwreck

On the Tuesday Roderick McIver learned much more of the story of the schooner *Jane*. The cutter had been searching the Minch for whisky smugglers and had sighted a large open boat beached in a quiet part of the Lewis coast. The customs men had landed and asked for details. They found an assorted crew under the command of a man who called himself George Sadwell. Naturally suspicious of an open boat with no apparent reason for being in these waters, the customs men asked who they were and where they were bound. At first the men said they were outward bound from Boston, but then the youngest of them, a Maltese ship's boy, followed McIver through a howling torrent of rain and asked for a private meeting. The boy had seemed nervous, almost afraid, so McIver took him to a quiet spot and asked what the matter was. He was astonished when the boy told him that some of the crew had murdered the ship's master and a sailor named Paterson. The boy wanted to turn King's evidence and confess exactly what had happened.

Mutiny on *Jane*

McIver asked for details and gradually unravelled the whole story. The men were all from the schooner *Jane*, owned by a Jewish man named

Leone. They were outward bound from Gibraltar to Salvador, in what was then known as the Brazils, with a mixed cargo of olives, sweet oil and beeswax. More importantly, *Jane* also carried about 38,100 Spanish dollars, or pieces of eight. The exact value in Sterling of these eight barrels of silver is problematical, but perhaps £10,000. The schooner had taken on two new men at Gibraltar, a cook and a mate. As was normal in the period, there were some arms on board in the shape of six muskets, usually kept to ward off pirates or to control a mutinous crew. Unfortunately, they would be put to other uses.

Jane left Gibraltar on 19 May 1821, with Thomas Johnston as master, a man from Shields named Peter Heaman as mate and a crew of three Britons and an Italian, plus the Maltese ship's boy, Andrew Camelier. Johnston was liked and respected as a shipmaster; he rarely touched alcohol and nobody had ever seen him drunk, which was something that could not be said for every British shipmaster.

At first the voyage went well; the weather was fine, so the crew slept on deck, with only the captain spending his time off watch in the cabin below. However, sailing with a small crew and thousands of pounds' worth of silver on board proved fatal. Two of the crew – Francois Gautiez, the French cook, and Peter Heaman, the mate – decided that they had a hankering for the pieces of eight. They plotted mutiny. Apart from the captain, Heaman was the only man on board who could navigate; he was the leading light of the mutiny. In such a compact craft it was impossible to keep a secret, so the other members of the crew, Strachan, Paterson and Smith, also heard of the plan but wanted no part in it. They were informed that they had no need to take part in the mutiny, but if they kept quiet and did not interfere they would be included when the silver was divided up.

On a calm 7 June, at six degrees north and seventeen days out into the Atlantic, the two mutineers acted. Captain Johnston had been on watch that night, with nineteen-year-old Peter Smith from

Arbroath and the Italian crewman, Johanna Dura. Johnston retired to bed in his cabin about midnight, as Heaman, James Paterson and Gautiez took the watch. The pirates did not waste time. Heaman and Gautiez both grabbed muskets and set to work. Heaman fired a shot into the captain's cabin, and when Paterson tried to interfere, Heaman attacked him.

'Murder!' Paterson yelled, 'Murder! God save my soul, for I am murdered now!'

That was a prophetic statement, as Heaman battered him to death with the butt end of the musket. Paterson fell headlong beside the main hatch, just as the captain emerged from his cabin.

'What is this?' Captain Johnston asked, staring at the fallen man and holding his forehead. Blood oozed from between his fingers. 'What is this?'

Without uttering a word, Gautiez grabbed Johnston and thumped him with his musket. The Captain yelled and fell, so Gautiez hit him again, and continued to hit him as Johnston writhed and moaned on the deck. Heaman joined in with his musket until Johnston lay a twitching and bloody heap.

Three crewmen – nineteen-year-old David Strachan, Peter Smith and twenty-five-year-old Johanna Dura – came up from the forecastle to see what was happening, but Heaman lifted an axe and met them at the head of the companionway. Dura ran on deck but then Heaman stepped forward. 'Don't come up,' he warned, brandishing the axe. 'Don't come up!' As the men retreated, Heaman slammed shut the hatch cover to secure them below deck. With the loyal hands out of the way, the pirates fastened a heavy chunk of iron to Paterson's coat and ordered the ship's boy to help throw the bodies overboard.

'Don't kill me,' Camelier pleaded, 'and I'll do it.'

They found some rocks from the ballast, placed them inside the captain's shirt and casually tossed the still moaning man overboard. Johnston sank at once, with only a few bubbles rising from the depths of the Atlantic to mark his passage. Gautiez appropriated Johnston's watch, while Heaman grabbed the chain for himself.

Early next morning, the mutineers nailed shut the hatch cover to keep Smith and Strachan below. Heaman descended to the aft cabin and started a fire in a copper kettle. He bored holes in the bulkhead so the smoke would billow into the forecastle. Next he ordered Camelier to make a paste with flour and water and seal all the cracks in the hatchway and deck above the forecastle so the smoke could not escape. Smith and Strachan were to be slowly suffocated.

The two men were kept prisoner in their smoky hell for thirty-six hours, no doubt wondering what was happening up on deck. After that time Heaman casually wondered if they were dead yet. Camelier said that he did not know.

Heaman ordered the hatchway opened and the fresh air wafted down, reviving the two trapped men. They looked up, disconsolate, scared but alive. Heaman looked down at them and ordered the hatch cover replaced and once more nailed secure. It was on the third day, and only after Dura pleaded for them to be spared, that Heaman finally released Smith and Strachan.

Scared, with their faces black with smoke, weak with hunger and thirst, both teenagers staggered up, but as soon as they arrived on deck, Gautiez tied them to the rail and told them they would be thrown overboard. They pleaded for their lives, reminding the pirates that they had known about the mutiny but had told no tales. Heaman eventually and grudgingly released both men. But there was a condition: Strachan and Smith had to promise to swear on the Bible that they would not tell anybody what had happened. Not surprisingly, they both did as they were asked. They stood at the binnacle, held the Bible and repeated: 'May God Almighty never save my soul if I ever reveal what has passed.'

With that detail out of the way, Camelier was ordered to wash the blood from the captain's cabin and the deck. As the Maltese boy scrubbed busily, Gautiez had the wheel and Heaman emptied the casks of pieces of eight. A number of little bags were sewn up for the coins.

There were promotions on board as Heaman made himself master and Gautiez the cook was made up to mate. But now he had taken command of the ship, Captain Heaman was undecided what to do next. For a few days they steered an erratic course as they debated where they should go. They finally decided to sail to the island of Lewis in Scotland. They sailed past Ulster to the island of Barra, where Gautiez donned Johnston's best green coat, ventured ashore and bought an open boat from Hugh MacNeill for £15. Renaming himself Captain Rodger, Heaman claimed he was outward bound from New York to Archangel.

They sailed *Jane* northward from Barra, up the Little Minch and into the Minch itself. On the evening of Saturday, 21 August 1821 they were not far to the east of Stornoway when they saw a cutter cruising nearby and Heaman immediately altered their plans. The pirates counted their loot and then loaded it into the open boat and parcelled it out with a tin pot – hardly the most romantic image of successful pirates. Each man gained around 6,300 pieces of eight: an astonishing sum of money. Gautiez ordered the ship's boy to scuttle the schooner so she would sink. Accordingly, Camelier took a crowbar and knocked holes in the hull of *Jane*; then they abandoned her in the Minch and took to the boat.

With *Jane* rolling and hopefully sinking in the choppy seas, Heaman steered the boat for the mainland, but the weather in the Minch is fickle at best; a sudden squall drove them westward toward Lewis. They beached in a deserted cove at Swordale, dragged the boat above the crashing surf and buried some thousands of pieces of eight under the Hebridean sand. What silver remained, the pirates slipped into the canvas bags they had made and divided amongst themselves. They hid the money in their clothing and wondered what to do for the best. It was obvious that they would be very conspicuous in Lewis, so they hoped to repair the boat and try again for the mainland.

Hanging at Leith

As soon as McIver heard Camelier's story, he called upon a number of the Lewismen to help secure the mutineers. He ordered his men to tie the crew up if they should try and escape. McIver also had the crew search for the pieces of eight and dig up those that had been buried. When the revenue cutter *Prince of Wales* next called at Stornoway, the pirates were put on board and transferred to Leith and then Calton Jail to await trial.

In November 1821 Peter Heaman and Francois Gautiez appeared before Sir John Connell, Knight Judge Admiral of Scotland, at the High Court in Edinburgh, charged with piracy and murder. Heaman claimed that it had been Captain Johnston who had shot Paterson, and then the rest of the crew had killed the captain in self-defence. Heaman said he did not know who had proposed burying the silver but all the crew had agreed to participate.

The jury tossed aside this weak story. They found Heaman and Gautiez guilty and Sir John Connell sentenced them to be taken back to jail and fed on bread and water until 9 January 1822, when they were to be hanged on Leith Sands. On that day an escort of dragoon guards arrived for them. They were the central attraction in a convoy that rolled down to the foot of Constitution Street, with magistrates in padded carriages there to watch the show. The pirates were hanged below the high-water mark, with the bells of South Leith Church clanging slowly, once a minute, and 40,000 to 50,000 people watching. That was the last execution for piracy in Scotland. The bodies of Heaman and Gautiez were coffined and, still with the dragoons as escort, taken back to Edinburgh and handed over to Dr Murray to be dissected.

There is a small postscript to this hanging. Heaman's widow had come from Shields to Edinburgh for the trial and was in terrible distress after her husband was hanged. The jury had a collection and raised three guineas to help her and her four children. This small act of compassion for the widow of an executed pirate shows the kindly heart that beat beneath the rough Scottish exterior.

6

Cotton Combinations

In the wake of the defeat of Napoleon Bonaparte in 1815, Scotland seethed with discontent. Peace brought unemployment and a swarm of paid-off men with no trade other than soldiering; the Clearances blighted the Highlands, while Establishment fears of a French-style revolution meant that repressive laws clamped down on town and country alike. Oppressed by the very people so many thousand Scots had bled and died for during twenty-two years of near-incessant wars with France, many working men became bitter and sought something more from life than never-ending poverty, without a voice or an opportunity to alter a flawed system.

Combinations to combat the masters

One method of resisting was to form combinations, an early name for trades union, where men who worked in the same industry united or combined together to resist wage cuts or any other form of repressive practice. However, sometimes the combinations replaced repression with other forms of tyranny. Based in west central Scotland, with

Paisley and Glasgow as the nerve centres, the cotton spinners' combinations of the 1820s and '30s were some of the most militant of them all, stretching well beyond their original idea of protecting wages and jobs, and entering the murky world of oppression, threats and murder.

At the end of the eighteenth century, thousands of Glasgow weavers responded to low wages and high food prices by staging a city-wide strike, and as the nineteenth century dawned, the mill owners and cotton masters were wary of a new era of combination among the cotton spinners. Paper workers, weavers and calico printers also showed more militant tendencies as their living standards were eroded. In 1812, when the employers tried to lower weavers' wages, the weavers appealed to the Justices of the Peace for help, quoting a law of 1661 that said Justices of the Peace could legally set wages and hours. The weavers won their case but the employers carried on in their own sweet way and so 40,000 weavers across Scotland went on strike. The authorities arrested the leaders of the strike and parliament hurriedly appealed the inconvenient JP Law.

Conditions continued to deteriorate for working people and they gathered in meetings to voice their protest. But they did more than talk: merchants' houses and mills were attacked and there was open talk of rebellion. Working men, as well as some of the middle orders, demanded the end of the Corn Laws, which kept bread prices artificially high, while protest groups campaigned for other radical improvements, including universal suffrage. The authorities responded with dragoons and special constables, not always with success. One outcome was the 1820 rising.

After the massacre at St Peter's Field in Manchester in England, the radicals became more militant and began drilling men with the prospect of an armed uprising. Posters proclaimed that a 'Scottish Provisional Government' had been created and what was arguably the world's first general strike spread across Scotland in April 1820. That same year, possibly inspired by *agents provocateurs* planted by the government, around 150 armed men marched across the Lowlands, to be scattered by cavalry at Bonnymuir, near Falkirk. The cavalry took a number of prisoners; three were hanged and one was decapitated after death.

However, the struggle continued, with tailors, colliers, weavers and building workers all trying to flex their muscle. Combinations were formed and strikes called, but always the government held the whip hand and smashed the strikes, so living conditions deteriorated and men became desperate.

Combinations and nobs

Despite the law, by 1816 the Glasgow Cotton Spinners' Union was well established and more militant than the employers liked. It was highly organised. If the masters (employers) tried to lower average wages by bringing in unskilled, non-combination labour, known as 'nobs', the combination would strongly advise the incomers to leave by handing them a card depicting a coffin with their name on it. In 1824 the Anti-Combination Acts were repealed, but the employers and authority in general, as well as the press, were very much against them.

There were violent clashes between combination men and the despised nobs, the combination men believing the authorities sided with the nobs. They may have had good reason for their beliefs; they spoke of a nob named McDade who had killed a combination man but whom the police released without charge. They men muttered about the unfairness of the courts and watched the actions of the masters with jaundiced eyes.

Around 1818 a master named Dunlop undercut the skilled spinners when he recruited cheap female labour for his factory at Broomward in Glasgow. This new attack on the working conditions of the skilled male spinners incensed the more militant of the combination. There were stories that some of the combination men had resorted to what they termed 'colliery' – they had tried to set the factory at Broomward on fire. It was an old method but in this instance it failed. There were other methods.

There were persistent rumours that combination men had broken into a house in Pollock's Land in Calton and murdered a woman named Macpherson. It had been a foolish murder, for the men were hunting for her daughter, who worked in Dunlop's mill. Again according to rumour, the combination paid for the murderers, Barney McKenay and Paton Dunlop, to be sent to America.

There were many other rumours and are sufficient facts to show that west central Scotland was in a ferment as the men of the combination attempted to hold on to their position while the masters used the forces of authority to stay in power. Rumours and police informants mentioned that men named Andrew Dunagh, Owen O'Callaghan and Stephen Campbell were paid to shoot a nob named McQuarrie. The attempt on McQuarrie's life on the Serpentine Walk on Glasgow Green but although a reward of £300 was offered the culprit was never arrested. McQuarrie recovered from his wounds, but not only nobs were at risk.

Shooting at a master

Although the masters could raise and lower wages, and hire and fire staff, they were not immune to retaliation. At about 10 p.m. on 16 December 1821, a Paisley manufacturer named William Orr was in his house when two men came to his door. As soon as Orr walked to the entrance somebody fired two shots at him and fled into the night. Both shots missed and the police dug the spent pistol balls from the wall where they had lodged, and hunted for suspects.

Four men were accused of the crime: Henry McConnell, who had once been employed in Orr's mill the infamous Owen O'Callaghan, and Hugh Lafferty and Malcolm Cameron. All four were seen running away from Orr's house, and when Callaghan was arrested he had a pistol in his possession, the calibre of which matched the bullets fired at Orr. John O'Donnell, who kept a public house in Paisley, had seen the four men together and had seen McConnell loading a pistol that same night. The judge and jury agreed that the four were guilty and they were sent to sunny Australia for their sins.

War on the streets of Glasgow

The collieries, intimidation and shootings continued. In 1825, Dunlop again caused trouble when he lowered wages. The combination called a strike. Dunlop brought in nob labour and the bitterness increased. On 30 March 1825, John Graham, a cotton spinner and a nob, left Dunlop's mill with a tight group including William Bell, John Campbell and some others. They walked up Clyde Street on their way home. All the men were a bit apprehensive, as there was a huge crowd of striking spinners blocking their path, shouting insults, yelling 'Nobs!' and chanting obscene and ugly songs.

One of the combination men slipped out of the crowd and stood slightly apart from the others. Although there was neither moonlight nor street lamps, it was not dark enough for the man to be hidden and Bell noticed him pull out a pistol, aim at Graham and fire. The report was distinct and the cloud of greasy white smoke hung in the air for a while, a screen behind which the shooter disappeared back into the crowd. That shot missed, but a second man named John Kean, stepped closer to Graham and shot him in the back. Graham fell, and the crowd gasped and then clustered around his body.

Bell watched as Kean withdrew a quick two paces, turned and ran along Clyde Street. Obviously a brave man, Bell pursued and caught him twenty yards down the road. Kean wheeled round and swung his pistol, catching Bell on the shoulder with the heavy steel barrel. Bell flinched but continued forward, knocking the pistol onto the ground; he grappled with Kean, who shouted threats, fought back violently and would probably have escaped if two men, including a nob named James Fraser, had not arrived to help.

After a few moments, Constables Fraser and Murray came along, but even with the five of them, Kean was a handful. The situation worsened when a man named McKell led some of the combination strikers in an attempt to free Kean. The police and nobs managed to wrestle Kean inside the yard of Dunlop's factory and banged the iron gate shut. McKell shook an angry fist in the face of James Fraser and threatened he would 'mind them afterwards'.

When the police questioned Graham, he said he had seen a man called George McDonald a few seconds after the shooting and thought he may have been one of the men who shot at him. At the Glasgow Circuit Court in April 1825, Kean was found guilty of attempted murder and McKell guilty of obstructing the police. Kean was sentenced to be whipped publicly in front of the jail and then transported for life, while McKell and another man named Lafferty were jailed for eighteen months with hard labour. John Kean left for Australia on *Marquis of Huntley* on 10 May 1826.

On a brighter note, after McKell was convicted the combination paid twelve shillings a week to his wife for the next eighteen months, and while Lafferty was in jail the combination supported his wife. When he was released, the combination paid for Lafferty's passage to the United States.

Judicial whippings were public events and not pleasant to watch. When a combination man named Archibald McNicoll was whipped through Johnstone for attempting to murder a nob named James Henderson, there were fears of a rescue attempt. McNicoll was tied to the back of the cart and trundled through the town, and to ensure the event was uninterrupted, there was an escort of two troops of dragoons, plus a body of infantry. McNicoll was given twenty lashes at School

Green, near where he tried to murder Henderson; twenty more at the Cross, the same at one end of the Square and a final fifteen at the opposite end of the Square. McNicoll took all seventy-five in silence, despite the bloody mess of his back. After his three-hour ordeal he was taken back to Paisley jail to await transport to Australia for his fourteen-year sentence.

There were many other incidents, some doubtless distorted by propaganda on one side or the other. There was the case of a combination man named Walker who shot and wounded a nob named William Brown; he pleaded guilty and was transported. There was an attack on a man named Carnie, who lost an eye when acid was thrown in his face in 1822. The police arrested a man named Peter Mellon for that nasty piece of work, but a jury found him not guilty and he walked free.

There were secret passwords, there was intimidation and there was money collected to pay for a passage to America for men who had fallen foul of the law. The stories were contradictory but if even half were true, the cotton spinners' combination was run like a Glasgow mafia.

There were rumours of a secret committee who were committed to destroying life and property; there was talk of a guard committee, who were the 'strong arm' men of the combination. They supervised the men who picketed the cotton mills that were bringing in nob labour. The guards could use persuasion or bribery with free drink to stop the nobs from working. If that did not work, they would resort to sterner action with fists or boots, or vitriol and gunfire. In the words of John Rosser, a sergeant of the guard, if the gentle methods failed, they could 'do as they liked' to the nobs. The guards and other combination men were paid for every nob they convinced not to work, by whatever method they chose. They worked in shifts of around six hours under a sergeant, and answered to a captain who was on the committee. Most of the names have been lost, but in the 1830s a man named Walter

Morrison was the master of the guards. During strikes, or when a man was dismissed for any combination connection, the association paid 'aliment' to him with money collected from the members.

The authorities watched the rising power of the combinations with some concern, and then in the late 1830s matters came to a head. In 1837 trade was depressed and some employers reduced wages. In 1838 the wage reduction became general and the combination called a strike, to which the masters responded by locking them out of work.

At this time Glasgow and west central Scotland were in ferment. The 280 men of the Glasgow police tried to protect the respectable and decent, while very aware of the growing poverty that stalked the streets. Demonstrators gathered around the fluttering flags of the combinations, vocal men gave rousing speeches, drums clattered in a heart-stopping call to action and the authorities muttered in fitful sleep as the country seemed destined to descend to anarchy. As trade slumped, masters lowered wages to keep the firms in profit or even in existence, but the combinations fought for a living wage every step of the way.

James Wood was a partner of Francis Wood and Co., cotton spinners of Bridgeton. When he lowered wages, his workers went on strike and on 12 April 1838 somebody threw a firebomb at his James Street house. The bomb, a five-inch-long canister filled with gunpowder and whale oil, caught in the window blind, so Wood caught it and threw it back, but a second bomb hit him as he did so. He closed the shutters hurriedly and called out 'murder' for help. When he looked out a few moments later, the street was empty.

The violence continued. Whenever managers employed nobs, the combination organised riots and mobs to wreak havoc outside the factory, and threw firebombs at the inside. A man named Thomas or Tammy Riddell was said to be prominent here.

Alexander Arthur, the manager of the Adelphi Mill at Adelphi Street in Hutchesontown, reduced wages from twenty-eight to twenty-four shillings a week but offered the established spinners the first chance of the jobs; they refused and walked out. When the nobs came to work on 5 May, the combination spinners pelted them with insults and stones. The nobs were so intimidated by the waiting combination crowd that they refused to leave the factory at the close of day. Arthur locked them in for their own safety and they slept inside the factory for some weeks. When David Gray and Edward Kean, two of the bravest of the nobs, ventured out, a group of combination men attacked them.

'We'll make you desist!' the combination men yelled, as they knocked the nobs to the ground and stuck in their heavy boots.

As well as attacking the nobs, the combinations moved against the masters. The proprietor of the Adelphi, Neill Thomson, fled the country for fear of the combination, while Arthur received threats in the post. He did not flinch.

Call for the cavalry

On 8 May 1837, at Oakbank, beyond Cowcaddens, the management took on about thirty new hands. An estimated 600 combination men gathered outside the factory, many armed with stout sticks. The combination men hissed and threw stones at the new hands and beat up all they could get hold of. The police sent six or seven criminal officers, plus ten uniformed men, to try and control the crowd, which was at its worst on the road between the mill and Cowcaddens. When some of the nobs fled into a house, the strikers followed and hammered on the doors and windows until the police pushed them away and escorted the nobs to safety. Nevertheless, the crowd was too dense to ensure proper protection. Sheriff Alison arranged for a squadron of the 9th Lancers to break up the mobs, but the combination learned of their approach and dispersed the crowd before the cavalry arrived.

There was also trouble at the Mile End factory, where Captain James Smart of the Calton Police was heavily involved in trying to keep the peace. He initially had ten men but doubled that as thousands of strikers and their supporters laid siege to the factory and abused the new hands, who again were unable to leave without a police escort. There were a number of arrests.

The factory of Hussey and Sons also cut wages; the combination men walked out on strike and the masters advertised for workers at lower wages. The combination men firebombed the building.

Sometimes the strong-arm men of the combination made house calls. Thomas Donaghy was a working spinner and on 29 June 1838 Thomas Riddell, the fire bomber, came to his Reed Street lodgings, together with a gang of followers. One was a loud-voiced man named Thomas Caffle. When Donaghy ignored the initial heavy banging on his door, the combination men grew vociferous.

'Let me in,' Caffle roared, 'and I'll tear the nob bugger's guts out!'

Donaghy decided it was best to keep his door firmly closed but Riddell kicked it in and burst into the house. Rather than run, Donaghy stood square in the middle of the floor with a pistol in his hand and said he would shoot the first man to come any closer. Riddell agreed to leave but his followers refused to budge. He asked Donaghy if he would join the strike. Donaghy agreed he would strike if they all left him in peace. They shook hands on it and left. Donaghy hoped that was the end of the incident, but the combination men returned within a few moments and demanded he hand over the pistol. Strangely, Donaghy agreed, and Riddell put the pistol in his pocket. In a spirit of mutual co-operation and trust, Riddell then asked Donaghy if he could buy him a drink; Donaghy sensibly refused. Next day Donaghy went to work as normal.

Among the masters who cut wages was a man named Houldsworth. The combination retaliated with a strike that extended to England, and which frightened Archibald Alison, the Sheriff of Lanarkshire, so much that he genuinely feared revolution; he clamped hard on any demonstrations. As usual, the master brought in large numbers of nob labour at lower wages, which increased tension and led to heightened resentment. Rather than mix with the growling, hungry combination men, the nobs who worked for Houldsworth were kept in a separate community. This was known as Houldsworth's Barracks and was in Cheapside, Anderston, in Glasgow. Many of the workers were not local but came from Ireland, England or other parts of the west of Scotland.

The murder of John Smith

The nobs were strongly advised to remain within these barracks, as angry and resentful combination men were on the prowl. On 22 July 1838 a nob named John Smith and his wife Margaret left the barracks to go into Glasgow. It was not a peaceful visit, for the combination men recognised him as a nob and jostled, hissed and insulted him. 'He's a blacknob,' somebody said.

The Smiths avoided the Green, for the combination men patrolled there looking for nobs. Bridgegate was also dangerous. The Smiths had shopped in Anderston Walk and around eleven at night were edging along Clyde Street toward the Broomielaw when somebody fired two shots. The bullets hit Smith in the side and he slumped to the ground. The man who fired the pistol did not linger, so by the time passers-by came to help, he was long gone. Margaret Smith, naturally agitated, screamed, 'Murder!' and tried to help her husband. She saw four people close behind her but could not identify any of them.

As usual in Glasgow, people did their best to help. Two labourers named John Duffy and James O'Donnell rushed forward and Smith said, weakly, 'Murder, murder; I'm shot.' Margaret was in deep distress, clapping her hands together and crying: 'Murder! My man's been shot.' Smith told O'Donnell he had been shot because he was a nob in Houldsworth's mill.

The helpers carried Smith to a local doctor and then bundled him in a coach that galloped to the Royal Infirmary, but he died on the Tuesday morning. The police made a number of quick arrests, but did not have enough evidence to hold anybody; However, did they have their theories.

The masters offered a £500 reward for information to arrest the murderer, and the government added £100 on top. That was a substantial amount for the murder of an ordinary man, and it indicated the crime was of more than usual importance. The political ramifications were substantial; if it could be proved that the killing was by a combination man, the whole structure of the combination could be discredited or perhaps destroyed.

Clandestine meeting

The prospect of so much money at a time of depression was attractive and two men, James Moat and James Murdoch, fell for the temptation. They arranged a clandestine meeting with Sheriff Alison in a gloomy vault in the depths beneath the Old College in Glasgow. Moat had been a spinner and a member of the combination, and had also been imprisoned for poaching a hare when he was unemployed. The whole affair smacked of cloak and dagger; Murdoch and Moat sneaked through the College Green and tapped on the back door, to be admitted in silence and secrecy.

According to later reports, which may well be apocryphal, Murdoch and Moat claimed that unless the combination got its way on pay and conditions, it planned to wipe out the nobs and the masters one by one. Murdoch and Moat also told Alison that Alexander Arthur was next in line to be murdered. That was sensationalism at its peak; an apparent plot of serial murder. If the informers said such things, they gave Alison exactly what he needed to take decisive action. It might have been these men who suggested that the combination had hired a man named William McLean, paying him the strange but substantial sum of £29 to commit murder.

Perhaps the informers spoke some of the truth. They did tell Alison that the combination strike committee would meet on Saturday night, 29 July, in William Smith's Black Boy Tavern in Glasgow, and confirmed the name of each man.

Armed with this information, Alison took the opportunity to break the strike and the combination. He had arrest warrants issued for the entire strike Executive Committee and organised a commando-style raid on the Black Boy Tavern. Alison may have been a stern enemy of the combination, but there was no doubting his courage. He worked in his office that Saturday and at nine at night he lifted his walking stick, whistled up Salmond, the procurator fiscal, and Nish, the sheriff officer, and marched across Glasgow to Black Boy Close, a bottle's throw from the Cross.

The raid on Black Boy Tavern

Black Boy Close was a horrible place: stinking, dark and a focal point for assaults, muggings and drunken brawls, but Alison was no fool. He had gathered together Captain Henry Miller and a stalwart score of policemen as insurance against trouble. Posting four men at the entrance of the close, Alison ordered them not to let anybody pass in either direction. He ordered four more to the back of the tavern and a dozen at the front, and marched boldly inside.

Alison was taking a risk. If the combination men were as militant and dangerous as Murdoch and Moat claimed, then he could have been thrusting into a den of pistol-wielding maniacs. In the event, there was no trouble. Alison and his men clattered up a wooden ladder to the upper floor of the tavern, but at first they could not find the committee anywhere. At length they found a room, where around ten men of the executive committee were peacefully sitting around a table, except one who was asleep on a sofa. They all looked much more like cotton spinners than violent revolutionaries. The combination men looked up in surprise at Alison's entrance, but when he brought up a bevy of police, the whole lot were arrested without a hint of resistance. A man named Richard McNeill was in the room next door, talking to his wife, and they arrested him too, as he had also been named as a committee man.

After Alison had decapitated the head of the combination, the workers held a meeting on Glasgow Green and voted to return to work, albeit on much reduced wages. With the executive under arrest, the violence in Glasgow stopped at once. There were no more reports of intimidation, riots or fire-raising.

Arresting the hit man

But Alison was not finished yet. He was now after the supposed murderer of Smith: William McLean. He issued a warrant for his arrest. James McDougall, a criminal officer of the Stirlingshire Police, went on the hunt. On 4 August 1837, together with a Glasgow officer named Donald McLean, he entered the house of McLean's father near Kirkintilloch. There was a man in the front room, busily writing a letter.

'What's your name?' McDougall asked.

The man put the letter in his pocket. 'John McIntyre,' he said.

'Come, sir,' McDougall replied, 'tell me your proper name.'

'William McLean,' came the answer.

'You are my prisoner, William McLean, and charged with murder.'

When McDougall escorted him out of the house, the erstwhile hit man was shaking with nerves.

The trial

In January 1838, four of the men arrested at the Black Boy Tavern – Thomas Hunter, Peter Hackett, Richard McNeill and James

Gibb – together with McLean, were tried at the High Court in Edinburgh. They were charged on a number of counts: creating an illegal conspiracy; conspiracy to set fire to Hussey and Sons' mill; conspiracy to send threatening letters and conspiracy to murder. Hunter was the president of the union, Peter Hackett was the treasurer, McNeill was secretary and Gibb his assistant, while McLean was a one-time member of the guard committee.

All the men pled not guilty.

The Lord Advocate said that, 'they had experienced the greatest possible difficulty in procuring persons to give evidence in this matter' and he had given to the witnesses 'an assurance of the fullest protection which the law could give both before and after trial'.

That statement strongly suggests that the combination members were intimidating the witnesses, or perhaps they were merely incensed at who had come to speak against the Committee, for James Moat, the informer, was a principal witness. Despite the defence arguing that Moat was hardly neutral as he stood to gain hundreds of pounds' reward money if the accused were convicted, he was allowed to give evidence.

Moat told the court that he had been a cotton spinner for upwards of twenty years and had sworn an oath to join the combination and not to reveal its proceedings. He had also been a member of the supply committee of the combination. He confirmed the existence of a secret committee, and mentioned the acid attack that had cost Carnie an eye. Moat named three men – Milne, George MacDonald and Keane – as being involved in the attack and said the committee paid them for their work. He confirmed the function of the guard committee as the sentinels and strong-arm men.

According to Moat, Alexander Arthur was disliked because of his 'bad actions' against his workers and therefore, the committee believed itself justified to use 'any measure'. Moat claimed that Richard McNeill had sent the written threats to Arthur.

James Murdoch, the other informer, added to the evidence against the executive and the combination. He said that men had to join the combination and pay their fees or the other men would tell 'clashes' – stories – to the masters about them and make their lives 'uncomfortable'. He spoke about a secret oath of the combination with special words taken from the Bible and secret signs so that members could recognise one another.

A spinner named William McGraw also gave evidence. He said he was also a member of the association but he did not have to make any secret oaths and the object was to have a 'just and lawful strike and to maintain their just and lawful rights when the masters reduced the wages'. He denied, 'so help me God,' that there was any secret bond to commit violence. He admitted that there was a guard committee, but said it was there to ensure that no striker received money – aliment – but still went to work. He added that the guards were allowed to persuade the new hands to strike by offering them a drink, but he had orders not to use any bad language to the new hands, let alone resort to violence.

Archibald Mackay was another combination member who denied any use of violence to the new hands. He gave his 'grave oath' that there was no proposal to use violence. He said that the cotton-spinning combination was blamed for violence that others committed.

The prosecution created a case against William McLean. Robert Christie kept a pub in the Gallowgate. McLean was an occasional customer and Christie heard him say he was 'going to death Mr Arthur'. Christie, an ex-spinner himself, tried to dissuade him but McLean said he was 'damned but he would'. On another occasion Christie was with McLean at Glasgow Green when McLean loudly threatened violence against Arthur. On the night of Smith's murder, Christie claimed that McLean had a pistol in his pocket.

Christie's evidence continued. There was the occasion when McLean and two companions kicked in the door of a house to get at the occupant. The woman of the house guessed they were set on violence and sank to her knees, begging for the life of her husband. As soon as he entered, McLean realised he was in the wrong house. The un-named man told them to get out; he said he would sort the door and say nothing to the police. McLean added, wryly, 'No wonder the wife cried, for it was an awfu' like thing to see three awfu' like ruffians like us coming in.'

After the murder of Smith, McLean was in Christie's pub and boasted he had 'made one bugger sleep'.

'Oh, William; what are you saying?' Christie asked.

McLean pointed to a notice that offered a reward for information leading to the murderer of Smith. 'D'ye see yon?'

'Yes,' Christie said, '£50 reward.'

'No, by God,' McLean boasted, '£500!'

Christie was shocked at the expression on McLean's face. He took hold of the front of his jacket. 'William, for the love of God leave my shop and make your escape, for you'll be apprehended!'

McLean turned away. 'Oh, damn it; there's nae down upon me [nobody is looking for me]. They are after another man to Liverpool.' A few moments later he held out his hand and said: 'There is the wee paw that did the trick.' He made a motion as if mimicking a man firing a pistol and walked away. 'I have done one bugger and will do some more of them.'

McLean also claimed to Christie that he had 'done Miller of Lancefield'. Miller was the proprietor of a spinning mill who some years previously had been badly beaten up. The culprit was never discovered. McLean added he 'wished to God there were three days of darkness for I would do for the buggers'. He also spoke about going to America, as the combination had already arranged passage as a steward on one of Hamilton and Brothers' vessels. He had spoken to James Hamilton of the shipping line about sailing on *Henry IV* as a steerage passenger, presumably in case the steward's job did not appear. James

Hamilton was quite aware that the combination helped pay the passage of a number of members, some with false names.

Christie believed that McLean had murdered Smith but did not tell the police, 'as perhaps McLean might have done me evil'.

The trial lasted eight days and the accused were sentenced to seven years' transportation, although they were found guilty only of conspiracy. The charge of murder was found not proven.

Thomas Riddell was caught in Manchester, brought back to Scotland and tried at the Glasgow Circuit Court, where he was found guilty of intimidation and sentenced to seven years' transportation.

The combination did not allow its executive to be martyrs and fought back through its own paper, *The Liberator*, and in 1840 they were pardoned. By that time the cotton combination was no more and the Glasgow cotton industry had all but vanished. Many of the combination men emigrated. In its time, the cotton combination had seen intimidation, fire-raising, threats, murder and one of Scotland's early hit men. Yet today it is virtually unknown.

7

The Poachers

The conflict between gamekeepers and poachers was ever-present throughout the nineteenth century, but when times were hard it could escalate into something approaching all-out war. It would be simplistic to claim it was a straight case of landed gentry against the down-trodden population, although there may well have been elements of class dispute in some instances. In others, it was a case of men who would be law-breakers in whichever environment they happened to live pitted against dedicated gamekeepers performing a dangerous job.

The early decades of the century were not easy times for the bulk of the Scottish population, with oppressive laws and reactionary politicians. The situation worsened in the 1840s, with terrible weather, a trade depression, poor harvests and potato blight leading to poverty, unemployment and despair. Not for nothing was that decade known as the 'hungry forties.'

Some families despaired, some emigrated, but some in the country-side turned to poaching. The Vickers family of Midlothian were one of the latter, but rather than sneak around with traps in the dark, they moved as a clan, fully armed with fowling piece and clubs, and challenged the gamekeepers to do their worst.

The Gorebridge Vickerses

On 18 October 1847, a night of wild winds and scudding clouds, the Vickers clan gathered their forces and recruited an ally in the person of William Beveridge. They all marched forth to the copses and policies of the Earl of Rosebery in the Carrington area. This is truly delightful countryside of immaculate fields and well-groomed forests, with small villages with a long farming history mingled with the mining settlements that tore wealth from the ground at the expense of the health and safety of the colliers. It was also a landscape dominated by wealthy landowners: the Earl of Rosebery; Robert Balfour Ramsay of Whitehill; the Marquis of Lothian, Dundas of Arniston and the Earl of Dalhousie.

In gathering an armed band to go poaching, the Vickers clan were putting themselves at considerable risk, for the law stated that if three or more armed poachers were found on land either enclosed or open, they were liable to sentences that varied from three years with hard labour to fourteen years' transportation.

On this occasion the Vickers expedition met with serious opposition. They entered Aitkendean Wood, about half a mile from Carrington and came face to face with four gamekeepers. The instant both forces met, they reacted. One group were poaching game, either in the hope of feeding their family or of selling the produce to make money for the same objective. The other group were performing their duty in looking after the game on the lands of their employers. Neither would back down.

When the poachers first realised they had been seen, Alexander Vickers aimed his shotgun at the keepers and squeezed the trigger. Most of the shot missed, but a number of pellets smacked into the buttocks and thighs of Robert Hume, the Earl of Dalhousie's game-keeper. Hume yelled, and the two forces closed in a flurry of blows. The gamekeepers knocked George Vickers down, as the poachers battered Archibald White, assistant keeper to Robert Dundas of Arniston, to the ground and put in the boot.

Both sides seem to have withdrawn then, carrying their wounded with them, but the Vickers family and Beveridge were later arrested and charged with night poaching and assault. Alexander Vickers, who had fired the gun, and John Vickers, who had carried out the assault on White, were sentenced to be transported for seven years and the others got eighteen months' imprisonment.

The Vickers family had lost a couple of their men, but the instinct to poach must have carried on down the generations.

Murder in Midlothian

John Fortune was a gamekeeper on the Rosebery Estate, a few miles south of Gorebridge in Midlothian, which is about fourteen miles south of Edinburgh. On the night of 15 December 1884 he was patrolling
the fields of Redside Farm, along with twenty-five-year-old John McDiarmid and James Grosset. McDiarmid was a rabbit trapper who lived on the estate but who had only worked there a couple of weeks, while Grosset was head gamekeeper of the Estate. Grosset had worked on the estate for twenty-nine years and was vastly experienced. Poaching had been prolific during the dark weeks of winter, so they were on the alert, but they did not expect serious trouble. They carried walking sticks but no firearms, and huddled into their jackets against the cold December wind.

At about half past two in the morning, the gamekeepers separated after a fruitless search. Each man went home, with Grosset returning to Rosebery farm steading and McDiarmid his near neighbour.

Fortune lived three miles away. Grosset was nearly home when he heard the sharp crack of a shotgun. He shouted out to Fortune, and sent his wife for McDiarmid, and all three men hurried toward the sound of the shot. They crossed the bridge at the overflow of the Edgelaw Reservoir toward the farm of Westerpark of Redside.

They followed the edge of a fence at an open field that sloped upward, and saw two armed men at the crest of the slope. The gamekeepers lay on their stomachs beside the fence, watching the poachers. At that time of night, there was nothing else the two men could be. The poachers slowly and cautiously approached across the field.

When the poachers were about fifteen yards away, the gamekeepers suddenly stood up. The two poachers backed off, still facing the gamekeepers and still holding their shotguns. In the soft glow of a nearly full moon, obscured only by scudding clouds, Grosset recognised them both: thirty-seven-year-old William Innes and a thirty-six-year-old miner with the familiar name of Robert Vickers.

'There is no use running or going on like that,' Grosset shouted, 'I know you, Innes.'

When they were about fifteen paces from the gamekeepers, the poachers stopped. Innes shouted for the gamekeepers to stand back. The keepers continued to advance and Innes spoke again, with his words quite clear to Grosset.: 'You take that one and I'll go for this bastard.'

Both men raised their shotguns and aimed. The second poacher, Robert Vickers, fired immediately.

At fifteen yards he could not miss, even in the bad light, and McDiarmid fell, badly wounded. Grosset bent to see if McDiarmid was dead, just as Innes fired again. Grosset winced as four pellets slammed into his back.

As Grosset staggered with the shock, Vickers fired his second barrel and hit Fortune.

'I am shot through the heart!' Fortune cried, as he lay on the ground. 'What will my poor wife, do?'

As Grosset moved to help Fortune, he thought he heard the poachers discussing him.

'Don't let him get off,' somebody said, 'load quick and shoot him.'

As Fortune lay dying, he whispered to Grosset, 'I would have got the little black rascal if the other had not done for me.'

Innes aimed directly at Grosset and fired the second barrel. Luckily the percussion cap was faulty and the gun misfired. The smell of gun smoke drifted in the night.

Grosset advised Fortune to try and keep still and quiet while he fetched help. He saw the poachers reloading their guns, their movements unhurried and professional, as their words drifted toward the gamekeepers.

'Load quick,' Innes said, 'and don't let that bastard get away. Give him another shot.'

Grosset was busy for the next few seconds, but he heard somebody say they would get him at the bridge. Despite the pain of his wounds, Grosset still outdistanced the poachers, crossed the bridge and ran to Edgelaw farm. The farmer, Robert Simpson, rushed to Gorebridge to find a doctor and sent the grieve William Brydon and one of the farm hands to search for the wounded gamekeepers. Brydon and the farm hand carried the wounded men back to Fortune's house.

Fortune died on 18 December 1884, but McDiarmid lingered for weeks and only succumbed to his wounds on 8 January 1885. Before he did so, he identified Robert Vickers as one of the poachers.

Sergeant Adamson of the Gorebridge police knew the Innes family and he knew Vickers. He had arrested Innes' brother Alexander in the nearby village of Loanhead and when he returned to Gorebridge he found William Innes in bed with a slight gunshot wound to the jaw. Adamson inspected the shotgun in the house and found fresh mud on it. He took Innes to the hospital and shortly afterward arrested Vickers in the street.

At the trial, witnesses claimed to have seen both poachers in a public house in the nearby village of Stobhill before ten on the night of the murders. However, Vickers claimed to have been in his own bed on the night of the murders, while Innes said he was at home all night. When he was asked about the wound to his jaw, Innes said that a man named Bernard had chapped on his door in the early morning of 15 December and he had accidentally banged against his shotgun, which went off.

A number of witnesses spoke for the poachers. There was John Wallace, a miner from Stobhill, who said he had accompanied Vickers to the pub early that evening. Wallace swore on oath that they were there until about half past ten. There was Helen Wilson, Vickers' next door neighbour. She happened to be out at about ten o'clock on the Saturday night of the murders. She thought she saw her husband beside a dry-stane dyke, so called out and waited for him, but it turned out to be Vickers. She saw him go into his own house and did not hear him come out again that night. There was Mrs Walkinshaw, who lived near Innes in Stobhill. She saw Innes come home around eleven at night. She was up around five in the morning to wake her three daughters for work and heard a shot from Innes' house. That tied in with Innes' own statement. When Mrs Walkinshaw investigated, Innes did not look as if he had been out during the night. Her husband confirmed her statements.

Despite the testimony of friends and neighbours, a jury at Edinburgh High Court found Innes and Vickers guilty of murder, albeit by a majority. Lord Young sentenced them to death, with the execution set to take place in Calton Jail on 31 March 1885.

Calton Jail was situated at the side of Calton Hill, which rose above the stern grey buildings and overlooked the tranquil streets of Edinburgh's New Town. A gibbet was built especially for the execution and positioned so that nobody could climb Calton Hill specifically to watch the event. Before they were hanged, Innes and Vickers confessed to the murders. Vickers claimed that Innes had been slightly drunk and had fancied having 'a shot'. He said that when Fortune came toward him he intended shooting him in the leg but because of the angle of the hill, he hit the keeper's stomach.

The Home Secretary rejected a 1,000-signature appeal and both men were hanged on 31 March. A crowd of around 5,000 gathered on the slopes of Calton Hill to try and watch the spectacle. Many were Gorebridge miners come to say a last farewell, but all they would see was the wooden roof of the building within which the two men were hanged.

Poaching continued.

8

Tommy on the Loose

When Rudyard Kipling wrote his poem 'Tommy', he was defending the ordinary soldier who guarded the largest empire the world had ever seen and probably will ever see. Kipling wrote of the trials and tribulations of private soldiers who were barred from public houses, mocked by civilians and refused entry to places of public entertainment. Yet even Kipling, a renowned champion of the man in the scarlet jacket, recognised the failings of the ordinary British soldier.

The words 'hustlin' drunken soldiers when they're goin' large a bit' augmented by 'sometimes our conduck isn't all your fancy paints' give an insight into the occasional troubles caused by the Army, who lived in garrisons the length and breadth of the country. The newspapers and sundry court reports were peppered with references to soldiers, acting singly, in small groups or en masse, who sometimes set the authority of the civilian world at naught and roared frustrated defiance to the bitter Scottish winds.

The civilians may well have viewed the soldiers as a breed apart, but they also walked wary of the men in the battered red coats. They had cause to. The British redcoat was often from the impoverished rural areas of Scotland, Wales, England or Ireland, or from the festering streets of some of the worst slums in western Europe. He could have been bred to violence and was trained to fight and kill. He was badly housed, poorly fed, savagely disciplined and could be sent to any of 100 trouble spots throughout the world at a few days' notice.

Those redcoats who survived were veterans of truly vicious wars, where they had faced disease and extremes of climate more dangerous than the human enemy, but where defeat in skirmish or battle may have meant annihilation or death by torture. The pages of nineteenth-century British military history are black-edged with horrors: the Kabul retreat of 1841; the massacre of Isandlwana in 1879; the jungle wars of Burma or Ashantiland; the scorching deserts of Sudan or the pitched battles of Chillianwala or Inkerman. Victory was never assured and life was hard, as the British soldiers faced some of the most warlike peoples in the world.

It was no wonder that the men sometimes overreacted when they were at home. Some regiments had reputations that preceded them. The 88th Foot were one such.

Connaught Rangers

In the early nineteenth century, the 88th Foot were garrisoned in Edinburgh. They were a truculent bunch and were prone to draw their bayonets and become involved in violent altercations with the local wild men. On Monday, 9 September 1817, four of them appeared before the sheriff charged with drunken rioting. The sheriff remarked that when an earlier Irish regiment had garrisoned the castle he had ordered them to leave their side arms behind when they left the barracks and there were so many of the 88th getting into trouble that he may do the same again. Other regiments did not work in such small numbers . . .

The riot in Perth

In 1843, while the Army was fighting in India and South Africa, the depot of the 68th Foot was ensconced in Perth barracks. They had arrived the previous winter, so by summer they knew the town well. On the evening of Wednesday, 24 May Perth celebrated the king's birthday in the traditional raucous style. It had long been accepted that the birthday of any monarch was an excuse for mischief and drunkenness, particularly among the youth of a town, and Perth was no exception. On this occasion the lads and young apprentices gathered in the town centre, around the Cross, St John Street, Skinnergate and George Street. They formed a disorderly mob and entertained themselves by knocking off the hats of anybody who passed and throwing fireworks, jeering at those they deemed worthy of abuse and generally acting as idle groups of teenagers have acted since time immemorial.

When a pair of soldiers happened to pass by this cheerful mob, they were treated no differently from anybody else. One of the soldiers was in civilian clothes and the other in undress uniform; both were greeted with insults and not always friendly banter. The men escaped to a High Street public house and remained there as the youths scoffed at them for running. The soldier in civilian clothes refused to re-emerge without the protection of a military picket, so his companion slid out the back door of the pub and ran to the barracks to call for help.

The 68th were not wont to leave any of their own in danger and a corporal led four men in a rescue mission down the hostile territory of darkest Perth. They wore side arms – bayonets – and in their scarlet uniforms were conspicuous targets for the mob. As the picket and the rescued man made their slow passage down the High Street, a large body of young boys gathered behind them, hissing, booing and throwing a choice selection of dead cats, vegetables and battered household utensils.

Not surprisingly the soldiers were irritated and fought back. They reached the Old Ship Close, turned around, drew their bayonets, stood against the wall and challenged the boys to do their worst. It was one thing to chase a moving target but quite another to run against the drawn bayonets of seven determined men; the mob pulled back, formed a semicircle around the soldiers and wondered what to do next. It was a stand-off between the youngsters and the redcoats.

By this time the police were aware of what was happening and Superintendent Boyle led four constables to relieve the beleaguered picket. The united strength of police and army forced through the mob toward the barracks. Another party of five soldiers joined them, and then a small group of police. The combined force managed to get the redcoats home safely, while also arresting eight of the mob.

Up to that point there was nothing extraordinary. There had been a minor disturbance which the police had controlled. However, the men of the 68th Foot did not agree. They growled at what they perceived as an insult to the regiment and they planned revenge. There were murmurs and whispers which reached Superintendent Boyle's ears and he sent word to Major Hoey, the senior officer of the garrison. No doubt the major did his best but angry British soldiers have their own methods of circumventing authority. Soldiers slipped out of barracks in ones and twos and threes. They walked awkwardly, with one arm straight down at their side, and when they reached the High Street they pulled short, stout sticks from their hiding places up their sleeves. The men had been busy; their weapons were not simple lengths of wood, but had been hollowed at the business end and weighed with lead so they were formidable weapons that could injure, maim or even kill.

By seven in the evening of Thursday, 25 May 1843, there was a large number of these stick-wielding soldiers gathered at the head of the High Street, as the nervous citizens of Perth gave them a wide berth and hurried home from their work. At some signal, the soldiers spread out across North Methven Street and moved slowly toward the barracks, shouting challenges, insulting civilians and pushing men and women out of their way. More soldiers slipped out of barracks to join them until there were about sixty-five men gathered. They ignored the pleas of the locals to return to where they belonged and then suddenly charged, lashing out with their sticks.

Civilians scattered as the men of the 68th swarmed along North Methven Street and down to the High Street Port, knocking people down, hacking with their iron-soled boots, crashing their cudgels on heads and shoulders of men, women and even children. They halted for a second to reorganise and then advanced in a body down the High Street. Some were drunk, others were plain angry and all were intent on creating as much mayhem as possible in Perth. They marched in formation, swinging their clubs, yelling, shouting and intimidating the populace.

The civilians could do little but hide. Shop owners put up shutters and hoped the solid wood would be protection enough; some men gathered their families and withdrew from the mob while others ran to the meagre police force for help. At length the soldiers reached the foot of the High Street and then things got worse.

The soldiers began to use their weapons in earnest. First they attacked the young men of the town, the group that had caused the trouble on the previous evening, and then they widened their scope of operations to include anybody and everybody. By that time most of the people of Perth had withdrawn indoors, but some brave men stood up to the soldiers, disarming a few and punching others to the ground.

At half past eight, Major Hoey sent a picket to control the riot, but rather than control the rioters, many of the men of the picket supported their colleagues. In the meantime the town authorities had not been idle. They gathered together all the police in the burgh, recruited a large number of special constables and marched to the High Street to try and contain the trouble. For a few moments the two sides eyed each other. The people of Perth were determined to reclaim their streets, but the 68th would never back down.

Then they met in a headlong charge; Donnybrook had come to Scotland. It was a full-scale battle in central Perth, as the specials with their long staffs waded into the drunken 68th Foot. As the forces of law arrived, more civilian men left their houses to aid their friends.

The conflict was vicious but ultimately the civilians won the day. Those of the rioters still on their feet were either arrested or fled back to the sanctuary of the barracks, while Major Hoey sent out two strong pickets armed with musket and bayonet, which arrived too late to stop the trouble. The police had to hold back a suddenly brave mob that wanted to tear the soldiers limb from limb. Instead the police escorted the soldiers back to barracks for everybody's safety. Perth counted the cost. Sixteen citizens were known to have been injured and thirteen soldiers were under arrest.

After the Lord Provost complained to Sir Neil Douglas, commander of the Army in Scotland, the 68th were moved to Stirling and the 88th Foot, the Connaught Rangers, took over the barracks. The 88th were also known as the Devil's Own and had a ferocious reputation in battle, but when they left Stirling the people said they had not caused any trouble. The people of Stirling gave no heed to the previous misbehaviour of the 68th and put the blame on the people of Perth.

When the case came to the High Court in July, five privates of the 68th were tried. Four were still in their teens and the fifth in his early twenties. All had been in the army for less than a year. The judge sentenced them to eighteen months with hard labour but added that in Perth Prison they would be taught to write and on their release they would return to their regiment.

There were other military riots in Scotland.

Mayhem in Hamilton

The nineteenth-century army was a strange creature. Each regiment was a world in itself, with its own traditions and history. As well as the regular British Army, there was the Indian Army, which until the Indian Mutiny of 1857 was the private army of the Honourable East India Company. There were also a great number of militia and volunteer regiments, roughly the equivalent of the Territorial Army. These formations were not always as well disciplined as the regulars. On one occasion in May 1860 some of the West Yorkshire Militia ran amuck in Hamilton.

The people of Hamilton did not much care for the West Yorkshire Militia. On 16 May 1860 one of their number, Thomas Ashton, barged into John Pillan's spirit shop in Castle Street, grabbed the money in the till and ran. He escaped with a lenient twenty days in jail. Other crimes were much more serious.

On Thursday, 25 May 1860, Mrs Agnes Maxwell of Camp Colliery, Dalziell, near Motherwell, was walking home from Hamilton. She was following a footpath along the bank of the Clyde and was nearing a dark wood at the Camp footbridge when she heard a noise behind her. She turned around, saw a group of men burst from the wood and tried to run, but they grabbed her, dragged her into the wood and sexually assaulted her. During the course of the attack she noticed that all five were members of the West Yorkshire Militia.

When the soldiers released Mrs Maxwell, she complained to the police and described her attackers as best she could. There was also a witness named Alexander Johnstone, who offered his help to the police.

The police began their search. On Saturday 25 May, Johnstone accompanied Constables Stewart and Maxwell through the streets of Hamilton, looking for the militiamen. All three were in plain clothes. When they were in Almada Street, near the barracks, they saw three hard-drinking militiamen. Johnstone thought he recognised one of the men, a private named Joseph Wilstonholm. Without revealing their occupations, the police invited the suspects into a pub for a drink. Once the militiamen were out of sight of their colleagues, the police arrested Wilstonholm. His companions watched, seething at the deception, but returned quietly to barracks.

With Wilstonholm dragged away and put safe under lock and key, Johnstone continued his search. He recognised a second of the rapists lounging close to the barracks and sought help to have him arrested. He found Inspector Gibb, who called on Sergeant McLeod and the burgh constable, a man named Smith, who arrested the man and took him inside a nearby house to be questioned. Unfortunately the militiamen were not happy at all to see another of their men jailed.

Wilstonholm's colleagues had watched from the barrack gate and surged forward to his rescue. They booted open the door of the house and poured inside, yelling their heads off. Taken by surprise, the police offered only slight resistance as the militiamen grabbed their comrade and rushed him back to barracks in roaring triumph. It took a few moments for the police to recover their equilibrium, but they straightened their uniforms, checked their helmets and marched to the barrack gates. The sentry had watched, but when Inspector Gibb requested entry, he barred the gate with his bayoneted rifle. Gibb demanded to see an officer, who reluctantly allowed him inside the barrack square, where Gibb asked to identify his suspect.

The officers called out the entire garrison and made them parade. The police walked along the ranks of sullen faces until they identified and arrested their man and escorted him toward the gate. However, the militiamen were not having this. They broke ranks and charged the police, knocking down and injuring Inspector Gibb, McLeod and Smith. There were around 200 militiamen involved in this riot, and they treated the orders of their officers and the police with equal contempt. The sergeant major ran to the barracks of the Light Dragoons for help, but the cavalrymen refused to come, as their officers believed they were too few in number to make any difference. That may or may not have been true; perhaps the cavalry officers did not fully trust their men to intervene against fellow soldiers.

When it became obvious that they could do nothing against hundreds of angry redcoats, the police withdrew, but they returned on Monday. They were now reinforced by Procurator Fiscal Dykes, together with Captain Mackay, who was the chief constable of the County Police; Superintendent Cullen of the Hamilton burgh police; John Thomson, messenger at arms; Sergeant Carmichael, Sergeant MacLeod and six police constables. Once again they arrested the suspected militiaman but once again his comrades made a rescue attempt, as they reached the barrack gates. Around forty of the soldiers threw a barrage of stones and followed with a charge with musket butts and boots. One of the constables fell in a mad flurry of blows; three more were injured as, faced with the Yorkshireman, the police withdrew to the guard room.

The soldiers followed, yelling oaths and threats. They knocked another policeman to the ground with a wild swing from a shovel and battered into the rest. Sergeant Carmichael of the police was badly injured and Sergeant McLeod lost two teeth and had the rest loosened by punches and kicks.

Captain Mackay was not a man to be intimidated; he drew the long blade from his sword stick and defended himself manfully, as the soldiers surged around the small knot of police. Again the redcoats tore their comrade from the hands of the police and began to jeer and yell despite anything the officers could do or say. The redcoats continued to cat-call for at least an hour after they had rescued their colleague but when they openly discussed launching a full-scale assault on the nearby police headquarters, Provost Mitchell called his own council of war.

The town's magistrates decided that the situation was serious and called out the army. As the cavalry had proved useless and the West Yorkshire Militia was mutinous, the authorities summoned the local volunteers: Number Two Company Hamilton Rifles. Within the hour, Captain Nisbet led ninety fully armed local men into the town and stationed them in and around the county police station, the jail and the County Hall. They waited for the West Yorkshires to emerge from the shelter of the barracks. It was a ludicrous situation, with two units of the British Army facing each other across the sights of their rifles in a small Scottish town. The next morning Number One Company Hamilton Rifles relieved their comrades, sword bayonets loose in their scabbards.

As the situation escalated to dangerous proportions, Sheriff Archibald Alison came hot foot from Glasgow, accompanied by a body of associates and officials, all concerned that Hamilton might see an armed encounter between two rival bodies of British infantry. Alison marched into Hamilton Barracks and demanded the suspect be handed over to him, together with any other men who may have been involved in the initial assault on Agnes Maxwell. Either the West Yorkshires had sobered up, or Alison's authority carried the day, for he emerged with four privates under the guard of a military escort. Superintendent Dewar and a body of police took the suspects to Glasgow by train and Hamilton slowly returned to normal.

The entire unit of West Yorkshires were taken to Edinburgh and put on parade in the castle. As they stood to attention, Agnes Maxwell walked around the ranks, scanning each man to see if he had attacked her. She identified a fifth man as having raped her, while Captain Mackay arrested a sergeant and seven privates for being involved in the attacks on the police, with another five men watched as possible suspects. The arrested men were taken to Hamilton jail and later the rioters were sentenced to three months. The rapists were given much longer sentences.

9
Wild Women

Although Scottish men have sometimes earned a reputation for being quick-tempered and stubborn in adversity, they are more than matched by their womenfolk. Scotswomen have not only to cope with a changeable climate and a volatile job market, they also have to deal with their men. No wonder they can sometimes be a little too ready to retaliate first. But Scotswomen could be equally unpleasant to their own gender. For example, there was Mary Smith of Dundee, who, in December 1826, was charged with poisoning one of her servants, apparently because the girl had the audacity to become pregnant. It was often wise to walk warily around a woman from Scotland.

Woman with a gun

Women were involved in just about every type of crime but it was unusual for a woman to use a firearm. However, it was not unknown. In 1878, Mary Ann Whittington, a good-looking young Englishwoman, was safely at home in Yorkshire when she met a handsome and personable Scotsman named Henry Summers.

The two formed a close friendship; so close that Mary believed they were to be married. When Summers had his wicked way with her and disappeared, Mary thought it best to follow him and travelled north to Edinburgh. She made inquiries and discovered that he lived in Cromwell Street in Leith, so she arrived at his door, knocked and was very disappointed when his current wife asked who she was and what she wanted.

Naturally angry, Mary bought a pistol and waited for Summers to come home. She ambushed him in the common stair leading to his house, pointed the pistol at him and pulled the trigger. Luckily for everybody concerned, she was not skilled with firearms and the percussion cap fell off, so there was no damage done. Perhaps she would have been better advised to tell his wife about their affair and leave any vengeance to her?

Another woman with a gun

There is an old saying that hell hath no fury like a woman scorned, and at the end of April 1897, James Allan of Ballochnie Farm by Airdrie witnessed the proof of this, up close and personal. He had gone to bed on Thursday, 29 April without any worries, but very early the next morning his bedroom door opened and a white figure appeared.

For a moment Allan stared, unable to work out who or what had entered his room. If he had been an imaginative man, he could have thought it was a ghost, for the intruder wore a shroud and a hood as if she were a corpse risen from the grave. However, Allan realised that the figure was much more dangerous than any supernatural apparition when it produced a six-chambered revolver and pointed it at him.

'You promised to marry me,' the figure said, in a woman's voice, 'and now you have put me away.'

The figure pulled the trigger of the revolver, but there was no shot. Allan jumped out of bed, grabbed the gun and wrestled the intruder to the ground. It was fortunate that the revolver was only half-cocked, or Allan could have been killed, but as it was, he was unhurt. The woman in white was forty-three-year-old Jane Ferguson, his housekeeper, whose employment he had decided to terminate at the end of the current term.

When Allan pushed Ferguson down, she fell awkwardly and dislocated her right shoulder, but still managed to jump up and grab a knife from the mantelpiece. Rather than continue her attack on Allan, Ferguson turned the blade on herself and attempted to cut her own throat. However, she proved as useless with the knife as with the pistol and only managed a few shallow cuts. Her next idea was to produce a bottle of poison and drink it, but that was only a trick, as the liquid inside was merely diluted vinegar.

Ferguson appeared in Glasgow Old Court in June, when it appeared that she and Allan had been intimate for some time. When Allan had tried to break off the relationship, Ferguson had become agitated. She said that she had only intended to scare Allan. Lord Young saw her injuries and her point of view and discharged her, with the good advice to avoid revolvers in future.

Other women used different weapons when they had domestic disputes.

Women with acid

Dundee was a shipbuilding centre of note in the nineteenth century, with firms such as Gourlay Brothers and Alexander Stephen & Sons producing vessels as good as any in the world. However, even successful families had their internal disagreements. One such was the Livie clan, who built boats, including whale boats, that worked in some of the most arduous conditions in the world.

When Christina Gauld married into the Livie family in 1881, she thought that life would be perfect, but unfortunately her marriage to

Stewart was anything but smooth. They were both drinkers and spent much of their time arguing, with the occasional separation to add variety. Christina would stay in the marriage home, while Stewart would run back to his mother on Exchange Street.

On 27 March 1888 they had a bitter quarrel, and as usual Stewart stomped out of the house and back to his mother's, leaving Christina with no money and bills to pay. She struggled on as best she could, but by Monday, 23 April she was at the end of her tether. Left with no option, Christina swallowed her pride and decided to ask her husband for money so she could pay the rent and buy food. She was naturally agitated when her sixteen-year-old brother met her as she walked to her in-laws' house, but they parted at the bottom of her mother-in-law's stair. No doubt Christina was nervous as she tapped on her in-laws' door, but she would not have expected the rough reception she got.

Christina was allowed inside and told her mother-in-law why she was there. Her sister-in-law, Lizzie, was also present, and both women combined forces and threw Christina out, telling her to get back to her own house. Surprised, Christina left, but she was too stubborn to stay away. She returned, only for the two Livie women to block her entrance. Christina was not disposed to take rejection quietly, but when she began to shout, Stewart Livie made his appearance. He physically ejected her from the house and told her to get back home. He also shoved her around a little. Christina left, but not for long. She ran to a chemist, bought a bottle of Salts of Sorrel poison and some vitriol, and was back at the Livie house in a short while. Again she knocked on the door and again she asked to speak to Stewart, but this time she held the small bottle of vitriol in her hand, ready to throw it over him.

Christina got into the house and refused to move. As before, she disturbed the household with her shouting and when Lizzie, her sister-in-law, came out of the kitchen, Christina followed her and held up the bottle.

'Oh, that's vitriol!' Lizzie yelled, backing away.

Lizzie's mother heard the shout and rushed to ensure her daughter was safe, but as soon as she entered the lobby, Christina threw the contents of the bottle at her.

Mrs Livie screamed as the liquid sprayed her clothes, with a small quantity landing on her face and burning her. Some also splashed onto Lizzie's clothes. The two women were in a panic as Christina left the house, probably equally upset but for a different reason. Lizzie rushed Mrs Livie to a doctor, who found her burns superficial, and then the Livies informed the police. Detective Herron arrested Christina. He found her very sick, having taken poison in an attempt to commit suicide. A doctor restored her to health and she was charged with throwing vitriol.

Christina appeared before Sheriff Campbell on 18 May. After listening to the case, he said that there had been faults on both sides and released her without charge.

Women as pickpockets, footpads and thieves

In the nineteenth century, women were adept at the gentle art of pocket-picking. This was a skill that required steel nerves, small hands and a delicate touch. For those reasons, children and women often made the best pickpockets, but they were not always successful. No doubt the best were never or seldom caught, but even so the courts were often infested with females who were known to have 'dipped' or picked somebody's pocket.

In the High Court on 24 January 1837, Catherine Burns was transported for seven years after being caught picking a handkerchief from the pocket of Alexander Macarter near Frederick Street in Edinburgh. That sounds a harsh sentence, but she would not have been sent to the High Court if this had been her first offence. Burns was 'habit and repute' a thief with previous convictions. She sailed on *Nautilus* for Van Diemen's Land.

At the same court, seven women were charged with robbery: Agnes Rutherford, Dorothy Barnes, Mary Bain, Mary McCallum and Ann, Janet and Joan Paterson. They had been in the house of Alexander Murray, husband of Janet Paterson, in North Fowlis Close, Edinburgh, and had attacked a man named Ebenezer Wilson. He was a farmer from Falahill near Lasswade in Midlothian on a trip to the capital, and was obviously not wise to the ways of city women. The female gang were accused of grabbing hold of him and robbing him of over £34, plus his snuff box. They pleaded not guilty. As the case against Janet Paterson depended on the evidence of her daughter, the crown withdrew the charges against her. Only Rutherford and Barnes were found guilty and they were sent to Australia for fourteen years.

Women often banded together to assault men. In January 1838 three girls – Janet McLean, Jean Blackwood and Mary Matheson – together with an elderly woman named Mary Gillespie were charged with assaulting and robbing a gentleman's servant in Edinburgh. Gillespie was released but the teenagers were sentenced to fourteen years' transportation.

Such attacks were more common than is often realised. To give one last example of women muggers, here is a snippet from 1878: Helen Brown was thirty-six and married to John Brown, although she had to do without her man as he was serving ten years for stabbing a man in a riot in Fraserburgh. Instead Helen teamed up with Margaret Park, who was one year older than her and married to a travelling chimney sweep. On 20 September 1878 near Monkshill at Fyvie in Aberdeenshire, the women ambushed and mugged a sheep dealer; both ended up in prison.

Family dispute

On 27 August 1883 four young women had a family gathering at 18 Hallside Street in Glasgow. There were three sisters – twenty-one-year-old Ann McKenzie, nineteen-year-old Catherine White and twenty-three-year-old Margaret Reid – and their sister-in-law, twenty-five-year-old Ann Murray, who had her six-month-old baby with her.

The women were drinking and laughing together, but when the drink took over the sisters began to argue with Ann Murray. Words escalated to blows and the three sisters made a frenzied attack on Murray. They knocked her down, stood on her and took turns to kick her in the groin and belly. When her husband, John, brother of the attackers came home, Murray lay in a pool of her own blood. He took her home but she died within the hour.

Although it was always the spectacular crimes that made the headlines, women, like men, were much more likely to be in trouble for petty offences. For example, in the Aberdeen Police Court in September 1880, Ann Low was fined ten shillings for being drunk and incapable; it was her second conviction for the same offence. At the same court, Ann Connor was found guilty of a breach of the peace in a house in West North Street. She was a habitual offender and was slapped with a fifteen-shilling fine. On the following Monday Jane Smith appeared before the Police Court, holding her baby in her arms. On the previous Saturday she had got herself drunk in East North Street and had used 'profane and abusive language'. She was fined seven shillings and sixpence. On that Monday, Margaret Smith, a known troublemaker with a foul temper, was found guilty of assaulting thirteen-year-old Elizabeth Bertram and was ordered to keep the peace for the next six months or forfeit a £2 bond. The next day, Ann Burke of Exchequer Court was fined a guinea for loitering for prostitution.

That same week, two married women, neighbours from Scott's Court in Regent Quay, were found fighting. The police separated them three times before eventually charging them, and at the termination of hostilities, the ground was scattered with handfuls of human hair that had been torn out by the roots. Both were given ten days in jail or a £1 fine.

Although many more men than women appeared in court, women were guilty of just about everything in the criminal spectrum. It was an ill thing to cross a Scotswoman in the nineteenth century.

10
The Navigators

When Robert Stephenson watched his famous *Rocket* chuff along the rails between Stockton and Darlington in September 1830, he could never have known what an impact his machine would make on the world. From faster and cheaper transport to the eventual demise of stagecoaches, railways changed the culture of the country and the world. Creating the railway network also caused major disruption, as the lines crossed rivers and moors and cut through hills and mountains in an amazing sequence of nineteenth-century engineering achievements.

The fearsome navvies

Backing the technical skills of the engineers was an army of labourers. Known as railway navigators, these men provided the muscle that made possible the inventor's dreams. The name navigator was inherited from the men who had dug the canals, or 'inland navigations', that preceded the railways as the most modern transport system. The term was soon shortened to 'navvy' and the world had a new word and a new demon.

The navvies were viewed with respect, with awe and, in some cases, with fear. When the Caledonian line was being built in the south of Scotland, 1,000 navvies were paid at Lockerbie. John Baird, the local Deputy Clerk of the Peace, was concerned that all the local lads copied the worst habits of these wild men. The youngsters were drinking, swearing, smoking and fighting – all renowned vices of the navigators.

The navvies, both canal and railway, soon earned a most unenviable reputation for violence and drunken brawls. They worked in gangs, often lived in encampments of tents or huts, and had their own dress code and culture, which excluded any outsider. They settled disputes by the boot, the fist and sometimes the sharpened edge of a spade. They had internal disputes, as Irish fought the Scots or English, or Highland and Lowland Scots fought each other in mass brawls that the tiny rural police forces were often powerless to quell. In one riot in Dumfriesshire, the Carlisle militia were called out. Sometimes the violence crossed the line and became murder.

Trouble in Gorebridge

In February 1846, the North British Railway was crossing the countryside of Midlothian, about ten miles south of Edinburgh, on its way to the Borders town of Hawick. As so often, the navvies were split along national lines – this time Scots and Irish. Wilson and Moore were the contractors who employed the Irish and they worked on the northern, Edinburgh section of the line. The Scots, with some English, were further south near the Border, with men named Graham and Sandison as the contractors. The two groups were mutually hostile.

Winter in Scotland can be harsh and that of 1846 was wet and dark and ugly. The navigators' living conditions were primitive, as they crushed into long wooden huts, shared beds and paid high prices for the privilege of eating swill from the 'tommy shops' – shops provided by the contractors, who recouped some of the worker' wages in return. The huts held up to twenty-four families in communal living, with no privacy and beds piled, bunk-bed style, one above the other. The line was difficult to build, with moors and hills and many cuttings, so there were casualties among the workforce and tension was high.

The navvies were paid on the last Saturday of the month and often vanished into the nearest pub to squander their wages in drink and joviality. In this occasion the Irish navvies were paid at the village of Gorebridge and when they came to reckon their wages, they thought they had been cheated.

The tommy shop system was always loaded against the workers. The men were overcharged for inferior food and, as many were illiterate and unable to count, they could not properly calculate how much they had already been cheated of. However, Somerville's pub was warm, the whisky was available and work was done for the time being. The men spent what they had left today, with scarcely a thought for tomorrow. They were in a relaxed state and ready for mischief when a packman came to call.

A packman was a travelling peddler. They were common in old Scotland and acted as bearers of news, as well as sellers of goods and trinkets. They were as much part of the community as farmers and millers, and were usually welcomed for the *craic* as much as for the exotic wares they carried to often isolated communities. This packman showed the drunken navvies the selection of watches he carried, allowed two to be passed around, and probably was not too surprised when his watches vanished into an Irish pocket.

Rather than argue his case with a bunch of muscular, half-drunken navvies, the packman asked the local police for help. Brave men, Sergeant Brown of the Railway Police and Constable Christie of the Edinburgh County Police walked into the pub, arrested two navvies and thrust them in the cells until they were sufficiently sober to question. That should have been the end of the matter, but the navvies were still seething at the perceived injustices of their lives and decided to free their imprisoned colleagues.

The figures stated in the press and the official documents vary, but between 150 and 300 navvies collected pickaxes, spades, billhooks and sundry other weapons, talked themselves into a fury and marched to the tiny police office in Gorebridge. Brown and Christie stood up to them for a while, but the navvies crashed in with boots, fists and evil intent. Seeing the apparent weakness of the police, the navvies smashed Constable Christie on the arm with the back of an axe. Despite that, Brown still refused to open the door of the cell that held his prisoners. Brown was a brave man, for even when a navvy mouthed foul oaths and threats as he held a pistol to his head, he refused to release the prisoners. The navvies ignored him, used their pickaxes to force open the door, and freed their comrades. They rampaged through the grey stone streets of the village, cheering and roaring in triumph.

At the same time as the navvies were disrupting Gorebridge, two more police officers, Constables John Veitch of the County Police and thirty-year-old Richard Pace of the Railway Police, were returning from a tour to check the local pubs. They were in the region of the tiny hamlet of Fushie Bridge when they heard the commotion ahead. They stopped to listen and possibly saw the flicker of torches as the coarse voices roared through the dim of the night. Knowing the temper of drunken navvies, the two police hid away behind a hedge, but they were either too slow or too noisy, for the navvies found them and hauled them out. There were a few moments of confused struggle and both police were injured. Veitch ran for his life but Pace was less lucky. Somebody cracked him on the head with the handle of a pick and the navvies followed up with a flurry of boots as he lay prostrate. He was only 100 paces from his home, where his wife must have heard the noise.

When the navvies tired of kicking the policeman, they shambled on their way toward Arniston Toll Bar. Once they were gone, two local youths emerged from the dark, inspected the injured constable and carried him home. They gave the alarm and ran for medical help, but it was too late. Although the local doctor did all he could, Constable Pace died in his own bed at six on the Sunday night, by which time police inquiries were in full swing.

Superintendent List of the county police whistled up two dozen of his own men, begged twenty-five more from Captain Haining of the City of Edinburgh police and sent them to Gorebridge to keep the peace and flush out the murderer. They arrested thirteen of the Irish navvies around midday, but there was no other work for them to do; the navvies had already dispersed. The police were not sure who amongst the prisoners had been involved in the murder.

However, other people apart from the police had heard of the attack and were gearing for battle. The navvies at the southern section of the line – mostly Scottish Highlanders but with a stiff leaven of English – decided that enough was enough: they would sort out these Irish once and for all. They used the excuse that the policeman was Scottish and so were they, but in reality the murder was probably only a trigger for animosity that was deep-seated and longstanding. It is possible that Highland navvies were second only to the Irish in their propensity for creating trouble; Highland navvies rioted in Stonehaven and murdered at least one other man in the north of Scotland.

The clans gathered; Highland, Lowland and English navvies. They met in pubs and drinking dens, reached out to the local colliers for reinforcements and laid their plans. By the Monday they were ready and marched north in a body 1,000 strong. There was nothing secretive about this advance. A piper played rousing tunes while the shrill scream of a bugle shrieked defiance to the morning as they tramped, bearing spades and pickaxe handles, clubs and cudgels, and all wearing the heavy, iron-shod boots that were weapons in their own right.

The people in the path of this army sent messengers to alert the police, who counted the numbers and posted urgent messages to

Edinburgh for more men. A coach and four galloped south from the capital, with the driver cracking his whip and the police packed inside, no doubt wondering what trouble awaited them. The superintendent knew that a handful of police would not be enough to deter hundreds of angry navvies, so he sent to Piershill Barracks for the cavalry. Shrill cavalry bugles called the men to mount and ride.

Sometime after nine on the Monday morning, the noisy navvy army halted at the paper mills at Newbattle near Lothianbridge, only a couple of miles outside Gorebridge. Either by chance or by pre-arrangement, 150 local colliers joined them. The combined force of perhaps 1,500 men marched to meet the foe. The Irish navvies were aware that the Scots were coming and gathered at their encampment at Crichton Moss, not far from the medieval Crichton Castle, where the Scots repelled an English Army in 1337. There was no desperate battle this time, for when the Irish saw how badly they were outnumbered they ran.

Left undefended, the six or so long huts and homes of the Irish at Crichton Moss were an easy target for the rampaging Scottish Army. They evicted any wives and children, then burned and destroyed, before moving on to a number of other Irish navvy settlements near Borthwick, which they treated the same way. The Scots fired the ruins, with the Irish wives sitting in disconsolate huddles, watching, knowing their men had deserted them. With the spoilage complete, the Scots turned on the overseers and contractors. Two overseers, Darbie O'Brien and Thomas Carrol, were brave or foolish enough to remain at home near the old farm steading at Crichton Moss and the Scottish navvies attacked both, but without inflicting major injuries.

However, they were not quite finished yet. Thomas Martin, one of the railway contractors, was lodging at the inn at Fushie Bridge, so the navvies hunted him as well. They barged into the inn, pushed aside the proprietor, Barbara Wilson, and cracked Martin over the legs with a stick. Martin ran for his life, leaving a portion of his clothing as a souvenir in the hands of the navvies. He fled to a cottage at nearby Catcune Mill, but the navvies followed and for a while debated whether they should set fire to the house. In the event they decided not to, called it a day and gradually dispersed.

Sheriff Speirs and the police had watched but had done nothing to halt the destruction. The sum of their actions was to inspect the smouldering remains of the Irishmen's winter quarters. When Sheriff Speirs clambered into a carriage and led sixty of the 4th Irish Dragoons from Piershill Barracks in Edinburgh, the navvies had already gone. Speirs stationed the cavalry around the smouldering camp in case there were further outbreaks. Some of the dragoons helped the police scour the public houses and inns on the route south and between them they arrested nineteen men, who were suspected of being involved in the burnings. More men were arrested the following day.

Although the Irish had been defeated, their fighting spirit remained intact. On the Wednesday an Irish navvy stabbed a Scottish navvy at Pathhead, about five miles east of Gorebridge, but the scuffle did not lead to further rioting.

Once they had recovered their nerve, the 200 Irish gathered again to march against the Scots, but the cavalry ranged before them tapped their swords and shook their heads. The Irish looked at the tall men on their tall horses, heard the broad Irish accents and decided not to bother.

When all the fire and fury settled down, Sheriff Speirs and the police resumed the hunt for the murderers of Constable Pace. As usual the navvies closed ranks and refused to help the investigation. It was a month before Speirs got a couple of names and issued descriptions of the men who had been blamed for the policeman's killing. Those named were Patrick Reilly and Peter Clark. Reilly was described as a stout man of about five feet seven or eight, aged around forty, with black whiskers turning to grey, a blue bonnet, the usual moleskin waistcoat jacket, waistcoat and trousers, and 'large navie boots'. Clark was apparently between thirty-five and forty, an inch or two taller than Reilly, with sandy hair and whiskers, a blue jacket and grey trousers, as well as the inevitable 'large navie boots.'

Despite knowing the names and having a fairly decent description, the police did not catch either man. The navigators would bicker and fight amongst themselves but rarely co-operated with the authorities.

On 12 May 1846, nine navvies appeared before the High Court in Edinburgh, charged with mobbing and rioting, fire-raising, malicious mischief and assault for their part in the burning of the Irish huts and the attack on the contractors and overseers. Eight had Highland names – McQueen, McKillop, McLean, Grant, Mackay, McCracken, Morrison and Shaw – and the ninth was plain Henry Brown. After hearing the evidence, the court dismissed McLean but sentenced the others to terms of imprisonment ranging from two years for Brown to eight months for Shaw. In June a further contingent of four Irish navvies appeared before the High Court; the Lord Justice Clerk transported them for seven years each.

That was only one riot among many that involved the railway navigators. Another, equally bloody, took place in the Borders.

A fair riot

If the world were to end tomorrow, either by some man-made calamity or by natural disaster, and fire and brimstone rained down upon the earth; if the ground was blanketed by thick smoke and the seas dried up; if there were seven billion dead and nothing was left except wasteland, then the next day two Scottish Borderers would crawl out from under the wreckage, dust themselves down and start to rebuild. That is to say: the Scottish Borderers are natural survivors. They were there before the Romans came and they were there when the Romans abandoned Britannia. They survived the periodic but savage raiding from the Norse, but most of all they survived centuries of raids and warfare from the English to the south, as well as internal Borders reiving and the odd family feud. The Scottish Borders was arguably the most fought-over area in Europe, with the town of Berwick-upon-Tweed changing hands a reputed eleven times before finally ending on the English side of the frontier.

The result of this history of stubborn resistance is a unique people, with a very strong sense of local identity. They are also a people well able to fend for themselves, which is an attribute that came in handy on 18 July 1849, when the railway navigators went on the rampage at St Boswells Fair. This was a cattle and horse fair, with up to 1,000 horses on show on the green at St Boswells, the largest village green in Scotland. The St Boswells Fair attracted a large number of muggers, or dealers in crockery, and gypsies from all four nations of Britain. There were also side-shows, fortune-tellers and the local pub; all in all, a splendid place for navvies to congregate once the day's work was done.

That day, two of the navvies had an argument in front of Mrs Brown's Inn, but the verbal conflict soon degenerated into a fist fight. When one of the men hammered the other into the dust and began to put in the boot, Constable John Guild of Hawick and Constable Moscript stepped in to stop serious injury. When the more successful navvy protested, Guild arrested him and escorted him toward the barn that acted as temporary police head station, jail and court house.

The barn had only a single entrance and a single window, so it was relatively secure, while a four-foot-high dry-stane dyke ran at the side. As so often, an arrest led to a riot, as the other navvies grabbed whatever weapons they could and gathered to rescue their colleague.

As the navvies gathered, they began to chant, 'Killing! Killing!', which must have unnerved the police, considering the reputation of these men.

The police barn came under siege, as around 300 navvies rammed against the door. In response to the navvy slogan, the police called out:

'Rally round, rally round, Irishmen!' They formed a tight formation to try and repel the navvy attack.

There were twenty-one police on duty at the fair, and about fourteen were inside the barn, so they were vastly outnumbered and in a bad way. Superintendent William Everett of the Roxburghshire Police had seen the navvies thrust his officers aside and rescue the prisoner. Everett moved to interfere but the navvies knocked him down and were cheerfully putting in the boot, but Everett rolled away, struggled to his feet and ran to the shelter of the barn.

The navvies tried to force their way into the temporary police head-quarters but the police formed a blue barrier at the doorway and battled with their long batons. They managed to grab John Murphy, one of the most forward of the attackers, and pushed him into the barn. Everett clambered on top of the dry-stane wall beside the barn and appealed to the crowd for better behaviour. When he suggested to Constable Guild that they might be best releasing Murphy, Guild wiped the blood that was pouring down his face and said, 'I'd rather die first!'

The navvies were surrounding the police, flailing at them with sticks and throwing stones and rocks whenever the notion took them. There was a rush at Everett, and grimy hands tried to haul him off his perch on the wall as the navvies gradually forced the police into the barn. A clout from a club temporarily dazed the superintendent, and then a stone cracked against the back of his head. The police made another arrest but then the navvies surged forward and kicked the door down, so that it imploded in a welter of splintered timber.

'Turn him out!' the navvies were roaring, 'turn him out!' As they tried to break through the creaking police lines to rescue the prisoner. At last Everett gave in and allowed the prisoner to go free. Immediately he emerged, the noise eased and most of the navvies began to withdraw. There were still a number of assaults, and Constable Andrew Kerr arrested a navvy named John O'Neil. That ignited the crowd to even more fury and some of them got inside the barn, where the fight continued.

The navvies knocked down a Lilliesleaf constable named Stirling, who shouted out 'Scotland!' as a cry for help. He lay on the ground, yelling, 'Scotland! Scotland!', as the navvies rained kicks on him with their mighty boots. Stirling added, 'You surely won't stand to see us all murdered!' Constable Guild had been badly hurt, with blood pouring from a number of wounds, and Constable Yule was also in a bad way.

The Borders way

At some time during this riot, the local people realised what was happening and banded together in the old traditional Borders fashion to resist an alien invasion. The two forces collided in a major riot, but the navvies were more used to violence and caused considerable casualties among the more peaceable locals. An old man brandished his walking stick and ran at the navvies but went down before a flurry of blows. A joiner named William Stenhouse from Melrose was knocked unconscious and a Melrose blacksmith named John Lauder tried to help Constable Yule. His son, William Lauder, also rushed to help but in the press father and son got separated. While John Lauder was injured, William fared far worse.

Lauder was around twenty-five years old and was a shepherd from Whitelee near Newtown. At least three navvies, including John Brady, Peter Lafferty and Thomas Wilson, surrounded Lauder, but he was a strong young man and was holding his own with an ordinary walking stick until Wilson came behind him and smashed him over the head with a bludgeon. When Lauder was on the ground, Wilson held his bludgeon with both hands and brought it down full force on the head of the helpless shepherd. Once Lauder was out of the way, the navvies moved on, leaving him lying prone on the ground.

When the dust had settled, John Lauder and other men carried William to Mrs Thomson's Inn, where he died without recovering consciousness.

As the trouble died away and the navigators left, the police arrested three more of them, and they picked up another suspect the following day. All the arrested men were taken from St Boswells to the much more secure accommodation of Jedburgh Jail.

As well as Lauder and Guild, John Yule of the Railway Police had a serious head injury and was badly bruised around his groin, William Everett was cut around the head, Constable James Johnston from Kelso had two broken ribs, and three more police were also injured. Lauder's father John was also badly hurt, as were four or five more of the volunteers. The worst of the wounded were also carried to Mrs Thomson's Inn, where they remained until they recovered.

On 4 October, three of the principal navvies accused of mobbing, rioting, assault and murder appeared at Jedburgh Circuit Court. They were Thomas Wilson, John Brady and Peter Rafferty (or Lifferty), also known as 'the Switcher'. The jury heard the evidence and found Wilson and Brady guilty of all the charges, while Rafferty was only found guilty of mobbing and rioting. Although the jury recommended mercy, the judge sentenced Wilson and Brady to death, while Rafferty was sent to Australia for fourteen years. Brady broke down in tears at the sentence but Wilson, a determined-looking man of about twenty from County Down, stared stonily at the judge, Lord Wood. The sentence on Brady was later commuted and he was transported instead.

A further eight navvies were tried for the riot and mobbing and were transported for seven years. Only the hanging remained to put a full stop on the riot.

Early on Thursday, 25 October 1849 the town of Jedburgh was drenched with rain that had begun the previous evening. Despite this a crowd of around 2,000 gathered, coming in from all the country districts on foot or horseback or cart, flicking the rain off their hats as they congregated around the Council House. In case there was any disorder, a guard of 200 local men stood with long batons, reinforced by sixty men of the 21st Foot, who stood at attention around the scaffold. In the background, weeping with rain, a black flag drooped above the jail, as a bell tolled its sombre message of an imminent execution. At eight in the morning, Thomas Wilson was brought out, his blue jacket and dull trousers shabby as he faced the crowd and the Roman Catholic priest.

Immediately before the noose was placed around his neck, Wilson shouted: 'I am going to be launched into eternity to face my God, and I am not going with a lie in my mouth. I lifted neither stick nor stone on the fair day. I am about to suffer for another man.' He was hanged a few moments later. There were a few Irish navigators present when his body was cut down at nine in the morning, and one woman, who the newspapers reported as having 'wept very much and very bitterly'.

Sometimes the navigators were the victims and not the aggressors . . .

The murder at Tomatin

Behind the tartan façade and the wealth-created bubble of huntin', shootin' and fishin', the life of the indigenous Highlander was one of struggle against a harsh climate and often challenging conditions. Working hours were long; wages were low and often nonexistent. The Highland economy depended on men and women leaving their native parishes to work elsewhere, either at the harvesting in the Lowlands, on east coast fishing boats or as navigators on the constantly expanding railway network.

When the railways inched north into the Highlands, many local men sought employment as navvies. In doing so they entered a different culture of itinerant labouring with men who lived by their own rules, slept in barrack-like huts, worked like Trojans in all weathers and were proud of their own ability. However, it was natural that having so many vital and physical men working and living in such close proximity for long spells led to frustration, irritation and explosions of temper and violence.

Such a case occurred in February 1896, when the navvies were working on the railway between Inverness and Aviemore.

Late on Saturday, 15 February 1896, the navvies were sitting inside a structure called Jack's Hut at Tomatin around seventeen miles south of Inverness. The hut was one of a number of similar structures used by the navvies as they worked on the railway line. The men had lived there for some months, so it was a second home. They were drinking, talking and joking at the end of the working week. All had spent the day working and were tired but happy. A Perthshire man names James Slater Mackintosh was drinking with an Irishman named Walter Powell. As the drink took hold, the words became heated and escalated to fists.

Ellen Jack, the wife of the hut keeper, heard the noise and opened the hut door to see what was happening. She had thought that the men were sober when they had returned from work, but now she saw a scrum of three men rolling and struggling on the floor. As well as Mackintosh and Powell, there was another Perthshire man involved, named Daniel Macmillan.

Powell stayed at another hut and earlier had come in to ask Mackintosh to accompany him to buy drink. They had searched their pockets, scraped together enough money and bought a bottle of whisky, but when they had got back to the hut, they had argued about who had paid the most.

Ellen Jack was a brave woman. She strode into the hut in the middle of the bearded, drinking men and helped Mackintosh to his feet. She ignored Mackintosh's fluent swearing, but smiled when Macmillan told him to hold his tongue because there was a woman in the hut. As she left, Ellen saw Mackintosh charge at Powell, fists flying. He knocked Powell to the ground and was kicking him with his heavy boots until Powell rolled under a table.

Mackintosh was clearly winning, but then Powell grabbed a poker and smacked him over the head. Powell roared, then pulled his clasp knife and stabbed Mackintosh five times in the back and once on the shoulder. When Daniel Macmillan tried to pull them apart, he was also stabbed in the thigh and hip, but was not seriously injured.

Powell either dropped the knife or it was knocked from his hand, for Ellen scooped it up from the floor and called in other navvies to help. By that time, Mackintosh was in a fighting fury; he felled the first two men with the whisky bottle but force of numbers told and he was overpowered and subdued. By the time the fight ended, Mackintosh lay dead on the floor. Other men also dragged Powell away. With the combatants pulled apart, Ellen left them to it and ran to fetch her husband. Alexander Jack arrived at the door of the hut but he was not a well man and thought it best not to interfere. The navvies may extend some courtesy to a woman, but that would not extend to a man.

Mackintosh was a mature man of fifty-six and had worked in the Highlands for years. He was later buried at Tomnahurich in Inverness. Powell was a muscular thirty-two and lived in Cardiff, although he was born in Belfast. He was a quiet man with no relatives and an inability to make friends easily. Until that day he had never been in trouble, while Mackintosh had a reputation for being violent when in drink. When the doctor examined Mackintosh's body, he found that the stab wounds were very shallow and certainly not fatal; he thought death had been caused by shock rather than the knife.

The local constable arrested Powell, handcuffed him and brought him by the mail coach to police headquarters in Inverness. When Powell arrived, he had a deep cut across his nose. Daniel Macmillan was taken to the Northern Infirmary in Inverness.

The case was held at the Circuit Court at Inverness Castle in front of Lord Low. After hearing all the evidence about the characters of the respective men and the events leading to the killing, the judge advised the jury that Powell had acted in self-defence and he was declared not guilty.

That sordid little tale took place in 1896, when the ferocious reputation of the navvies was a dim memory. They flourished in the great days of rail expansion and by the latter decades of the century were still hard and hard-drinking men, but nothing like the fearsome creatures of mid-century. The legend, however, remains.

11
Duel

Cardenden does not advertise its place in Scottish history. It is a pleasant former mining town about four miles north-west of Kirkcaldy in Fife, but in 1826 Cardenden was the centre of national attention as the site of the last fatal duel in the country.

Duelling was an ancient system of settling a quarrel between gentlemen, usually over some point of honour. It may have begun with the chivalric practices of medieval knights, but escalated in the seventeenth and eighteenth centuries when gentlemen settled their differences across the hilts of swords. Pistols gradually replaced swords and the traditional meeting was along the long barrel of a finely balanced gun. However, despite the appeal to honour and the code of gentlemen, if one protagonist in a duel killed the other, he was as guilty of murder as if he had plunged a knife through his rival's heart in some festering Edinburgh close.

Pistols at dawn

Early on the morning of 23 August 1826 two gentlemen stood face to face in the East Park at the farm of Cardenbarns, just outside Cardenden, which was part of the estate of Raith. One of the men was George Morgan, and the other was David Landale. George Morgan was a banker in Kirkcaldy, while Landale was a linen merchant in the same town. Both carried long pistols and both were determined to kill or be killed. As was usual in these circumstances, there were seconds in attendance: William Milie attended to Landale and Lieutenant Milne of the Royal Navy cared for Morgan. The seconds were there to ensure that the proper procedures were carried out and neither of the principals had an unfair advantage over the other. Two doctors were also there to try and patch up anybody who was merely wounded rather than having had his head blown off.

Before taking his place in the firing line, Landale offered a peace deal; he said that if Morgan apologised he would consider the matter ended. Morgan refused point-blank. After ascertaining that both protagonists wished to continue, the seconds allowed the duel to take place.

In most duels, there were no fatalities. The affair was over after an exchange of shots, and honour was satisfied; the men had proved their commitment and courage, and life continued as before. In this case, Landale shot Morgan in the right side, under his upraised arm. The ball travelled right through Morgan's body end exited at his left armpit. Morgan stood for a few seconds and then collapsed.

Leaving his defeated adversary lying on the ground with the doctors clustered round, Landale's second hustled him away from the duelling ground, away from Cardenden and away from Fife.

However, duelling was illegal and the authorities started their search for the man who was technically and legally the murderer. Although Landale was nowhere to be found, the police contacted

Morgan's second, Lieutenant Milne, and asked where the duellist might be. Lieutenant Milne asked Milie, who said that Landale was not running from the law and would attend the court without question as soon as he was summoned.

It was now that the police began to investigate both duellists to find out what caused the fatal dispute.

Cause of the quarrel

Landale was known as an honourable merchant and a gentleman. A few months before the duel, he had written to the Bank of Scotland requesting a business loan. The bank asked Morgan, as a banker, his opinion of Landale's security, and was told that 'he considered the security of D. Landale and Co. quite good' and he 'employed many people and had always adhered steadily to the bank'. Accordingly Landale was offered a £5,000 loan, with a clause that said he could not withdraw more than £3,000 unless he checked with the bank first. Landale had to give security for £5,000 to obtain the loan. However, once he had reviewed the terms, Landale decided not to take the loan and he withdrew his business from the Bank of Scotland.

Morgan seemed to take Landale's purely business decision as a personal slight and he revealed details of Landale's finances to a number of other merchants in Kirkcaldy. As a result, some people, including a man who had been a longstanding friend and business associate, withdrew his financial support and would no longer act as security to Landale's company. Landale wrote a letter explaining why he had withdrawn his business from the bank, but rather than treating the matter as confidential, the bank manager showed the letter to Morgan, who once again took it as a personal slight.

From that time, Morgan began a campaign of abuse toward Landale, insulting him verbally in the streets of Kirkcaldy and sending him a number of very ugly letters. One letter called Landale a liar, which was one of the worst insults possible for a gentleman of the period. Morgan turned the blame around and demanded an apology from Landale for what he called, 'your false unfounded and ungentlemanlike expressions regarding me'. Morgan signed the letter, 'George Morgan, Lieutenant, half pay 77th Regiment of Foot'.

Presumably Morgan had intended to intimidate Landale with the reminder than he had been an army officer before changing career to the financial sector. Morgan seemed to want a duel with Landale, but he had been informed that the challenger in such cases was liable to be transported, so he tried to provoke Landale into issuing the challenge. It was claimed that he gave the following somewhat stilted speech: 'I will assault Mr Landale publicly for the purpose of forcing him to challenge me.'

When Landale heard of Morgan's intentions, he must have walked the streets of Kirkcaldy in the daily expectation of being attacked. Publicly, Landale scoffed at the notion that one gentleman would act in such a manner toward another, and refused to alter his normal routine. He rejected advice that he should carry a weapon. He may have heard that Morgan had asked William Todd, the Kirkcaldy blacksmith, to make him some dozens of pistol bullets, but if so he disregarded that story as well.

At length Morgan and Landale came face to face on the street. Morgan had been in Cumming's bookshop when he saw Landale pass. He left immediately, lifted his umbrella and thumped Landale over the shoulders, saying, 'Take that, sir!' with the threat, 'By God, sir, you shall have more of this yet!'

'What you have done now is wrong,' James Cumming told Morgan, who merely shrugged.

'You are a coward, sir,' Landale said, as he gathered his dignity and withdrew, 'a poor silly coward.'

Under such provocation, Landale could either cringe or retaliate, and he chose the latter. He wrote a letter and gave it to his friend,

William Milie, to hand to Morgan. 'I must request,' it said, 'that you meet me tomorrow morning at 7 o'clock … and give me the satisfaction which as a gentleman I am entitled to'. He also added that he would happily accept an apology instead. Morgan refused to apologise.

There were a few minor difficulties for Landale. For a start, he did not own pistols, so he took the ferry over the Forth to buy a pair in Thomson's gun shop on Edinburgh's Princes Street. Secondly, he had never fired a shot in his life, while Morgan was an ex-army officer and would be experienced in such matters. Morgan had seen action in the Peninsular War and had the reputation of an aggressive, hot-tempered and ill-mannered man. He would be a formidable figure to face across the short distance that duelling required.

The seconds, Milie and Milne, tried to smooth things over. They met in the George Inn in Kirkcaldy and tried to seek mutual ground, but when Milne read out a letter from Morgan, it made no mention of an apology. The two parted without any agreement and not on the best of terms.

No apology

At half past five in the morning of 23 September, Landale, Milie and Dr Smith got into a carriage at Kirkcaldy and drove to Cardenden. On the journey, Milie asked if Landale would still accept an apology.

'By all means,' Landale said. 'I do not want Morgan's life. I only want an apology for the insult he has put upon me.'

While Morgan and Lieutenant Milne were on their way to the ground in a post-chaise, Morgan told Milne that he had 'horsewhipped' Landale. That was the first Milne had heard about the incident with the umbrella and he was not pleased.

Morgan and his party arrived at the chosen ground a few moments later. Again Landale said he would accept an apology, but Morgan said: 'No, no apology!'

They tossed a coin to see which second should choose the ground and Milne won; they loaded the pistols and took six paces each, turned and faced each other. There would be birds singing in the growing light of dawn. Lieutenant Milne gave the fatal words: 'Gentlemen, are you ready?'

At the word 'ready', Morgan raised his pistol, but Milie rebuked him: 'Mr Morgan, that's not fair – drop your pistol until the word "fire" is given.'

Morgan obeyed at once.

'Fire!'

At the word 'fire' both parties raised their pistols, took very quick aim or none at all, and squeezed the triggers. The double crack of the pistols was so close together the seconds heard only a single sound.

It was a cold-blooded, calculated act of courage and butchery. The pistols fired and the greasy white smoke hung amidst the chill air of the September morning as both men stood still, staring at each other. After about ten seconds, Morgan crumpled to the ground. His blood stained the green grass. Ignoring Milne's request for him to stay, Milie hustled Landale away. Landale travelled as far as the Lake District and changed his name, but as soon as the court asked him to appear he did the honourable thing and came north again. He was well aware that it was a murder trial and he could be hanged if he was found guilty, but he was a genuine gentleman and faced up to the consequences of his actions.

The case came to the Perth Circuit Court in September 1826, with Henry Cockburn defending. After a five-hour trial the judge, Lord Gillies, advised the jury to find Landale not guilty; they agreed and he walked free. Despite the law frowning upon duelling, there had been not a single conviction of murder as a result of a duel in Scotland since at least 1700.

The Morgan–Landale affair is said to have been the last real duel in Scotland, and Landale's pistols are held in the museum at Kirkcaldy. A small cairn marks the site of the duel. A quarter of a century later, Landale's daughter married Morgan's niece. Life continued . . .

12

The Dundee Museum Robbery

The building housing the McManus Museum and Galleries dominates Albert Square in the centre of Dundee. It is iconic, a splendid example of Victorian Gothic architecture, and it is quite rightly loved by the population of the city. Built to commemorate the life and death of Prince Albert, consort of Queen Victoria, it sits in its own space and is guarded by a phalanx of statues; it is a place to be visited again and again. Yet in the middle of the 1870s, this museum was the scene of a break-in that brought scandal to the city and ended up with the downfall of the Superintendent of Police.

Break-in

About half past ten on the night of 11 November 1875, the duty constable in central Dundee tested the south door of the McManus and found it secure. He continued on his beat and returned one hour later. This time he found the door was open a crack. Naturally suspicious, he hurried to tell his sergeant, who woke up the curator. His name was Reid and he lived in the north part of the building. Reid helped the police search the museum. There had been an extensive burglary, with about £1,000 worth of objects stolen.

Shortly before, there had been a presentation of silver plate to Provost Robertson; there were nine pieces of silver and nine crystal fruit dishes. These had been exhibited in a glass case on the ground floor, within easy distance of the windows on the south wall. The robber had made straight for the case but rather than break the glass, which would have been noisy and might have alerted Reid, he had pressed the wooden door until he had broken the lock. After that he had removed the plate but left the crystal behind. The plate alone was worth around £600.

Not yet content, the robber had run up the splendid staircase to the second floor, where he broke open two more cabinets, one at the window and another further in the shadows of the gallery. He had been selective: the window case held a valuable selection of gold watches and various coins and jewellery, together with antique weapons. To make it worse, the museum did not own the articles, which were on loan from a man named Jason Goodchild. After an attempt to force the lock, the thief had discarded any caution and had simply broken the glass and delved into the treasures beneath. He had then moved to the inner cabinet.

To judge by the marks and scrapes on the woodwork, the thief had attempted to pick the lock, but he had either grown impatient or knew he lacked the skill, so he simply forced the cabinet open. Once again the contents of the case were not part of the museum collection; this time South Kensington Museum owned then. They were silver artworks intended to be used by students, but the robber would have been disappointed when he found out they were not made of real silver but were merely copies of the originals.

The thief had chosen his night well; the full moon ensured there was no need for a lantern, whose tell-tale light might have alerted any passer-by. The police believed he had hidden inside the museum while it was still open, carefully selected the objects he fancied and walked out, although Reid said he had seen nobody when he had doused the gas lamps at nine that night. If the thief had not left the door open when he had left, the robbery would not have been discovered until morning.

Investigation

The police immediately began their investigations. Their first clue came when a couple of men told them that around midnight they had seen a man on Constitution Road carrying a sack. One of the men had inadvertently bumped into the sack carrier and heard it jangle. The police were interested and when they heard the description they recognised the man; it was someone they knew well. He was a riveter and his name was Peter Graham. When the police arrived at his house in Scott's Close, Nethergate, at about one in the morning, Graham was out, but the key was still in the lock. An hour later, Graham was in bed and the police turned the key, entered the house and arrested him there and then.

At this point, there was a twist. Graham neither admitted nor denied that he had been involved in the theft, but offered to guide the police to the stolen items and the culprits, for the meagre reward of £150. Strangely the police did not immediately accept his kind offer, but they pressed their questioning further. Graham proved suspiciously helpful. He claimed that there had been three men in the robbery, two from Leeds and one from Dundee. The police gave a collective nod, locked the door of his cell and left him to stew.

With their prime suspect safely in custody, the police continued to trawl for anybody else who looked suspicious. They picked up a smart Londoner on Reform Street, asked him a few questions and let him go. They sent patrols out to the roads leading out of Dundee, stopped and questioned anybody who happened to be walking at that late hour, but made no further progress. As soon as daylight permitted, detectives searched the outskirts of Dundee for any trace of the stolen objects, but without success.

The detectives split into two groups, with Lieutenant Hill commanding the east side of Dundee and Inspector Lamb the west. While Lamb had no initial success, ex-Bailie Brownlee advised Hill to investigate the railway tunnel that ran through the Law, the hill that dominates Dundee. At first Hill was sceptical, as the tunnel seemed too obvious a place for a professional to hide his loot. However, Brownlee was persuasive and Hill eventually agreed.

Treasure in the tunnel

He started from the south, shining a lantern ahead of him into the dense damp darkness. Near the northern end of the tunnel the lantern light glimmered on an area of disturbed ground, and there was evidence of something having been recently buried, but Perhaps the oil in the lamp was running low, for Hill did not investigate further. He had been sceptical all the time, so instead of pursuing the search he turned his attention to Camperdown Woods, where he found nothing. He decided belatedly to return to the tunnel.

While Hill had wasted his time in Camperdown, Inspector Lamb had entered the railway tunnel. He found the broken ground and ordered his men to dig two feet into the ground near the footprints. There was a shout of triumph as the spade clinked on something solid, and within minutes the police hauled out most of the stolen objects. When he met Hill at the entrance of the tunnel, Lamb had two sacks full of recovered items. Although the silver dessert service presented to Provost Robertson had been damaged in transit, nearly everything had been found. Only a couple of rings were still missing.

The events created immense curiosity and a number of questions. Crowds rushed to visit the museum as never before and probably never since, with an estimated 10,000 people crushing into the McManus in the course of the next week. The questions rang round Dundee: how had Peter Graham, if it was he, entered the museum unseen? How was the loot carried through Dundee without the police intercepting the thief? Why was there not sufficient security set on Provost Robertson's testimonial plate? And, possibly even more intriguing, how had the police located the stolen objects so quickly?

Councillor Jobson of the Free Library Committee, who ran the museum, had suggested that the museum should have better lighting for Robertson's testimonial plate but Robertson himself had rejected the proposal.

Bribing the robber

There was speculation that the police had accepted Graham's offer to help them find the loot in return for £150 and a quick release. However, on Saturday, 13 November, Graham appeared before the Police Court and was charged with the robbery.

The museum hastily appointed a watchman while the police continued their investigations, still concentrating on Peter Graham. They thoroughly searched his house and found a screwdriver under his bed. When they tested it on the museum cases in the museum, they found the head of the screwdriver exactly matched the scratches.

Next they took Graham's mother, Mary Gray, aside and questioned her. She told them that she, and not Graham, had left the key in the door. She left it there so her cab driver husband could get home easily when he returned from working late. More worrying was her frank admission that Graham had been given £100 in return for information that led to the recovery of the stolen items. Graham had given the money to her, and was disagreeably surprised when he had been charged with the robbery; he had expected to be released on the Saturday morning. Mary Gray deposited the money securely in a bank, so it was safe from thieves until her son was released from prison.

Mrs Gray was a very respectable woman and had run her lodging house in Scott's Close for many years. Not only did she help her second husband, Graham's stepfather, but when Graham had returned home from Barrow-in-Furness because of ill health, she searched for a mill job to help support him as well.

When news spread that Graham had been bribed, the Dundee public wondered what sort of police force they had. On Thursday, 16 December, there was a public meeting at the Kinnaird Hall in the city. Interest was so great that the hall was packed to capacity and other men waited outside. Two days later Peter Graham was charged with the theft.

In the statement he made to the police he said he had been in several pubs on the night in question, but he believed that two men from Leeds had committed the robbery. After a series of interviews with Superintendent Mackay and a selection of detectives, he said, he was asked to reveal the whereabouts of the stolen goods on the tacit understanding that he would be paid £100 and be released, as long as he left Dundee. He was given a cheque for that amount, he said, and informed the police where the museum objects were hidden.

On the Saturday morning, £100 in notes was exchanged for the cheque but rather than release Graham, the police remitted his case to the Procurator Fiscal. To the public in Dundee, this whole series of transactions smacked of bribery and corruption. They wanted their police force to be both moral and respectable, and considered that offering bribes was wrong. It is possible that they also considered that the superintendent of police should keep his word, even to a criminal. On 1 December the Dundee Police Committee met and decided to launch an inquiry into the entire police establishment of the city. The upshot of the report of Charles Carnegie, the Inspector of Constabulary, was that Superintendent Mackay, a long-serving stalwart, was asked to retire. Other minor matters were also revealed, such as the fact that policemen who had broken the law were discharged before their appearance in court and recorded as labourers. That way the record of the Dundee police appeared pristine, with no serving officers charged with an offence.

On 17 January 1876 Graham appeared before the High Court in Edinburgh, charged with the robbery. The judge made a lot of the fact that the police had supplied him with drink when he was in custody, and after confirming that Graham had been bribed, he directed the jury to find him not guilty.

The career of Peter Graham

Peter Graham did not disappear from history after his acquittal. In June he was arrested for an alleged burglary at the railway station in Fyvie in Aberdeenshire. He had given the name Philip Clark when he was arrested but the police knew who he was. He was tried in Aberdeen but once again escaped, as there was insufficient evidence against him. He left the court smiling and dashed into the nearest pub in the Castlegate.

He was no sooner freed from that case than he returned to Dundee and was immediately in trouble again, this time accused of assault and theft. He complained that his fame invited men to seek his company, while claiming that the police sought to arrest him on any pretext. He may have been correct. At the end of June there was a break-in at Ogilvie's public house in West Dock Street and Graham was again arrested on suspicion. The police hauled him out of bed at four in the morning but once again the prosecution could not find enough evidence and he was released. Only a fortnight later, he was again in police custody after a shop-breaking in Greenmarket.

This time Constable John Ross had been watching Graham, as he was acting suspiciously in Fish Street. Ross saw Graham carrying something and challenged him; Graham ran up Fish Street, but Ross caught him as he dived into Scott's Close. Graham tried to smash a bottle of beer over Ross's head, but the policeman knocked it out of his hand and wrestled Graham to the ground. Ross blew his whistle and when two more police arrived Graham was overpowered and arrested. Stolen goods from the shop were found in his possession.

At the Dundee Circuit Court in October, the prosecution found out that Graham broke a window in the loft above the shop, used a ladder to descend from the loft to the shop and cleaned the place of everything valuable. He pleaded not guilty but this time the judge had no doubt and sent him down for fifteen months with hard labour.

After his release, Graham spent time in the Glasgow area. In December 1878 he was back in trouble, accused of shop-breaking in Lancashire. He gave his name as Peter Cramm, but was recognised. He was sentenced to a hefty five years' penal servitude.

More trouble at the museum

While Graham was pursuing his criminal career, the museum was also having an interesting time. In the early morning of 10 May 1877, despite the extra precaution of a watchman patrolling the museum, there was another break-in. This time the burglars hit the north-west side of the building, opposite Panmure Street, sometime between midnight and one in the morning. They waited until the beat constable was at the furthest distance from their target, broke the lower half of a window and slipped inside. The interior was dark, but they must have known where they were going, for they headed to the first floor and smashed the glass of two display cases that contained valuable coins and jewellery. Once again, Jason Goodchild's collection of antique watches was rifled. However, the burglars had made a slight miscalculation in not carrying anything to break the glass. They had to punch through the glass; with the result that they left a spatter of blood on the case and all over the floor. Apart from that small mistake, the thieves had chosen their target well. Once they had grabbed what they were after, they scampered back downstairs.

The watchman, William Ramsay, was patrolling the picture gallery at the time of the robbery. Ramsay had spent twenty-five years as a turnkey in Dundee Prison and had a reputation as a reliable man. He came across the broken cases at around one in the morning. As many of Goodchild's valuable objects had been left behind, Ramsay guessed that the thieves had heard him coming and had fled. He immediately alerted the management and the police, and then busied himself with a thorough inspection of the building. There was nothing else missing. The museum valued the missing items at around £30; Goodchild thought them worth rather more, estimating their value at around £100.

The police found traces of oil on the steps, but believed they came from Ramsay's lamp rather than anything the burglars had carried. More importantly they also found spots of blood on the pavement and followed the gory trail along Meadowside and Barrack Street to an address in Butcher's Row. They interrogated the inhabitants of the house but found nothing. As usual in these circumstances, the detectives checked pawnshops in case any of the stolen objects were handed in. They also used their extensive network of informers, one of whom whispered the name James Cameron to them. It seemed that Cameron had been seen drinking in various Dundee pubs and had boasted he would soon be known for some famous crime. On the night of the robbery he had left the pub just before midnight and had not returned to his Princes Street home but had walked to Broughty and caught the ferry to Fife. The Dundee police investigated Cameron's life and found that he had been in the United States more than once, and his relatives there would no doubt be pleased to welcome him back, particularly if he brought some new wealth with him.

The Dundee police asked the police in Glasgow to watch for Cameron, in case he should try and sign articles on a ship bound for the United States, but there was no sign of him. They sent his details to the other Scottish police forces. The description was fairly clear, saying he was a twenty-five-year-old native of Dundee, five-feet-eight-inches tall, sturdy with short, dark brown hair and large blue eyes. He had clean-shaven cheeks but a two-inch beard on his chin, high cheekbones and a fresh complexion. Cameron had been involved in industrial accidents: a machine had damaged his left hand, crushing two fingers, while he had lost half a finger on his right hand.

The police knew exactly what he had been wearing. Cameron was dressed in dark tweed, with either a tweed cap or a black felt hat. Lacking cheap photography, the nineteenth-century police still had the ability to send an image across the country.

The descriptions obviously worked. On 18 May, the Edinburgh police telegraphed their colleagues in Dundee and told them that Cameron was in their city. Sergeant Gamble knew Cameron by sight and travelled from Dundee. He teamed up with the local detective Stevenson and they made their arrest. Cameron was sporting thick bandages on both hands and walking openly down the Canongate. He recognised the two men following him as police, took to his heels and fled. Gamble expected that and followed, down a steep close that led to the Cowgate, where he arrested him. When the police searched Cameron, they found an antique French watch and other valuables in his possession, so there was little doubt that he was the culprit. The High Court judge shared that opinion and Cameron was given eighteen months in jail.

With Cameron and Graham both in custody and a new superintendent of police in charge, Dundee museum could look forward to a more peaceful period, but these episodes reveal both the weaknesses and strengths of the police of the period, as well as a glimpse into the lives of professional thieves.

13

Murder in the Family

In nineteenth-century Scotland, people were more likely to be murdered by family members than by strangers. Mothers murdered their children, wives their husbands, and husbands their wives. This chapter looks at some of the many murders that took place within the family.

Religious murder

There is something in the psyche of many Scots that embraces the spiritual side of life. This can be very positive for most people, opening a door to a completely different dimension and allowing access to all the benefits of the major religions. However, for others, there is a dark side that can lead to prejudice, bigotry, violence and even murder. When a man living in the lonely stretches of the Highlands, where the long, brooding winters can lead to introspection and introversion, the risk of the negativity of religious fervour may be intense.

On Friday, 19 June 1868, a shepherd named Kenneth Campbell beat his wife to death. Campbell lived at Ribigill Farm, a few miles from the village of Tongue in Sutherland. The name of the farm tells of the Norse influence in this part of Scotland. At one time this area had been populous but Lord Reay and then the Duke of Sutherland had cleared the people to make way for sheep, so Campbell lived in a place sad with memories of the departed. He was a middle-aged man of muscular build and strong religious convictions, and was married to forty-year-old Assynt woman Margaret. The Campbells had four children, the youngest of whom was only one year old. A servant named Williamina Campbell also lived with them, and there was an occasional visitor or a fellow worker from the vast Lettermore Estate.

Kenneth Campbell was well known in the area. He was a quiet man, a good worker and kind to his family. He had long been interested in religion but around April of 1868 he had begun to pay far more attention to spiritual matters. At the beginning of June he attended a Free Church communion and came away saying that he was worried about the state of his soul.

On Sunday, 14 June, a local man, Graham Rae, arrived to stay with the Campbell family for the week. He had known Campbell for around three years and thought him a 'quiet, reserved man'. On the Friday evening 'about the darkening', Campbell held his usual family religious service and then everybody went to bed. Rae was awoken by a terrible noise coming from the Campbells' bedroom. The first thing he heard was Campbell's voice, roaring at Margaret. Rae thought it best to go for help rather than try and tackle the obviously irate Campbell himself, so he dressed hurriedly and left the farm. The last thing he heard was the tinkle and crash of shattering glass from the Campbells' bedroom.

Rae was not the only person disturbed by the noise. Williamina Campbell had gone to her bed in the closet around ten, but Campbell's shouting also broke her sleep. Unlike Rae, she remained in bed and listened to what was being said. She heard Campbell shouting out for Donald McKay, the shepherd at Inch Kinloch, a settlement a few miles away, far too distant for Campbell's voice to carry. Even more disturbing was the fact that Campbell was saying that he was in hell. That was enough for Williamina; she opened the window and slipped out into the cool dark of the night.

'Leave me alone'

As she passed the kitchen window, she heard Campbell's loud ranting and Margaret crying out, 'Leave me alone, leave me!' Williamina scurried to the front of the house, opened the door and peered in. She could not see Campbell but heard his voice, alternatively preaching passages from the Bible or roaring that he was lost in hell. There were other sounds as well, as if Campbell was 'banging his two fists together'. Williamina decided she would not return that night. She saw a figure approaching, realised it was Ann Campbell, the daughter, and both women made for Inch Kenneth in the dim light of the Highland night. They did not get that far. As they stumbled over the rough ground, they saw three shadowy men hurrying toward them: Graham Rae, Donald McKay and John Munro.

When Graham Rae had left the farm, he had run to Inch Kinloch, three miles away, and roused the two shepherds who lived there: Munro and McKay. They rose groggily as Rae told them that Kenneth Campbell was 'wrong in his mind'. The three men ran back to Ribigill, picked up Ann and Williamina, and hoped they were not too late to get the Campbells sorted out. They were too late. It was around four in the morning when they reached Ribigill, and even before they entered they heard Campbell's voice.

'I am Christ!' Campbell said. 'Christ was crucified and I was crucified alongside Him.'

After that, Campbell began to sing what Munro thought must be a psalm, although he recognised neither the words nor the tune. The singing ended with a loud prayer.

As soon as the party entered the house, they found the body of Margaret lying in a bloody heap on the floor behind the front door. Campbell stood behind her, blocking the door of the passage, as naked as the day he was born.

'Have mercy on my soul', Campbell roared. 'I am Christ and if you shake hands with me you will be saved.'

He stretched his hand out, but Munro was having none of it and did not respond. Campbell was ranting, the Gaelic words echoing around the house above the still, silent body of his wife. As soon as Munro refused his gesture, Campbell withdrew inside the kitchen and said he would 'knock out your brains if you come nearer'.

He tried his best to keep his word and swung a wild fist, but Munro blocked the blow and closed with the naked man. His companions joined him and bore Campbell to the ground. As two of them held Campbell tight, Munro fetched a rope and tied him hand and foot so he was helpless, but still vociferous. He lay on the kitchen floor for some time, alternating between total silence and wild raving.

As soon as the men had bound the naked Campbell, Williamina and John Munro lifted the body of Margaret and carried it into the kitchen. Williamina noticed that Margaret's face was swollen and 'quite black'.

Rae left the farm again, running to fetch Dr Robert Black at Tongue, about seven miles away by track and moorland. Dr Black examined the body of Margaret Campbell and found a sickening list of injuries. There was a wound over one eye that may have been caused by a fall, but more likely by some blunt instrument. Six of her ribs were splintered and shattered; her heart was torn open; her spleen was burst, her liver ruptured and she was a mass of bruises. In his professional opinion, Kenneth Campbell had knocked her down and kicked her to death.

When Constable Donald Stewart escorted Kenneth Campbell to jail in Dornoch, he said that Campbell ranted the entire time, saying that he would go to heaven even though he had killed his wife, for Margaret had been Judas and if he had not killed her he would have gone to hell. When Campbell was held in jail, Dr Robert Souter examined him; Campbell told him that on Friday lightning had come from heaven and gone through his body. As he spoke, Campbell tore off his clothes, said that a voice from heaven had ordered him to show Christ crucified, and threw himself onto the ground with his arms outstretched.

He also said that heaven had told him his wife was a 'perfect harlot'. Staring right into the doctor's eyes, he said that while he was in bed, heaven had ordered him to tell Margaret that he was Christ crucified, and once she had acknowledged that he was to destroy her.

The case was heard before Lord Ardmillan and Lord Jerviswood at the High Court in Edinburgh. Campbell was found not guilty for reasons of insanity and he was committed to a lunatic asylum.

Other wife murderers were less brutal but more cynical.

The bigamous husband

Bigamy was not an unusual crime in the nineteenth century, and murder was more common than might be supposed, but the combination of both was seldom encountered. However, it did happen.

William Bennison was an Irishman and like many others in the troubled 1830s, he made the short hop to Scotland in search of work. He was around twenty years old and not a classically handsome man, for he had a sallow complexion and bushy whiskers, but women seemed to like him, or perhaps he just liked them. Although he frequently moved between Scotland and Ireland, he settled in Paisley, where in 1839 he met a lovely young lady called Jane Hamilton. Bennison was so infatuated with Jane that he forgot to tell her one or two minor things.

For a start, he forgot to tell Jane that he was already married. On 5 November 1838 he had married an equally lovely lady named Mary

Mullen, in Tavanagh near Portadown in County Armagh. He also forgot to tell Jane that as soon as he had married Mary he had vanished for eighteen months on some mysterious errand of his own. The third thing he neglected to mention was that he had dragged his reluctant Irish wife with him to Scotland, and the fourth was that he had beaten and bruised her as a form of persuasion. Finally, he had forgotten to say that Mary had disappeared from the knowledge of her friends and family. All they knew was that they had last seen her wearing a blue mantle.

Given these insignificant omissions, Bennison and Jane's marriage seemed doomed from the outset. Bennison remained with his alternative wife for a few months, and then had to make the trip back over to Ireland. Jane moved into her mother's house, where her sister Ellen also lived, and waited patiently for her husband. When Bennison came back, he was dressed in mourning black and spun a story that he had travelled back with his sister, Mary, but she had fallen sick on the boat and died on their way to Airdrie.

Without any suspicion, Jane asked, 'Why Airdrie?' Bennison replied that her late master, a man for whom she had worked, lived there. However, Bennison tried to prove his affection for his wife by giving her some clothes that had belonged to his sister Mary, including a mantle of fine blue cloth.

There was one disturbing incident in Paisley. Jane and Bennison visited the Wesleyan chapel for Sunday service and a stranger approached them, holding out his hand. Bennison said he had never met the man before, but the stranger looked puzzled and said, 'I think I know your face. Was it not you who buried your wife in Airdrie?'

Bennison denied he had done any such thing. He walked quickly away and out of the chapel, leaving the man staring. Jane had not heard the conversation but her sister Ellen had; at the time she thought nothing of it.

Not long afterwards Mr and Mrs Bennison left Paisley for Portadown in Ireland and met some of Bennison's family. Strangely, they mentioned Bennison's supposedly deceased sister Mary as being alive and well. Naturally Jane enquired further about the woman who had died of seasickness and her loving husband gave the glib answer that she had only been his sister in the Lord. There was also some talk about another wife, but Jane had either not been privy to the whole conversation, or not been sufficiently interested to take note. She mentioned the fact to Ellen as a casual piece of gossip, but without any details.

Bennison spent some time back in Paisley and then returned to Ireland. Jane told him to take the blue mantle and other clothes back with him. She said that as they had not belonged to his sister, they must have belonged to another woman. Ellen thought that Jane meant she had no wish to wear the clothes of a previous wife. Shortly after that the Bennisons moved to Leith Walk in Edinburgh. Apart from the puzzling question of a first wife, they were a happy couple who rarely quarrelled and soon their marriage was blessed by the arrival of a daughter. If they did have disagreements, they centred on Bennison's frequent absences in the evening. Jane wished to spend more time with her husband but he preferred to go to Methodist prayer meetings rather than worship with his family.

The Bennisons were not alone in their Leith Walk home; they shared with a Mrs Alison Moffat. In the winter of 1849, Jane took a cold, which stayed with her throughout the dark months, but which Mrs Moffat thought eased with the warmer spring weather. Bennison disagreed: he said that her condition was deteriorating.

Ellen had a more serious reason for disagreeing with Bennison, for she had often seen him in the company of a young bonnet-maker named Margaret Robertson, whom he also sat close to at his Methodist meetings. Perhaps mindful of her sister's delicate state of health, Ellen did not tell Jane about Margaret. However, Ellen was not the only person with eyes; many of the neighbours had also seen Bennison and Margaret Robertson together.

About Saturday, 13 April 1850, Bennison informed Ellen that he was very concerned about Jane's health; he said he believed she was dying. Ellen rushed over to Leith Walk and found that Jane was very weak and had been violently ill. Jane had severe stomach ache and was very thirsty but she threw up anything given to her. A neighbour, Mrs Turnbull, came to help, but her ministrations failed to ease Jane's pain. Ellen thought that Bennison was quite calm, considering that his wife was in such straits, and a bit premature in ordering funeral clothes. He wrote letters inviting people to Jane's funeral while she was still alive. Although he paced the house as if anxious, he hardly approached Jane's bed.

The neighbours were very surprised that Jane had taken so sick so suddenly, and were more surprised when Bennison gave up hope for her and refused to call a doctor. 'I've no notion for doctors,' he told Mrs Porteous, a neighbour, but quickly contradicted himself by saying that he had already consulted one, who had said there was nothing he could do. Bennison told another neighbour, Agnes Turnbull, that Jane was 'going home to glory'.

Yet another friend, Euphemia Ingram, was equally unhappy. When Bennison had made some porridge and potatoes for Jane, Euphemia had inadvertently fed both to a dog. The dog sickened and died, so she immediately wondered what Bennison had put in the porridge. In a period when poisoning unwanted relatives was not uncommon, suspicion seemed quite close to the surface of many people's thoughts.

Jane obviously disagreed with her husband's opinion of doctors, for on Sunday, 14 April 1850, she asked him to call the doctor again. Bennison said that Dr Gillespie would return but he was expensive and could not help. Despite Bennison's words, Dr Gillespie eventually saw Jane; he said she was very weak and had been vomiting. He prescribed mustard poultice and wine and left the house. Jane grew worse; she sickened quickly and around midnight that same day, she died.

She died alone, for her husband had left the house in her final moments. He claimed he had met the doctor at their front door and told him Jane was gone and there was no need to enter.

Immediately after Jane died, Bennison removed her wedding ring and rushed to arrange the funeral for the following Wednesday. 'There is no point in losing more time,' he said. Then he left the house for that of Margaret and Mrs Robertson, although he did come back home from time to time. Ellen stayed beside her sister. Strangely, Margaret Robertson came into the Leith Walk house where Jane's body lay.

Ellen was not at all happy about the manner of Jane's death and wondered what had caused it. When she suggested to Bennison that there should be a post-mortem, Bennison 'got agitated at the moment' and claimed that 'his feelings would not stand it'. He tried delaying tactics: he said he would bring a doctor, but then claimed that neither of the local medical men were available until evening. The doctor did not turn up and then Bennison said he would not pay for an autopsy and, anyway, the church would disapprove.

Ellen was not the only person who was suspicious. Bennison had bought arsenic and ammonia from a local chemist called McDonald; he was not a silent man, so rumours soon spread that Bennison had poisoned his wife. On Friday, 19 April, a criminal officer named John Fallon and a sheriff officer named George Ferguson came to the Leith Walk house. Fallon pulled Bennison from his bed and arrested him. He also took away the porridge pot, some wrapping paper and a tub into which Jane had been sick. Next day Ferguson brought Bennison back to the house and examined it thoroughly for rats, including the cellar and the lower cellar, but although there were a number of holes, there was no trace of rats.

When Jane's stomach contents were analysed, the contents included arsenic, but the doctors were sure that there were no traces of poison in the porridge pot. However, there were traces in the paper that Ferguson had carried away. Bennison did not deny that there had been poison in the paper, but claimed he had bought it to kill rats, and he had given the packet to Jane and had not seen it since.

The police took Bennison aside and questioned him. He claimed he had never been married before, and had never known a woman named Mary Mullen. He later altered his statement to say he had been married to Mary Mullen but thought she had died when he was seeking work in Scotland. For that reason, he believed he was free to marry Jane Hamilton. When he had moved back to Ireland, he had discovered that Mary was still alive and lived with her for a while. He had come back to Scotland with her and she had suddenly taken ill and died and was buried in Airdrie. He also said that he had told Jane about her but asked that she keep the matter secret.

When the case came to court, Margaret Robertson denied any romantic liaison with Bennison and claimed that they only attended the same Methodist church and spoke solely of religious matters. Margaret also said that she had come to Bennison's house at the invitation of Jane, who was obviously not present to deny or confirm the fact.

The court found Bennison guilty of both murder and bigamy, and he was sentenced to be hanged. On Friday, 16 August, he was executed at Libberton's Wynd on the High Street in Edinburgh. Two hundred and fifty police kept back the crowd, but there was no disorder. Before he died Bennison confessed that he had put arsenic in his wife's porridge and he had an 'interest' in young Margaret Robertson, but she was innocent of anything. However, this confession still left the gaping question: did he murder his first wife in Airdrie? The answer will never be known.

Present for the wife

Sometimes men went to great lengths to rid themselves of an unwanted wife, but few went to such lengths as David Macrae of Tain. Macrae was a contractor and his wife Rebecca suffered from mental health problems. In 1873, Rebecca was in Saughton Hall Asylum, just outside Edinburgh, but Macrae decided he no longer wanted to be married to her.

As the couple were hundreds of miles apart, Macrae decided to murder Rebecca by post. Accordingly, he made up a lethal package to send to her. He found a stout box and placed a loaded pistol inside, with the hammer fully cocked and a percussion cap in position on the nipple. He added over four pounds of gunpowder and a large amount of broken glass. He tied a string to the trigger of the revolver and attached the other end to the inside of the box lid. The idea was that when Rebecca lifted the lid, the string would pull the trigger of the revolver so the hammer would fall on the percussion cap. The resulting spark would ignite the powder, which would explode and spread the broken glass into the face of Rebecca. Together with the exploding gunpowder, the glass could cause terrible injuries, or even kill her.

Macrae was aware that Rebecca may not open such a large packet until she thought she knew what the contents were. He circumvented her suspicion by sending her a letter in advance, telling her that he was sending her a box containing some of her mother's clothes, but she had to pick it up at Waverley Station. Rebecca was not so easily fooled. She must have had her suspicions about her husband, for when she saw the box she asked one of the railwaymen to help her open it, and told him her worries.

The railwayman managed to open the box safely; the pistol did not fire. When Rebecca saw the lethal contents, she immediately told the police. Macrae was charged but failed to attend his court hearing and was outlawed.

Domestic violence was not all one-sided. Wives were sometimes guilty of murdering their husbands . . .

Fatal triangle

Arbroath is one of the most interesting small towns of Scotland. It hugs the coast of Angus, about twenty miles north of Dundee, and centres on its harbour. Even today, when so many coastal towns have succumbed to gentrification and tourism, Arbroath has a working fishing fleet. The aroma of the sea permeates the area, mingled with the characteristic scent of the famous Arbroath Smokies – smoked haddock – that are created here.

In the nineteenth century, Arbroath had a much larger fishing fleet, as well as trading ships that sailed along the British coast and over to the Baltic. It was a busy, thriving town with a great deal of character. However, in common with every other community in Scotland, it also had its share of intrigue and crime.

On Saturday, 21 January 1843, John Cromarty, one of the many Arbroath seamen, came home for the last time. He lived on the Marketgate with his wife, Agnes. They had an interesting marriage, and she had brought him nine children, of whom six survived, which was a good average for the time. She was also pregnant again. But he was now around sixty-five and she had just turned thirty; she sometimes had a hankering for a younger man.

Cromarty was two days back from a five-month-long voyage, where his last port had been Riga in the Baltic. He had been drinking with a friend named David Durward and he weaved a little unsteadily as he made his way to the house, to find a number of people already there. As well as his wife, there was a crowd of his friends and a man named James Connell. Cromarty was no friend of Connell; he was a blacksmith in his twenties who worked at the harbour. Much more important, Agnes had become attached to him when Cromarty was away at sea.

She had taken him in as a lodger, but the good people of Arbroath knew that their relationship was far more intimate than that.

It was about nine at night when Cromarty arrived home, obviously a little the worse for wear. Not surprisingly, his friends advised that he go to bed, but he was a stubborn seaman and continued to down his whisky as the night wore on. He insisted on remaining awake until all the guests had departed. By that time it was around midnight. Cromarty was alone with his wife and the persistent and handsome James Connell.

Very early the next morning, Agnes Cromarty woke the Marketgate with her cries, as she wailed that her husband was dead. Among the first to be called out of bed were David and Margaret Smith, a married couple. When Mrs Smith hurried into her kitchen and saw Agnes Cromarty and Connell sitting together beside her fire, her husband told her, 'Jack is gone.'

Death was fairly common in any fishing community, and as Cromarty was not a young man, there was no sense of horror. Margaret Smith asked Agnes when it had happened.

'A while ago', Agnes told her.

Margaret Smith and Agnes hurried over to Cromarty's house, but when they reached the front door, Agnes refused to go in. She asked Margaret to get a candle and look at the corpse saying, 'I cannot go.'

Margaret Smith found old John Cromarty lying dead on his bed with a nightcap on his head. She called out to Agnes that she would need help to dress the body and make it decent, so another neighbour named Mrs Caroline Mather came to help. All this time Connell remained in the room, not saying much. Connell eventually helped by lifting the feet and legs of the old man so the women could take off his night shirt. Margaret Smith noticed that the sheets were wet with urine, while Caroline Mather was more concerned with the fresh blood on Cromarty's forehead, the fact that his face was swollen and the scratches on his chest. Agnes explained that her husband had fallen on his face when he was returning from the pub the previous night.

Mrs Mather asked why Agnes had not called a doctor, but was told, 'What use is a doctor to a dead man?'

Later on, Margaret Smith asked Agnes how Cromarty had died, and she gave two different versions. At first she said that Cromarty was chasing her, fell and banged his head; later, she said he had died alone in his bed. She told James Smith, Margaret Smith's stepson, that Cromarty had died 'through the effects of drink'. That same day Agnes asked for a coffin to be made; she hoped to bury her husband on the Tuesday.

James Smith was not impressed by the behaviour of Connell, who spoke casually of his work and laughed as he watched the corpse being prepared for burial. However, there was somebody else who might have known exactly what had happened.

William Cromarty was nine years old and the son of the dead man. It was some time before he told people that he had witnessed his father's death, but when he did, he caused quite a stir. He said that he had been in bed and had heard his father singing. His bed was in a recess in the wall, with no bed curtains or any other impediment to stop him witnessing everything. He had heard something that he thought was the table falling and looked over to see what the noise was. William said his father had been sitting on a chair beside the fire and Connell hit him on the head with something iron and sharp – maybe the fireside tongs. His father gave a 'wild roar' and fell down right away.

As Cromarty lay bleeding on the floor, Agnes Cromarty said, 'That will do for the old bugger,' and stood at the door as if to prevent anybody else from entering. Connell made sure that Cromarty was dead by strangling the semi-conscious or unconscious man. As a blacksmith, Connell certainly had the strength to deal with Cromarty, and the suspected intimate relationship with Agnes would provide sufficient motive.

Once Cromarty was dead, Connell took off the old man's boots and he and Agnes carried the body to the bed. Once there, Connell took off Cromarty's jacket.

A few moments later, according to William Cromarty, Agnes and Connell left the house. Not knowing what else to do, William turned over and tried to go to sleep. He was wakened as his mother and Connell returned with Mr and Mrs Smith.

The police were not inclined to believe Agnes' story, particularly as there was no evidence that Cromarty had fallen and banged his head.

The case came to court in July 1843. Agnes Cromarty gave a slightly different version of events. She said that Cromarty and some other seamen had been at a meeting in Hill Street, where he had fallen down. He had fallen again when he was in the house and she had to put him to bed. According to Agnes, she asked Connell for help. Connell had been lying on his bed fully clothed but had refused to help, saying, 'If the old cankered bugger will not go to bed, I will not do it.'

Only when her husband was in bed, Agnes claimed, did she lie beside him, and when she woke at about three in the morning, she found that he had died.

Doctor Traill had examined the body and said that the throat was discoloured and the skin twisted, as if somebody had strangled Cromarty with a neck cloth, while the marks on his face were 'more likely' to have been produced by blows than a fall. Traill believed that Cromarty had been strangled. Another witness, Ann Berry, was the servant of a cow-feeder. She had twice brought milk to Cromarty's house while he was at sea, and had found Agnes Cromarty in bed with Connell; there was no doubt the pair were lovers.

As far as the character of Connell was concerned, a number of witnesses agreed that Connell, from the island of Lismore in the Inner Hebrides, was a very quiet and well-behaved young man who had never been in any trouble – until now, at least.

The defence discounted the evidence of William, partly because he was so young, partly because William had believed that Connell had killed his father by a blow on the head, with the strangulation being an extra, and partly because William had not immediately run to tell anybody that his father had been murdered. Without the evidence of the only eyewitness, the jury could not convict. They found the case not proven: Agnes and Connell walked free.

14

The Siege of John Street

Shootings were not common in Scottish cities, so even a single gunshot could create consternation. When a gunman shot five people and stabbed a police inspector to death, the public were entitled to be shocked and alarmed. Such a series of events happened in Dundee in 1893.

Brain injuries

John Street was an ordinary residential area off Dudhope Crescent Road, just to the north of the city centre, yet it became the background to one of the city's most sensational crimes. In common with many Dundee streets, John Street was composed of four-storey-high tenements, mostly leased out to tenants. In 1893 one of the tenants at number 15 was a strongly built gas stoker named John Farley. He was an Irishman from County Cavan who had travelled around Britain as well as Russia and the United States before settling in Dundee. For all his burly appearance, he was not as healthy and fit as he had once been. About five years previously he had been working on a rescue operation in Glasgow when an explosion had knocked him aside. He was under the care of a doctor, who said he had ague and brain injuries, which seem to have had an adverse effect on him.

In the summer of 1892 Farley, together with his Irish wife Mary, their fifteen-year-old daughter and their four-year-old son, moved into an attic flat on John Street. They occupied one of three houses at the stair head. Farley spent his time with his son or searching for a job, while his wife and daughter worked in a jute mill. After a year of fruitless searching, Farley decided he should sail to America to find work.

It is possible that the neighbours breathed a heartfelt sigh of relief at the thought of Farley leaving the street, for he was not the easiest of men to live near. While his wife and daughter were liked for their respectable demeanour and regular working hours, Farley was thought of as strange and erratic. Farley often told his wife that the neighbours disliked him, and perhaps they had cause, for when Mrs Farley was working, he would annoy the women who lived in the stair. Rather than walking downstairs in the conventional manner, he would jump down step after step, chanting 'Jack the Ripper' at each step, and encouraging his son to do the same. In 1893, Jack the Ripper was still vivid in the public imagination; his crimes were still fresh and he had never been caught.

Naturally the local children heard his chants and joined in, so when Farley walked the streets he would be surrounded by a gaggle of youngsters, all calling him Jack the Ripper, which he found irritating. In time he became very frustrated with his jeering following and swore at their mothers, saying he would 'do for' them or shoot them. Farley was only ever aggressive to the women who lived in his stair, never to the men and never to anybody else, so when the women complained to the factor, a man named Walker, he thought they were exaggerating.

The morning of 15 August 1893 was like any other. Both Farley women went to work and Farley took his son for a walk around the locality. His wife and daughter came home for lunch at two and left again at three; all this was the normal routine. As soon as they left, Farley took their son out of the house for another walk. On the landing immediately beneath his flat there was a group of women talking. They were Mrs Leckie, who lived there, Mrs Isabella Norrie, who lived in the same close, and her daughter, Mrs Catherine Miller, who lived across the road. As he passed, Farley gave some objectionable remark, and Mrs Leckie retorted that it was a peculiar thing that women could not stand at their own door without interference. Miller, only a week out of hospital after giving birth, held her baby and said nothing.

'The man is coming back'

That seemed to close the matter, as Farley took his son down the remainder of the stairs. However, he had no sooner reached street level than he seemed to change his mind, turned around and came back upstairs. Young Robina Chaplin was playing on the second-floor landing and saw Farley remount the stairs. She shouted up the stairs: 'The man is coming back.'

Farley bounded up the stairs and rushed into his flat. He pulled out a locked wooden box from behind his bed and grabbed the revolver that was inside, loaded it quickly and ran out of the house. According to the gossiping women, he was in 'an excited state' as he rushed back down the stairs with the revolver in his hand. When he reached the three women, he aimed at Mrs Norrie, swore loudly and shot her in the stomach. Mrs Norrie fell, screaming out, 'Murder!'

'Now you, bitch – it's your turn next,' Farley said, and aimed at Catherine Miller, who stood paralysed with fear, holding her child close for protection. Farley shot her twice, with one bullet entering her stomach and the other her thigh, and then he looked for Mrs Leckie, but she had escaped, screaming 'Murder!' at the top of her voice as she fled down the stairs. Farley saw the youngster Robina Chaplin and fired at her too, the sound of the shots loud and echoing in the confines of the stair. Either he was a poor shot or Robina was very agile, for he missed completely and she escaped into her own house.

Either satisfied with his work, or because he had a moment of sanity, Farley ran back home and locked the door. Naturally the shooting and screaming had attracted attention and there was something like panic in the stair as women, children and a few men ran around with no real idea what to do. Nobody had any experience of dealing with a crazed gunman.

The first to act were the boys who could be found in any Dundee street. Attracted to the commotion like flies to rotten meat, they heard what had happened and, high with excitement, ran to the Bell Street police station and gabbled their news to the bemused officer at the desk. He did not believe a word and was about to throw them out when he heard the blast of a police whistle and a man ran into the station with exactly the same story. Three policemen grabbed their helmets and truncheons and ran the short distance to John Street. They were not alone, for the sound of shots and screaming had drawn a crowd of spectators. Police from the surrounding beats congregated to do their bit. Women were screaming, children were spreading tales about Jack the Ripper and men were wondering how best to look after their families.

In many places, the populace would have stood back and let the police do the work alone, but Dundee was a unique town. When brave constables – John Anderson, William Dickson and a third named Clark – got ready to mount the steps, they were joined by two local men, a street cleaner named John Wishart and a butcher named Andrew Coyle. These five men pounded up the stairs to Farley's door and demanded admittance. Farley refused, saying he would shoot the first man who tried to enter.

'You're the buggers I want'

'Come on – you're the buggers I want,' he said, and he emptied his revolver at the locked door. The first shot hit Wishart in the right arm. He staggered back, out of the fight. Then it was Anderson, shot in the jaw by a bullet that lodged against the bone and in the left arm. Then a bullet slammed into Dickson's shoulder. The shooting ended, possibly as Farley reloaded, and the assault party withdrew downstairs, bearing their walking wounded with them. Farley had won that round.

As a fleet of taxi-cabs took the injured to the infirmary, the crowd murmured their disquiet and offered imaginative ideas about how to end the siege of John Street. One favoured plan was to recruit the fire brigade and a powerful hose, but there were no details of who would carry the hose to the door or how it was to be applied.

News of the incident spread; the crowds that gathered in John Street spilled into Dudhope Crescent, blocking the roads and disrupting traffic. Deputy Chief Constable Lamb gathered together a team of police and led them from Bell Street to try and solve the problem. Rather than crash up the stairs, Lamb ordered his men to move quietly so they arrived on the top storey without Farley being aware of their presence. Perhaps that worked, as the tall police in their heavy boots tiptoed up the stone steps in the echoing dark of the close.

The other inhabitants of the attic were quietly evacuated and a constable moved in to the flat immediately below to watch in case Farley should try and clamber down the drain pipe. By that time Lamb had tried the door to see if it was open; it was not. Farley knew the police were on the landing outside his house; whenever they came to the door his footsteps sounded inside, as if he was prepared to defend his abode. His flat was small; it had only a single window at the side of the building that faced Cochrane Street. Occasionally he came to this window and gestured to the crowd, which surged back in case he opened fire. When his young son appeared at the window, many in the crowd wondered about the boy's safety.

'I'll kill as many of them as I can.'

At one point Farley opened the window and shouted, 'Come up on the slates and come in!' He pointed something at the crowd. There was a moment of panic before a woman realised that Farley held only a walking stick. The anxiety subsided; the crowd eased back, wondering what would happen next.

Shortly after four in the afternoon, Lamb sent for Farley's wife and daughter. He ordered Mary Farley inside the flat with instructions to grab the revolver from her husband and throw it out the window. Farley allowed her in, but did not let her near the gun. When she asked him to hand it over, he replied, 'No,' adding, 'I'll kill as many of them as I can.'

When the police accused her of not following their instructions properly, and of hardly spending any time in the house, Mary Farley responded by saying her husband would probably submit himself quietly if they all withdrew and left him alone.

The next person to try was Walker, the factor. He was sure his previous friendship with Farley would protect him, so he used a master key to step inside the flat. Farley immediately faced him and said, 'I don't want to take your blood, Mr Walker, but don't come in.' Walker thought that discretion was better than a bullet in the head and sensibly withdrew.

Lamb decided that he had only one option remaining: rush the door, chance the revolver and overpower Farley. In these days, long before body armour was thought of, and with professional negotiators far in the future, the policeman on the spot had to improvise as best he could. Lamb collected a number of chairs and had the police hold them in front of them as makeshift protection against bullets. A short search found a long plank of wood that would serve as a battering ram and the police were as ready as they could be. There seemed no thought of using Walker's key to open the door; perhaps Lamb thought the rushed approach would be more effective.

Inspector David McBey was selected to lead the assault; he was a distinctive figure in his civilian suit and bowler hat, with neatly trimmed whiskers and a calm demeanour. McBey was a Kincardine man who had been a farm servant before he joined the police when he was twenty-one. Now aged forty-one, he had experience as both a uniformed officer and a plain clothes detective. He was known for his bravery, having been rewarded for rescuing three women from a house fire a few years previously.

'I'm stabbed'

At a signal from Lamb, McBey led the police in a charge. He crashed through the door and bundled into the flat. Farley was waiting for them in the lobby, half dressed. He was in a fighter's crouch and in his right hand he held his revolver; in his left a long knife. McBey did not hesitate. Holding his chair high in front of him, he closed with Farley. He banged the chair against the gunman, who staggered back a step, recovered and thrust his knife into the inspector's stomach.

'I'm stabbed!' McBey yelled, as he slumped to the ground.

The other police piled in and leaped on top of Farley, who slashed left and right with the knife but did not fire his revolver. The blade ripped through the trousers of Constable Patterson, but he did not hold back. The police bore Farley to the ground, truncheons hammering until at least one splintered on Farley's bloody and broken head, and they overpowered the gunman. The police removed both the gun and the knife before they snapped on the handcuffs. From the time of the first shot until Farley was subdued, about an hour and a half had passed which was considered poor work at the time.

The revolver was found to be empty, but the knife had proved effective. With a six-inch-long blade, sharpened on both sides, it was an evil thing. Inspector McBey was in a half crouch, bleeding profusely onto the floor.

News of Farley's capture and the stabbing of Inspector McBey spread around the town, so the crowd in John Street swelled larger than ever. They waited outside in their hundreds when the police brought their prisoner out of the close. Even when his wrists were each handcuffed to a policeman, and with Lamb holding the back of his shirt, Farley looked defiant. He was the tallest man there, with blood pouring from his head where the police had been liberal with their truncheons, and his shirt and trousers shredded in the struggle, yet he still roared abuse at imaginary enemies.

'Lynch the bugger!'

The crowd were not kind. They mustered around Farley and his police escort, yelling, 'Lynch the bugger!' and at one point they seemed to surge forward as if they intended to put their words into action. The police manhandled their prisoner to Bell Street, while the crowd followed, shouted threats and pointed excitedly, as if the whole episode had been some bloody spectacle laid on for their own entertainment. More people waited around the Bell Street station; they grasped the iron railings and gaped at the blood-smeared man as the police bundled him inside. 'Lynch him!' they chanted.

Farley turned around as he was thrust between the square pillars at the gate. 'Three cheers for Ireland!' he retorted and he was bundled inside.

The crowd responded with a cheer, but for the police, not for Ireland.

As Farley was taken into Bell Street, Inspector McBey had his own painful journey. His wound prevented him from walking, so he had to be half carried down the narrow stairs of the close to Mrs Chaplin's house. A sheet was torn from the bed as a makeshift bandage, but the blood from the wound seeped through. An ambulance arrived around five and pushed through the crowds that still packed John Street. The ambulance men lay McBey on a stretcher and manoeuvred him down the steep, narrow stairs and into the ambulance. What remained of the crowd watched in a hushed silence. The ambulance took him to the infirmary, but he died on the following Saturday. Farley was now a murderer.

When Farley appeared in court, he said little but howled a lot, which alarmed those people present. When a number of medical doctors gave their opinion that he was insane, the judge ordered that he should be detained at Perth Penitentiary at Her Majesty's pleasure. The explosion in Glasgow had damaged him more than anybody could then understand.

15

The Curse of Drink

In the nineteenth century, much of Scotland's culture revolved around drink. So did much of Scotland's crime. In February 1834, the Dundee Police Commission stated, 'There is hardly a crime committed or a riot perpetrated but what may be referred to the intemperate use of ardent spirits and that mostly in the night time.' They were in the best position to make that judgement, as they could see the spread of drinking establishments.

One gallon of whisky per person per year

According to the historian T.C. Smout, in the 1830s the average adult in Scotland drank a gallon of whisky a year – that was legal whisky, on which duty had been paid. There were also around 700 illicit stills unearthed every year, so nobody will ever know how many hundreds were undetected. With no legal age restrictions on drinking alcohol, the nineteenth-century public house was an institution. With so many thousands of the population living in unbelievable squalor, the pub was somewhere to escape to, a simple source of pleasure in a life of monotony, poverty and hardship. In 1843, Dundee alone had 500 pubs and the city fathers were so concerned about the drunkenness that they proposed cutting the number by half.

Drinking was a way of life to many of the working class, and to many who would think themselves above that level as well. There were a number of different types of public house, from the opulent gin palace to the lowest laigh house that would give a hole-in-the-wall a bad name. The pamphleteer Citizen of Edinburgh, who admittedly wrote from a temperance viewpoint, spoke of 'the disgraceful quantity and the disgusting quality of the public houses' in some areas of the Old Town, with the 'stream of whisky and the stream of moral abomination … equal in length and … depth'. In the mid-nineteenth century, the Canongate was known as 'Whisky Way' because of the number of public houses there.

That blaspheming mob of drunk or half-drunk wretches

Many of the Old Town pubs were situated underground and were known as 'shades', 'potato-pits', 'coffins' or 'caves' – highly evocative terms that are not likely to invite a high class of clientele. These underground pubs were often little more than boxes with wooden partitions separating them from their neighbours. They were not known for their social niceties, with a mixture of men and women, and lighting provided by gas lamps. Citizen writes of 'soldiers staggering through that blaspheming mob of drunk or half-drunk wretches, male and female … strumpets gaudy with the gaudiest plumes of their proclaimed profession hanging upon military arms'.

These underground coffins also acted as brothels, with the less dedicated police turning a blind eye to the illegal operations and accepting free drink. But Glasgow also had its illegal drinking places, known as shebeens.

By the late nineteenth century there were three different classes of shebeen in Glasgow. They often took the place of licensed public houses over the weekends, when the law closed all pubs from midnight on Saturday until nine on Monday morning. Naturally this gap in the refreshment market led to entrepreneurs opening up their own drinking establishments all around the city, so there were hundreds of illegal dens, mainly small but some surprisingly large. The shebeens were classified as 'swell', second class and third class.

Shebeens

The swell shebeens were often located in the better quarters of the city, such as the West End or Kelvinside. They were typically inside the quality Glasgow tenements, and tolerated or even accepted by the other denizens of the common stair. These top-class shebeens were customarily open from around eleven at night for a couple of hours every day and for a longer time on Sundays. Not surprisingly, they catered to middle-class men: bankers, stockbrokers and managers; they sold fairly high quality drink. They were generally run by women who used their daughters or other female relatives as barmaids, so the service was good and behaviour inside the shebeens was impeccable.

Beneath this level of shebeen were the much more numerous second-class establishments that could be found in most places across Glasgow. They catered for clerks and small merchants, hard-working artisans and shopkeepers. In these dark rooms, beer cost sixpence a pint and whisky fourpence a gill, but it was not the best quality Glenlivet and might burn the lining from the drinker's mouth.

Unlike the upmarket West End shebeens, these establishments had occasional bouts of trouble and the police raided from time to time. When the police became officially aware of these places, the proprietor would move to another address not too far away and start again.

The third-class shebeens were terrible places in the worst areas of old Glasgow – the Trongate, Saltmarket and other disreputable parts of the East End. There were a huge number of these establishments and they sold rotgut whisky that was often methylated spirits with a touch of rough whisky added for flavouring. Many of these places were infested by thieves, pickpockets and petty thugs, with cheap prostitutes common. There was petty crime aplenty but the police only raided if there was serious trouble.

The Forbes Mackenzie Act, which banned Sunday drinking, was blamed for the existence of illegal drinking dens. In the early years there were fewer regulations and some pubs were best avoided.

Children and drink

On Monday, 27 October 1823, Sergeant Stewart of the Edinburgh police was inspecting the public houses in Bell's Wynd, which led from the High Street to Tron Square. One of the pubs was owned by a man named Adam Wood, so it was known as Wood's Inn. Stewart strode straight in and saw a group of eight youngsters seated around a table, polishing off a mutchkin of whisky. A mutchkin was about a quarter of a Scots pint, or three-quarters of an imperial pint. The oldest of the boys was thirteen and all were already known to the police as thieves, pickpockets and troublemakers.

As Stewart watched, one boy, whose age he estimated at around eight years, poured himself a glass of whisky and downed it in a single draught, then poured a second and finished that as well. One of his companions, at perhaps ten years old, ordered half a mutchkin and drank it down there and then.

Stewart arrested the whole lot, but as they had not committed any new crimes, they merely had to provide surety for their future good behaviour. At their age that was surely not possible. Adam Wood was fined a hefty five guineas for harbouring 'disorderly persons'.

The age of the boys was immaterial; their criminal past was all that mattered.

The reek of peat

For much of the nineteenth century, there was a war waged throughout Scotland. The government wished to tax all whisky made in the country, but many of the whisky distillers did not agree. From Orkney to the Rhins of Galloway, glens and cottages, caves and moorland became home to illicit distillers who manufactured tens of thousands of gallons of whisky, smuggled it to the towns and cities and lived off the proceeds. They were prepared to fight for their livelihood and often carried weapons as they transported the peat reek – the illicit whisky.

Opposing the distillers were the Excisemen. These hard-pressed and hard-working officers faced tremendous odds as they tried to stem a flood of whisky to earn revenue for the government. They were badly paid, but supplemented their income with a bonus for every gallon of illicit whisky they captured. To equalise the odds, by the 1820s they were reinforced by military patrols and occasional help from the navy.

Encounters between whisky smugglers and Excisemen could often be bloody.

Distilling in Caithness

From 1803 until 1814, and again for 100 days in 1815, Britain was engaged in a very intense war against Napoleonic France. The nation strained every nerve to withstand Bonaparte, who was arguably one of the world's greatest military commanders and one of the most dangerous men Europe has ever produced. The army and navy were stretched to breaking point. Every year saw battles on land or sea. Reputations were made and broken, and families lived with the constant fear of hearing about a loved one filling a grave in some corner of a foreign field that would be forever Scotland. Throughout this period, the whisky wars raged at home, causing the government grief and losing the country valuable revenue.

On 13 January 1812, as Bonaparte contemplated invading Russia and a new war between Britain and the United States loomed on the Atlantic horizon, Caithness witnessed a skirmish in the whisky wars.

Robert Harper was the Collector of Customs at Thurso, and that day he took two of his officers, Walter Steel and George Milne, to Ballanloid near Halkirk, about seven miles to the south. As usual in such cases, an informer had tipped them off about an illegal still. The house was leased by a woman named Bell Henderson, but when the Excisemen entered, Angus Grant, distiller and member of the Caithness Militia, together with his brother William and Alexander Gunn, were there with Henderson. They were all sitting around the fire, smoking and talking, while the peat smoke filled the house and the still bubbled away merrily.

As soon as they stepped in, the Excisemen began work. Milne made a grab for the head of the still, but without hesitation William Grant lifted a pitchfork and lunged at him. At the same time Grant shouted to Bell Henderson to douse the fire with a bucket of water. A violent struggle began, as the four distillers lifted bludgeons and attacked the Excisemen. The Excisemen began a hasty retreat but the distillers knocked Milne and Harper to the ground and stuck in the boot. The Excisemen struggled to their feet and fled with neither dignity nor an attempt at resistance.

Henderson's house was at the head of a small lane, which had a patch of bog land at the bottom end. Already injured with a bludgeon, Harper was slower than the rest; he made heavy weather of the soft ground and the distillers caught him and knocked him down again. As he lay helpless in the mud, the distillers set about him with their bludgeons. One of the distillers flicked off Harper's hat and they cracked him over his unprotected head until he was unconscious. Leaving him there, the distillers chased after the remainder of the

Excisemen. Harper returned to consciousness but was unable to move, so he was still lying there when the distillers returned. He groaned and tried to rise as they discussed what to do to him.

'We should break his legs and leave him,' somebody said, and the blows rained onto the backs of his knees.

Harper struggled to his side as the bludgeons hammered down. He saw Angus Grant watching, and offered him five guineas if he would help him into the house. Grant was more mercenary than humanitarian, for he lifted Harper, but the instant he realised that the Exciseman did not have any money with him, he dropped him again and walked away.

Harper lay for a while but eventually struggled, half crawling, to a nearby cottage, where Joseph McKay proved far more hospitable. McKay put Harper to bed and fetched a doctor. After hovering on the brink of death, Harper was able to leave the croft after eight days, although one of his legs was permanently damaged.

The Grants and Gunn were arrested and came to trial at Inverness in April that year. All were sentenced to twelve months in Inverness jail and then banished from Scotland for seven years. Bell Henderson was not arrested.

Other Excisemen were in just as much danger.

Smuggling in Ayrshire

In the early morning of 26 January 1816, Walter Graham, Supervisor of Excise at Ayr, took a party of men to Glenbuck, three miles east of Muirkirk, to quash any illicit distillation they found there. It was a typical January day – raw, cold, with a westerly wind and snow on the high ground – but Graham was quite cheerful and gathered his men together. Either by the aid of an informant, or because they were skilled in the art of detecting, the Excisemen found two stills. All the equipment was in two houses, the home of William MacPhilimy, a labourer, and the home of Mary Scott, his mother-in-law. After destroying most of the equipment, the Excisemen loaded what remained onto a cart to take it over to Muirkirk, high in the interior of the county.

That was a lonely road across rough moorland and about halfway over, a gang of around twenty men rose from the snow-covered heather and surrounded the cart. The men were armed with stout clubs, pokers and other weapons. Graham immediately recognised the leader as William MacPhilimy, but he was ably backed by his wife, also called Mary. MacPhilimy brandished his club, and loudly and obscenely demanded the return of their property. Walter Graham was obviously a brave man and replied that he was legally obliged to do his duty. Graham's words only excited the smugglers, who made a charge on the cart. They felled one of the Excisemen, William Duncan, and set about him with their sticks. MacPhilimy held him down and shouted out, 'Murder the bugger!'

James Clark, an Exciseman from Catrine, ran to help Duncan but the crowd attacked him as well and the clubs rose and fell, cracking him around the head; he reeled back. Another Exciseman, Thomas Cuthbert, was also knocked to the ground; he heard Mary MacPhilimy roar that she would 'tear out Duncan's entrails with her teeth'.

Another young smuggler took a swing at Graham and missed, but Mary MacPhilimy smacked him on the side of the head with her poker. As Graham staggered, the young smuggler smashed him again so he fell.

The smugglers gave three cheers as all the Excisemen lay prone on the blood-smeared snow. The Excisemen could only watch and nurse their wounds as the smugglers took control of the cart and rolled it away. Duncan was the worst injured; he was bruised all down his left side, with cuts on the head and both arms. However, the Excisemen had the last word. They called for help, took the smugglers to court and in May 1816 both William and Mary MacPhilimy were transported for seven years.

There were many more cases.

Distilling in Perthshire

On the afternoon of 6 March 1819, Dugald Cameron, Officer of Excise, left his base at Stirling to search for illicit stills on the Braes of Dunning and Hills of Blackford. He was not just patrolling on the off-chance of coming across something, for, as so often happened, an informer had whispered to him that there was more than one still along the banks of the Struie river; he even had some precise directions as to where he might be successful.

Cameron rode to the exact spot and found a camouflaged bothy with a large still inside. There was a man in the bothy, but as soon as he saw Cameron approach he took to his heels and ran into the heather. Cameron shouted, 'I am an Excise officer!' and followed, but the distiller escaped; he obviously knew the local area like the label on a whisky bottle.

Cameron inspected his find and was impressed. The distiller could make up to sixty gallons of whisky at the one time, and the still was complete with the worm or coil which was the hardest piece of equipment for the distiller to make, a number of tuns to hold the finished product, some empty dishes and a copper head, as well as a quantity of mash. It was a very good haul that would deal a severe blow to the distiller.

As Cameron took off his hat and began to destroy the equipment the man who had run returned, soon joined by another distiller. A few moments later a further two men came into the bothy behind him. Cameron recognised two of the incomers as David Barnet of Auchterarder and John Brown of Dunning but he did not know the others. Brown wore a short blue coat, while Barnet was in his waistcoat and trousers. All four men watched him destroying their livelihood for a while and then one said, quite casually, 'Murder the bastard.'

Cameron turned, but too late. Barnet lifted an empty bottle and smashed him over the head, while Brown lifted a spade and cracked the edge against his skull. The Exciseman staggered and all four of the distillers jumped on him. Somebody was hammering at him with a stick, another man with a stone and all the time the boots and fists were pounding in. Cameron kept his feet, put his arms over his head and tried to get away. He struggled out of the bothy and headed westward, where he could see a ploughman at work. However, the distillers followed him, still intent on violence.

The ploughman, William Rutherford, saw the lone man running toward him, with the distillers in pursuit. Their shouting and yelling frightened Rutherford's horses, so he was struggling to hold them in check. He had just got them under control when three of the distillers caught Cameron and the beating began again. Brown swung the spade again as somebody yelled out, 'Break his legs!'

Rutherford dropped the plough and ran over. 'If you kill the man, you will rue it!' he shouted. The distillers glanced at him and stopped, panting, only to grab Cameron by the cloak and drag him over the rough ground back inside the bothy, where the assault continued. Brown still wielded the spade and two others hauled Cameron's cloak away, threw him to the ground and thumped him with the stick and the stone as he lay there attempting to shield the more vulnerable parts of his body. When the distillers grew tired of beating up the Exciseman, they went through his pockets and found his commission from the Excise. They asked him to pay for the damage he had done to their property and robbed him of what valuables they could find.

With their anger assuaged, the distillers bundled Cameron, now only semi-conscious, onto a farm cart and trundled him along a track, tipped him out and left him in the heather. It was some time later – Cameron never knew how long – that a couple of men found him and sent a boy to fetch a barrow. The men placed him into the barrow and wheeled him to a farm-house. He lay near the fire for a while, vomiting blood, but the farmer said there was no room at the inn for Excisemen: get out of my house. Somebody threw him onto the back of another cart and drove him to a public house, but his troubles were still not over. The innkeeper took one look at Cameron, realised that he was an Exciseman, and told the cart driver to take him away and drown him, 'to prevent him doing any more mischief'.

The driver continued on the road toward Forgandenny, but either he became tired of trying to find a home for the injured Exciseman, or he took fright when somebody came toward him, for after a while he threw Cameron out of the cart. Cameron lay at the side of the road, groaning, bleeding and in too much pain to try to rise.

Another man stumbled upon him in the verge, and this time Cameron had found his Good Samaritan. This stranger called on some help and physically carried Cameron to the public house in Forgandenny, where he was washed and put to bed. He remained there for upwards of ten days, with Doctor Chalmers attending him regularly. The doctor found two deep wounds on the top of his head and extensive bruising down Cameron's left side, on his shoulders, his arms and his left leg. Chalmers estimated that Cameron would be bedridden for around a week.

Naturally Cameron reported the matter, and Brown and Barnet were arrested. They were each given eighteen months in Perth and told to find £40 surety for their good behaviour for a further three years.

Braemar smugglers

No part of Scotland was free from illicit distillers but the central Highlands were arguably their home territory. From Glenlivet to the hills around Braemar, whisky men and women ruled the land, and the Excise ventured there at their own risk.

On 25 April 1826, when the whisky wars were at their height, William Stevenson and Richard McLachlan, two Excisemen, patrolled the local hills. They were not alone, for they were accompanied by old George McHardy, the ground officer of the local landowner,

Farquharson of Invercauld. As always, they were looking for illicit stills, but in this remote area to the north of Braemar, the hills were anything but lonely, and even less friendly.

As they penetrated along the road into the great bald mountains, they smelled the distinctive perfume of peat smoke on the crisp air. It was an indication that there could be a still nearby, so they looked around and saw a blue drift of smoke above a hut that was otherwise well camouflaged amongst the grey-green slopes.

The Excisemen left the road and advanced cautiously toward the hut, brushing through the dry heather and rough grass. When they were around 200 yards away, two armed men emerged from cover, fired a shot each and ran into the hut; they may only have been sentries, for a few moments later a dozen men ran out. By that time the Excisemen were only about 150 yards away. The shots had sobered them and they had considered retiring, but the advent of the twelve men helped them reach their decision.

Many of the dozen were carrying long muskets; others had bludgeons or heavy sticks. The Excisemen turned back to the road, but the distillers were hill men, tough and agile on the heather. They ran after the Excisemen, shouting 'Halloa!' and firing their muskets. Stevenson thought he heard fifteen distinct reports, heard the zip and whine of the shots, and saw the balls thump into the ground around them. Somebody shouted, 'Take aim and shoot the buggers!' Then one of the distillers threw a stone that felled Stevenson to the heather. Before he could rise a host of excited and armed distillers surrounded him.

Stevenson looked around him; many of the distillers had blackened their faces so they would not be recognised; others had their coats turned inside out so the colour would not be ascertained. McLachlan was about eighty yards away and running hard for safety but McHardy had remained loyally with Stevenson. Ignoring the jeering distillers, he helped the Exciseman to his feet and supported him down the rough slope. The distillers were having none of that: three of them leaped forward and knocked Stevenson back down again, and hammered their boots into him as he lay prone on the ground. He struggled up again, and together with McHardy made for the road, but the distillers opened fire once more, with the shots cutting the heather stalks and making a peculiarly ugly thump sound as they hit the ground in front of the retreating men.

'If you go for the road, we will shoot you!'

The warning was clear. The Excisemen stopped running. They had intended to travel toward Crathie Kirk, but the distillers obviously had other ideas. Stevenson looked around again. Most of the distillers were close by, flaunting their cudgels, but three stood at the rear, watching and reloading their long muskets. The situation was grim. It was McHardy's turn to leave them, as McLachlan joined Stevenson and the two struggled miles across the rough countryside with the distillers dogging them, firing the occasional shot, and now and then rushing to knock one or the other down, land a few kicks and withdraw again. The distillers knew the Excisemen by name and by sight, and added threats and insults to the joy of the day.

Eventually, at about five in the evening, the Excisemen staggered thankfully into Ogilvy's public house, collapsed onto chairs and ordered half a mutchkin of whisky, followed by tea.

Stevenson had a broken head and blood was flowing down his face. Sundry kicks had left him bruised and sore. There was no doctor available, so Stevenson had to endure his various aches and pains until the next day, when he walked the eight miles back to Ballater. Once he was there, Dr Andrew Robertson examined and bled him. Robertson said that he had a large swelling on the side of his head, as well as his bruises, while McLachlan was also bruised and battered.

As he reached the streets of Ballater, Stevenson recognised one of the men who had attacked him: Charles Lamond. He was fairly sure that a man named John Smith had also been involved, as he was a close companion of Lamont's. McLachlan was surer about Smith, which was perhaps not surprising, as Smith had attacked him. Turning his coat inside out had not been sufficient disguise to conceal Smith's identity.

Smith and Lamont were brought to the High Court in July 1826 charged with wilfully and maliciously shooting at officers of Excise. Both pleaded not guilty. Lamond stated that he had been working with his father's carts and Smith said he never left his home at all.

Charles Lamond was found guilty; he had been recognised by both the Excisemen and had played a major part in the assaults. He was transported for fourteen years, sailing on *Albion* that September. The charge against Smith was not proven and he walked free.

Illicit stills in the city

Although the early decades of the nineteenth century saw a virtual war between the Excise and illicit distillers – with the army and even the navy patrolling parts of the Highlands – illegal distilling was not confined to remote glens and smugglers openly walked the city streets. For instance, in December 1824 the good people of Dundee were warned that, 'A number of vagabonds now infest the town, attempting to dispose of deleterious compounds under the tempting descriptions of smuggled whisky and brandy.'

Sometimes there were even stills operating within the cities.

In the autumn and winter of 1857, the Edinburgh police and revenue officers suspected that there was a distiller working in the suburbs of the city. The revenue officers were meticulous in their searching, and assiduous in their pursuit of distillers. They listened to the quiet words of informers in the dark corners of the city, and followed crooked leads to their goals. With a whisper here and a murmur there, helped by promises and threats, the Excisemen slowly closed in on one area of Edinburgh. In December David Smith, the

Supervisor of the First Edinburgh District of Inland Revenue, led a small team into Restalrig and, following the word of a friend, he came across the illicit still in the district of Marionville.

Smith and his men found two vats dug into the ground, each one holding an impressive 1,000 gallons of wash (the raw form of whisky, after fermentation but before distillation). The Excisemen also found gallons of whisky already made and some eighty gallons of low wine (whisky after the first distillation). The distiller had the Highland name of James Stuart and he was fined £30, while his equipment was destroyed and his wash poured away.

These episodes are only a few from hundreds of similar cases that occurred in Scotland, and probably still do occur. The struggle to ensure every gallon of Scottish whisky pays revenue to the government is ongoing.

16
The Poisoners

If any crime could be termed as archetypical of the nineteenth century, it would be poisoning. The Madeleine Smith case from Glasgow is too famous to be repeated, but it was only one of scores, possibly hundreds, across the country. Some of the less well known are related here.

Murder on the Broomielaw packet

When *Comet* became Europe's first seagoing steamship, as she chugged through the Firth of Clyde, she started a completely new mode of travel. From that day in 1812, steamships crossed and re-crossed the seas off the Scottish west coast. They carried vital goods to and from the islands and isolated coastal communities, and provided easier transport for people travelling for business or pleasure. Of course they also provided opportunities for crime.

Robert Lamont was a married man, a farmer and merchant from Ballygarten on the Hebridean island of Ulva. In December 1828, he was a passenger sailing to Glasgow to collect a consignment of goods. Together with his brother John, he boarded *Toward Castle* at

Lochgilphead and stood on deck, enjoying the winter scenery until they passed the Kyles of Bute. *Toward Castle* had been built in 1822 and was a 101-foot-long paddle steamer with an open deck and two masts. She was a popular vessel, with passenger facilities on her lower deck.

As the winter wind chilled them, the Lamonts nodded to a friend of theirs, a hawker's wife named Catherine McPhail. They asked why she looked so downcast. She explained that an Exciseman had just taken a gallon of illicit whisky from her, which had cost her dear. The Lamonts sympathised as they went below to find something to eat; they were directed to a small eating cabin with room for only half a dozen passengers.

A few minutes later a man and woman entered the cabin, also looking for food. Robert Lamont invited them to sit at the table and within a few moments everybody was in happy conversation. The newcomers were John and Catherine Steuart and they proved very cheerful companions. John left them to go back on deck, but Robert called him back, saying he had 'fallen in fine company' and said he should get a share of what was going on'.

The group polished off a bottle of porter and then began on the ale, but Robert thought the price, at nine pence a bottle, was a bit steep. He said he would only spend up to four pence more on drink that day. Mrs Steuart accepted the money and ran to the deck to buy another bottle; she returned with the ale and with Catherine McPhail, who joined them at the table. Mrs McPhail said she never drank when she was 'from home' but she soon lost her scruples amidst the cheery company and helped them finish off a gill of whisky. Her daughter, a young woman named Margaret McPhail, looked into the room and squeezed in at the end of the table.

As was not uncommon, the company shared a single glass for the ale, passing it around between them. Mrs McPhail drank first and said, 'That's the most abominable ale I have ever tasted in my life,' but she had a swallow straight from the bottle as well. She thought that the ale in the bottle had a different, less bitter taste than the ale in the glass.

Mrs Steuart said to her, 'Drink that, Mistress.'

'I wouldn't drink that for fifty pounds,' Mrs McPhail told her.

'Damn my soul but you must drink it,' Mrs Steuart said.

Mrs McPhail took a couple of sips and passed the rest to young Margaret, who drank it.

John Steuart said he would try it anyway.

As he put the glass to his lips, his wife pushed his arm down, laughing, and said, 'No, you blackguard! You must not fill yourself drunk!'

Mrs Steuart grabbed for the tumbler and, as they struggled for it, the contents spilled down the front of Steuart. The loss of the drink angered him and he began to shout at his wife. He raised his hand to slap her, but controlled himself and calmed down, albeit with a number of hard glares. Mrs Steuart filled the tumbler again and handed it to Robert Lamont, saying, 'This is your drink; you must drink it.'

Robert drank it straight away and John Lamont also had some, but he preferred whisky to ale, so did not have more than a few mouthfuls.

Young Margaret began to feel ill, so with a laughing remark about seasickness, Mrs McPhail took her onto the deck, but she was not well herself, despite the bracing December air and the smooth passage of the paddle steamer. Shortly afterward John Lamont walked back to the deck, leaving the others in convivial companionship. He did not return down below until they were berthed at the Broomielaw in Glasgow, and by then a massive change had come over Robert Lamont. He was sitting with his head between his knees, unable to move. John knew that he was not drunk, and wondered about foul play. He tapped the outside of Robert's jacket and realised that his pocket book, which held a substantial wad of bank notes, was missing.

Naturally upset, John ran to find the captain and told him that Robert had been robbed. He checked his brother's other pockets without success, but Captain Stuart found the pocket book on the floor. It was empty but a few letters were scattered around. The captain took both Steuarts and Mrs McPhail into custody on suspicion of the robbery. John Steuart was in the water closet and pretended to be drunk, but Captain Stuart had seen enough drunken passengers to know that he was faking. As *Toward Castle* chugged up the Clyde toward Glasgow, John also began to feel very nauseous and had to run up on deck, where he was violently sick.

When they arrived at the Broomielaw, the captain sent for three doctors, but Robert Lamont died on board the ship at half past five the next morning. The doctors suspected poison, and John agreed, mentioned his own nausea and said he must have been poisoned as well. One of the doctors helped with some medicine, but the symptoms persisted for hours.

When Constable McPherson searched the Steuarts in Glasgow, a bottle was found in John Steuart's pocket. It was empty but smelled of laudanum. Dr Corkindale and Dr Fleming examined the contents of Robert Lamont's stomach and thought he had been poisoned with laudanum; the smell was very distinctive. The police found a bundle of bank notes in Steuart's possession, yet when he boarded *Toward Castle* he had been flat broke. Steuart also had a black purse with distinctive embroidered ornamentation that Lamont's daughter later identified as being her work.

When the case came to the High Court in Edinburgh in July 1829, the prosecution brought in a surprise witness. His name was Malcolm Logan, and he had shared a cell with John Steuart in Edinburgh's Tolbooth. Steuart had spoken a lot as he was waiting for his trial, and had said he had intended to 'do' the 'smuggling woman' – that being Catherine McPhail. When the 'Highland man' – John Lamont – came along, he had switched victims. According to Logan, it was Mrs Steuart who had added the laudanum to the ale, but Steuart who had robbed Lamont as he sat stupefied in the cabin. Mrs Steuart had the laudanum in a small square bottle. Once he had emptied most of it into Lamont's glass of ale, Steuart said he went into the water closet and filled the bottle with water. Again according to Logan, Steuart claimed that he carried the laudanum with him for the sole purpose of 'giving the doctor' to anybody he met.

By that he meant he would add the laudanum, the medicine or 'doctor' to the drink of anybody who was worth robbing. During that period many people used a few drops of laudanum as a substitute for alcohol. It was a quicker method of becoming so stupefied that the miseries of life were temporarily forgotten.

Gruer McGruer was the criminal officer who escorted Steuart from Glasgow Bridewell to the Council Chambers to be questioned. McGruer said that on the journey Steuart confessed that his real name was not Steuart and he had previously been convicted of sheep stealing and had broken out of Stranraer jail. In his declaration, Steuart claimed that he was an Irishman and a blacksmith to trade, but had not followed his proper work for the last eighteen months. He had married his wife about six months ago at Gretna Green, and they travelled throughout Scotland and England searching for work.

The jury found both the Steuarts guilty of murder and robbery. Lord Pitmully sentenced them to be hanged.

There is a sinister postscript to this case. Before he was executed, Steuart confessed that Lamont was not his first victim. He said that he had drugged and robbed, and perhaps murdered, an unknown number of other victims during his criminal career. As his murders were nearly contemporary with the much better known killing spree of Burke and Hare, the Edinburgh body-snatchers, Steuart's name has all but faded from memory, but one phrase of his is still in common usage. When something is added to a drink to make it stronger, people still say that the drink was 'doctored'. Steuart's words have passed into everyday speech; a legacy from a murderer.

The Eaglesham Poisoner

Poisoning was possibly less common than stabbing or using a bludgeon, but it was still widespread and was used by both men and women to a surprising degree. Poison of various types was readily available in chemists' and grocers' shops, with few questions asked. At a time when houses could be infested with vermin, buying rat poison was normal practice, while arsenic could be used as a cleaning agent.

Most often poisoning was a domestic issue, with a wife administering some noxious substance to her husband, or less often a husband to his wife. That was probably because poison was intimate, and easy to administer in a household situation.

In an age before photography and with very imperfect records kept, people could disappear with greater ease than they can now, so a criminal wanted by one name in one city could move location and adopt a different name halfway across the country. It is entirely possible that unsolved murders were committed by the same person under different guises. That was the case with John or Jack Thomson, otherwise known as Peter Walker. He changed his name but kept to the same *modus operandi*, and it was this latter failing that caught him out.

In the summer of 1857 Scotland was rocked by the trial of Madeleine Smith, a wealthy young woman from Glasgow who took a lover and reputedly poisoned him. Smith became infamous and details of the alleged murder were published in every newspaper in the land and discussed at breakfast tables, in public houses and probably everywhere else that people gathered to gossip about the latest scandal. One of the many people intrigued by the story was John Thomson. It is possible that the story of Madeleine Smith inspired him to murder. He certainly asked questions about her methods and where he could buy poison.

Whether or not Smith influenced Thomson, he first murdered twenty-seven-year-old Agnes Montgomery and escaped scot free.

Then he attempted to murder two other people in Glasgow, failed and was caught, tried and convicted of both crimes. If the trial of Madeleine Smith had not attracted so much attention, Thomson's attempted treble murder may have been better known. As it is, history has consigned it to the dustbin of neglect.

In the autumn of 1857, when the interest in Smith's trial was at its height, twenty-six-year-old Thomson was working as an itinerant tailor. He found lodgings with his current employer, James Watson, on the ground floor of a tenement block. At that time Thomson was also interested in a young woman named Agnes Montgomery, who just happened to live in the same stair, and whose sister was married to Watson.

Agnes Montgomery was a fit and healthy woman who enjoyed her work as a reeler in the local mill, and had scarcely had a day off in her life. She was a popular woman, usually known as Aggie. Although Thomson and Agnes shared some history, she did not think as highly of him as he did of her. At one time Thomson had told Agnes that he had a fine Bible, but when she asked to see it he had produced what Agnes called 'a wee old-fashioned one with pictures'. She called him 'a cursed liar'. On another occasion Agnes and a woman named Janet Dollar had argued with Thomson and thrown water over him. Thomson had been angry at that and had said he 'would be upsides with the buggers for that'. Finally he had asked Agnes to marry him, but she had laughed him to scorn. After that incident, Thomson had taken the huff and had not spoken to her for some days.

On Saturday, 12 September, Thomson met a young lad named John Ferguson, who worked for the local carrier. Thomson handed Ferguson a note and asked him to hand it to Hugh Hart's chemist shop. Although Ferguson did not read the note, he found out later it was for sixpence worth of prussic acid. The acid came in a small glass phial. The next day, Sunday, 13 September, Thomson had tea in the Watson house as normal, and then went outside.

It was quite normal for Thomson to spend time with Agnes Montgomery in the evenings, or even to go back to work for a while. That evening a neighbour, David Clarkson, saw Thomson meet Agnes and both walked happily into her house. It was hard for the pair not to meet, as Agnes lived in a single-roomed flat on the second floor of the tenement. Not long after he saw Thomson go into Agnes' house, Clarkson heard a 'great rumble and desperate thrash on the floor'. Clarkson 'wondered at such behaviour on the Sabbath' but did nothing; a few moments later he heard Thomson leave the flat and lock the door.

Mrs Janet Wilson came into the house from the church about ten minutes after Thomson had left. At about quarter past five a baker named Jamie Fulton and a man named Muir came to the house looking for Thomson. Janet said she had no idea where he was. After she had eaten, Janet left the house with her daughter, young Jeanie, and again met Muir and Fulton, who were still looking for Thomson. As Janet came to the bottom of the common stair she met a woman named Mrs MacDonald, who said she had heard somebody moaning. Janet told her that it would be her aunt, Nannie Montgomery, who was not well, or Jeannie Clarkson, who lived upstairs in the same stair.

As she returned home shortly after, Janet also heard the moaning and thought that it came from her sister Agnes' house. She decided to investigate and climbed the stairs, but Agnes' door was locked and the key was missing.

'Aggie!' Janet called. 'Aggie, open the door!'

There was no answer, except for the low moaning.

Janet tried rattling the handle and banging on the door, but Agnes did not come, so Janet fetched a key and at around twenty past five she entered. The house was tidy and neat, with the kettle in place but no food prepared. Agnes was sitting with her head on the table, one arm hanging at her side and one in her lap. Janet raised Agnes's head; she was drooling from the mouth and her hair, normally immaculate, was in a complete mess.

'Aggie! Aggie, what's this?' Janet tried to get sense from her sister, but Agnes just stared straight ahead, her eyes unfocused. She said nothing. 'Have you been taking anything?' Janet asked.

Agnes opened her mouth wide, as if she was trying to be sick and Janet thrust three fingers down her throat to try and help. Instead Agnes bit down hard and did not release until she yawned widely in another attempt to vomit.

By now Janet was scared and sent a neighbour for the doctor. She put Agnes to bed, worried that her sister's face was swollen and discoloured, and her breathing was laboured. Thomson came into the house and asked what the matter was. He seemed concerned.

When the doctor arrived, he prescribed a hot toddy of whisky and said there was something wrong with Agnes' stomach. He prescribed more whisky and tried to bleed her, but failed. When he left to attend to another patient, Janet washed Agnes' face and bathed her upper body with spirits. Agnes turned paler as the evening ran on. Her lips lost their colour as the blood drained away.

About six in the evening the doctor returned. He visited Agnes, but only for a short while. Agnes had died.

When Janet stripped the house after the death, she found no money, although it was well known that Agnes' sailor brother, Finlay Montgomery, sent her £4 every second month. Agnes picked the money up at Jamaica Bridge six times a year. There was no secret; she often spoke of collecting her brother's money. What Janet did find was a small bottle marked *poison* which Agnes had used to combat the toothache from which she suffered. Janet also found a tumbler that had a film of some white powder on it that she did not recognise.

After the funeral, James Watson said Thomson was the last person in Agnes' house before she took ill. Thomson claimed that Agnes had been breaking sticks for the fire when he left her, which seemed a little strange, but might explain some of the strange noises that were heard. Watson also saw Thomson after Agnes' death in the garden, where a quantity of glass from a broken phial and the key to Agnes' door was later found. When Watson spoke of Agnes' death, Thomson said he was truly sorry as 'he never knew a girl he thought more of'. The Watsons, husband and wife, thought that Thomson was never quite himself when he spoke of the death of Agnes. They thought he hung his head and the blood drained from his face.

Very soon after the death, Watson lost an envelope with £1 inside. He openly accused the lodger. Thomson did not deny the theft but immediately paid the money, after which Watson ordered him out of the house. However, that was not the end of Thomson's venture into the gentle art of poisoning. On 26 September 1857, he tried again.

Thomson took lodgings in the house of Archibald and Agnes Mason in John Street in Glasgow. He proved a very amiable guest, charming the Masons with his smile and his habit of calling Mrs Mason 'mother', but his agenda had nothing to do with happy families. On 25 September he got into the house after eleven at night, when Mr Mason was in bed, but his wife was still up. He began a conversation and suggested they take a drink together.

'You'd be all the better of a glass, as you've been working all day,' Thomson said.

The Masons agreed, sociable people that they were, and Thomson lifted a black pint bottle and poured out two tumblers of whisky. Archibald Mason had a sip but he was not a heavy drinker and suffered no ill effects. His wife took a hearty third of the glass and a few moments later felt 'a queerness all through my system'. She began to feel dizzy and could not focus on anything. She tried to go downstairs with a bundle of clothes but dropped them and could hardly stand, so she had to crawl up the stairs.

Thomson met her at the top and offered her more whisky.

'Oh John, that's no' good whisky,' Mrs Mason said, but Thomson insisted it was the best Paisley whisky. She crawled into the main room, and Thomson and her husband joined her.

'I'm very ill,' Mrs Mason said and when Thomson said that she had eaten something that disagreed with her, she said that she had only drunk his whisky. She was ill for days, shivering and being sick. Thomson remained in the house, but with the Madeleine Smith case fresh in his mind, Mr Mason took a sample from the whisky bottle to Dr George Miller in George Street, who told him it contained prussic acid.

In the meantime Thomson offered Mrs Mason more whisky and told her that he had drunk the remainder of the whisky in the glass with no bad effects. He was still in the house when the police came to arrest him. A few days later, the police took the bottle of whisky away and found it was laced with prussic acid.

Nearly simultaneously with the drama at the Masons' house, young Jeannie Watson told her mother that she had seen 'Jack' give 'Aggie' something from a bottle and 'she fa'd doon'. Jeannie had also seen Thomson smash a small bottle in the garden and told her that if she did not tell he would 'give me a bawbee'. Mrs Watson immediately visited the police and told Detective Alexander Christy that she suspected Thomson of stealing £1 and of murdering Agnes Montgomery. On 30 September Agnes' body was disinterred and Dr Daniel McKinley performed an autopsy. He said that she had died of prussic acid poisoning.

The case came to court in December and Thomson was found guilty and sentenced to death. The police could find no motive for the murders and Thomson showed no remorse. He had no grudge against Agnes Montgomery and was on very friendly terms with the Masons. In fact, he had attended Agnes' funeral and remained in the Masons' house as Mrs Mason suffered the effects of his poisoning. Was he a true psychopath with no feelings whatever, or was he fascinated by the process of poisoning?

A few days after his conviction, Thomson admitted his guilt but claimed he had murdered Agnes for her money. Shortly before his execution he changed his story and told the prison chaplain that 'in reality he had no motive whatsoever; he was impelled by an influence for which he could not account'. He added that when he was a boy in Tarbert he had murdered another youngster by pushing him into a quarry; although he did not know why.

Thomson was hanged in front of the County Buildings in Paisley at eight o'clock on 14 January 1858. William Calcraft, probably the most famous hangman of the age, performed the execution, but cut down the corpse with nearly as much callousness as Thomson himself had shown, to the annoyance of the crowd. They nearly rioted, which was perhaps a fitting send-off but far better than Thomson deserved.

Mrs Beaton's household mismanagement

Usually a poisoner only targeted a single victim, but sometimes there was an exception, where a number of people were affected.

Such a case occurred in Moray in July 1896. The motive seems to have been jealousy or perhaps a bitter revenge. Ellen Beaton was the housekeeper for Thomas Hay at Rheeves Farm, not far south of Elgin in Moray; she was in her mid-thirties, a sturdy, capable woman who managed her charges well and brooked no interference from outside. Like so many Scotswomen, she was also of an independent turn of mind.

Thomas Hay was a hospitable man who liked to entertain and on 12 July 1896 he invited a number of people to dine with him. Including the farm servants, who ate at Hay's table, there were nine people in the house, but when Hay asked Mrs Beaton to prepare the food she refused point-blank.

'This is my night off,' she told him, 'and I am going out.'

Hay was used to her shows of independence, so he shrugged it off and said he would get another cook for the night instead. That seemed a reasonable compromise but Beaton did not agree.

'You will not do that as long as I am in the house,' she said, and stomped off in a fury.

Despite his housekeeper's tantrum, Hay continued with his second plan and called in a local woman named Mrs Forsyth, who had a reputation as a decent cook. When Mrs Forsyth arrived, Hay installed her in the kitchen and he checked periodically to ensure she knew what she was doing. As usual, the kitchen was bright, with a fire in the range and a pot of something bubbling away merrily. Hay had a sneaky look in the pot in case Mrs Beaton had decided to change her mind and prepare something special, but it was only barley so he lost interest.

As Hay left the kitchen, Mrs Forsyth was washing the vegetables for the meal. Mrs Beaton came in and immediately accosted Mrs Forsyth. The two women had a heated argument, but although Hay heard, he thought it best to leave them to it. Mrs Beaton asked who had sent her there, and when Mrs Forsyth told her that it was Hay who had invited her, Mrs Beaton got even angrier. She ordered Mrs Forsyth to return the way she had come. Mrs Forsyth refused, and Mrs Beaton grabbed a knife and a porridge spurtle, made threatening gestures and demanded that she go. Not surprisingly, Mrs Forsyth sent for Hay, who calmed things down and then promised he would dismiss Mrs Beaton on Monday morning.

Mrs Beaton stomped upstairs in a rage and remained there until Hay left the kitchen. When she returned, she did not speak to Mrs Forsyth but opened a deep cupboard. Mrs Forsyth heard the rustle of paper, as if she was moving a bag, then she left the kitchen for one of the other rooms before once more returning to the kitchen. Still without speaking to Mrs Forsyth, Mrs Beaton lifted a ladle from the dresser and began to stir the pot of soup.

By two in the afternoon all the guests had arrived and were seated around the table. There was William Hay Bisset, who worked in a local distillery, and his wife Margaret; there was a Dykeside farm servant named James Forsyth, and Jane his wife; a brewer from the village of Longmorn named John Grant and finally a young girl whose name has not been recorded.

Mrs Forsyth brought them a tureen of broth as a first course, but Hay was not pleased. He thought it tasted a bit bitter and his guests were less than impressed. They had only a few spoonfuls and began to feel sick. One at a time they ran from the room and vomited as soon as they got outside. Hay was soon as sick as the rest.

Mrs Forsyth also served the soup to James Forsyth and Alexander Hardy, two of the farm servants, and John Ellis, a coachman, all of whom ate around the kitchen table. Lastly she had some soup herself. She thought it tasted peculiar, but moments later she had more to worry about as she threw it all up, together with all the other contents of her stomach. Unable to continue as cook, Mrs Forsyth was escorted home, but it was not until nine that evening that she stopped vomiting.

Hay sent a servant to Forres for Dr Fyfe, who hurried over as soon as he could. He had a quick look at his patients, pumped out their stomachs and issued an emetic. Dr Fyfe thought they had been poisoned and he searched the house for anything that could have been responsible. He found a paper packet of 'Kearney's Infallible Powder' in a kitchen cupboard. This powder, also known as 'Kearney's Infallible Compound for Destroying Rats', was a well-known product and in common use. While Hay was searching, the patients gradually recovered and the worst of the illness passed by nine that night.

On the following Monday, Chief Constable Mair of the Elginshire police came to Rheeves Farm. He questioned Mrs Beaton, who said, 'I have nothing to do with it. I have been ill myself since Thursday or Friday.'

In February, Hay had bought a packet of Kearney's Powder, and had promptly forgotten all about it. A former servant named Isabella Garrow said that there had been three packets of rat poison but she had already used about half.

The rat poison and the remaining contents of the porridge pot were sent to Dr Henry Littlejohn in Edinburgh to be examined. He found that there was a large amount of arsenic in the broth, with a grain and three-quarters in every bowl: quarter of a grain more would have been sufficient to kill a grown man. Kearney's Powder was over half pure arsenic.

Mrs Beaton was arrested and jailed for fifteen months for administering poison. Her name has been entirely forgotten, but if she had been successful, she might have been one of the most famous mass murderers of the century.

17
Rural Murders

Although by the middle of the century, more Scots lived in towns and cities than in the countryside, there was still a sizeable rural population. Sometimes they did not see eye to eye with their neighbours.

'They are worse than brutes': murder in the bothy

The Agricultural Revolution brought change to Scotland as drastic as the Industrial Revolution did. The old days of communal farming disappeared and with them the proliferation of tiny holdings and a land swarming with people. In their place came enclosures with large, extremely well-managed farms that produced far higher yields of crops. These scientific farms still worked to the iron rhythm of the seasons, but they needed men as cogs in the farming machine. The farm workers – or farm servants, in the parlance of the period – had a definite ranking system, from the halflin, who was a boy in his teens who had not yet achieved the full status of a man, right up to the grieve, who was the farm overseer.

It was common for the married men to have farm cottages for the term they were employed, while unmarried farm servants lived together in barrack or dormitory-like accommodation, known as bothies. The men ate, got ready for work, often spent any leisure time and slept in the bothy. As can be imagined, with a collection of hard young men working long hours in all weathers and living in often isolated situations, tensions could build and tempers could fray, with sometimes tragic consequences.

In most farm steadings, as in many places of employment anywhere, there would be one man who was the target of cruel humour. He may have been the oldest man, or the youngest, or the quietest, or have come from outside the area. He would always be thought of as the 'other' and tormenting him would act as a bonding agent for the others; he was the gel that held the workers together.

The 300-acre farm of New Mains of Ury sat just north of Stonehaven and only a crow's call from the main road north to Aberdeen. It was situated on a seaward-facing slope, so on a clear day the servants could look up from their labours and enjoy the view over Stonehaven and the cold blue of the North Sea. The workers lived in a bothy and a neat row of four cottages around 150 yards from the farmhouse. As usual, the unmarried men lived in the bothy, with the married couples and families housed in the stone cottages next door.

In 1893 the foreman was twenty-two-year-old George McCondach. However, it was not a happy place to work, with the men frequently arguing among themselves. Robert Smith, who had been a cattleman at the farm for three years, was particularly affected by the tense atmosphere. Smith was illegitimate and a Laurencekirk man. He was about thirty-two, married with four children, and lived in a cottar house at the farm. Not tall, he had red hair, with a moustache and side whiskers. He was known as a 'capital worker and a most obliging servant', who was steady and sober but a bit 'excitable' and disliked the 'bantering' that was common currency of speech among the farm workers.

Smith had constant arguments with McCondach, a young halflin named William Robertson and Thomas Mitchell, the third horseman. McCondach in particular used to 'boo' at Smith and only a few days before the incident in question, Smith had threatened: 'That's the last day you will roar at me, Geordie.'

McCondach, a muscular young man, ignored the remark as bombast and laughed at the cattleman. McCondach was young for a foreman, but he had held that position for the past year. He was a local man from Dunnottar, well known and well liked in the area. 'Booing' meant exactly that: shouting out or hissing 'boo' to inform a man that he was not popular.

The taunting had begun when William Smith, the tenant of the farm, bought an extra gun and asked Robert Smith to look after it for him. That simple request gave some of the other workers the impression that Robert Smith was some kind of favourite and they termed him 'the factor', along with other less repeatable words. Once Robertson said, 'If the master kent as much about you as Brodie kens, you would not be about the farm for long.' Brodie was another of the farm workers.

There may also have been talk of Robert Smith's wife taking firewood to which she had no right, and he was concerned that the horsemen were stealing oilcake for their horses that should have gone to his cattle. There was name-calling as well – 'bullhead' and 'cow killer' – and the tormentors occasionally smeared the handles of his barrow with cow dung and covered the chimney of his house with a bag so smoke filled the room where his wife and children lived.

Eventually the verbal bullying got under Smith's skin and he asked the farmer if he could terminate his employment, as 'the loon' – Robertson – had called him a thief. Farmer Smith refused but promised to look into the matter; he never did. He thought it a trivial matter. Robert Smith complained to the police; they did not pursue the case. The tormenting grew worse: the three men who bullied him placed a turnip on a wall beside him, threw stones at it and said, 'What would they gie for a bat at the bugger's head?'

Simple stuff, but when constantly repeated it frustrated an essentially quiet man who wanted only to be left in peace.

On the morning of 16 May 1893, Smith rose early and drove a herd of cattle to the park (field), as his job required. On the way he passed the bothy door, where McCondach shouted out, 'Would you put a stop to me?'

'I would damned quick do that,' Smith replied. He continued, as Thomas Mitchell called out, 'Boo!' to him and McCondach echoed, 'Boo!'

With the cattle in the park, Smith returned home, dressed himself in a check tweed jacket and dark striped trousers, put his cap neatly on his head and lifted two shotguns, his own and the gun he was looking after for Farmer Smith. He nodded to his wife. 'It'll be nae warning tae them,' he said, cryptically, 'but it'll be a warning tae ithers.' And then he walked out of his cottage. He came next door into the bothy with two guns and shot McCondach dead, while also badly wounding William Robertson.

The killing shocked the local community and slowly more details emerged. At about quarter to five in the morning, three men, McCondach, Robertson and young Charles Gordon were in the bothy getting ready for work. They walked to the stables and got the horses prepared, as they always did, and returned to the bothy. As Robertson made the morning porridge, Gordon washed his face and McCondach sat near to the fireplace with his back to the door, lacing his boots. It was about half past five when Robert Smith strode through the outer door to the bothy, with a single-barrelled shotgun in one hand and a double-barrelled in the other.

Smith walked through the inner door of the bothy, positioned the double-barrelled shotgun between his knees and aimed the single-barrelled weapon at the foreman, who had not yet turned around.

'Pass you by, Charlie'

'Now, Condie,' he said, as the three men in the bothy stared at him in alarm. Smith gestured to Gordon and told him, 'Pass you by, Charlie. I won't touch you, as I have nothing against you.'

As soon as he had spoken, Smith aimed the shotgun. 'Now, Condie,' he said again.

McCondach turned around just as Smith fired. The entire charge of one barrel smashed into the side of the foreman's face, so half his head was blown off and spattered against the inside wall of the bothy in a mess of blood and brains and splinters of bone.

Obviously Gordon was a sensible man, for he did not hesitate but fled past Smith and into the cool morning air. The sound of his heavy boots echoed from the stone walls of the cottages next door.

'Now for the loon,' Smith said.

Seventeen-year-old Robertson was a trifle slower on his feet than Gordon, but he squeezed out as Smith laid down his empty shotgun and lifted the double-barrelled weapon.

Robertson ran as McCondach switched guns, but he did not go far. He ran straight to the cottage where Adam Robb lived, only two houses from the bothy, but the door was locked and Robb did not immediately open to Robertson's desperate hammering.

Smith had followed; he stood at the door of the bothy, aimed and fired. Luckily the charge of a shotgun spreads with distance and only a few pellets hit Robertson's right arm, with the majority crashing into the wooden frame of the door. Robertson must have yelled; he realised that Robb was not going to answer the door and moved to John Brodie's cottage next door, hammering desperately on the door, as Smith stepped closer and aimed again.

'Brodie!' Robertson pleaded. 'Brodie!' And then: 'Oh, Geordie!'

Smith fired the second barrel. This time his aim was better and the full charge smacked into Robertson's back. The force of the shot knocked the youth face down on the ground. He lay there, semi-conscious with something in the region of 200 lead pellets in his back, shoulder and arm.

Brodie, a horseman, yanked his door open and saw Robertson sprawled on the ground, and then Smith holding the shotgun.

'Oh, Rob,' he said, 'this is a terrible job you have been in this morning.'

'I'll put a stop to them crying at me,' Smith said, 'and if I had that bugger Tam I'd give him the same.'

He looked at Robertson, shrugged, told Brodie that he had nothing against him, and said, 'They cried for my heid up upon a dyke to get a pin in it but I'll gie them a heid.' And then he calmly returned to his cottage beside the bothy.

'Oh, Rob,' his wife said, 'you should have thought of your wife and children before you did this.'

'I could have died happy and shot them down like hares,' Smith replied. He reloaded the shotguns, said a calm goodbye to his family and left the house.

Annie Dunbar, who lived at East Lodge of Ury, had seen some of what happened. 'Oh, cattleman' she said to Smith, 'for the sake of your wife and children, lay down these guns.'

'I am prepared for anything this morning,' Smith replied and walked on.

In the meantime, Brodie helped the wounded Robertson into the bothy. The halflin was placed face down on his own bed, where he lay in torment, wondering if he would live or die.

'I've just shot two of your men'

Naturally, the reports of the guns were heard around the farm, particularly in the quiet of the early morning, but Smith often rose early to shoot a few crows, so nobody thought it unusual. It was a little later that Stuart Smith, the farmer's son, saw Robert Smith near the cart shed.

'I've just shot two of your men,' Robert Smith said, as casually as if he was merely passing the time of day.

Stuart Smith made a non-committal remark and walked away. Even when two cattlemen told him what had happened he found it hard to believe.

'Oh nonsense,' he said, 'that can't be.' When the cattlemen insisted that they were not joking, Stuart Smith was appalled and asked for details. As soon as he realised the truth he hurried to Robert Smith, who was walking around the farm carrying both guns, and asked for the double-barrelled shotgun, which was his own property. Robert Smith handed it over without any argument. When Robert Smith began to move toward the stables, Stuart Smith followed and advised him to give up the single-barrelled shotgun as well.

Robert Smith was more hesitant about that, but complied and said he was 'going for a travel' and would be 'down by'.

Two of the farm servants had run to the police so Charles George, Chief Constable of Kincardineshire, and Inspector John Farquharson arrived at the farm. They called on the farm workers and as many local volunteers as they could to organise a search party for Robert Smith. Working in pairs in case Smith proved violent, the men scoured the immediate area, gradually extending the area of the search. Two men, George McGregor and William Caird, checked the cliff path that led to Stonehaven. They found the fugitive outside the wall of the churchyard of Cowie, near the edge of the cliff and looking out to sea.

'Hulloa, cattler,' McGregor called out. 'What in the world have you done?'

'Oh it can't be helped now,' Smith told him. 'I dinnae care; it will be a warning to others.'

'You'll have to go to jail,' McGregor warned, but Smith did not appear concerned.

'That will be better, for I have been in purgatory the last nine months.'

When McGregor and Caird asked him to come with them, he agreed at once.

'It's a fine morning, Condie,' he said with a smile, as they met George McCondach, the father of the first man Smith had shot. Smith seemed dazed or perhaps in shock and asked to return to the farm so he could change his clothes. He was not allowed that luxury and McGregor escorted him to Stonehaven police station, where he walked quietly into a cell and sat down.

'I want another man yet,' he remarked to the police. 'I want Mitchell.'

Inspector Farquharson charged him with murder. 'They deserved it,' Smith replied, 'I will die happy. If it was not for Stuart Smith, I would have cleared the lot. I laid them over like rats.'

The next day, when he was asked if he felt guilty about murdering one man and seriously wounding another, Smith replied: 'I think no more of shooting these characters than I would of shooting brute beasts. They are worse than brutes, for if you treat a beast kindly you will receive kindness in return.' He was taken to Craiginches jail in Aberdeen in handcuffs.

As soon as she heard of her husband's actions, Smith's wife left New Mains of Ury and returned to her parents' house in Stonehaven; she was as much in shock as Robert Smith seemed to be.

The trial was held in Aberdeen Circuit Court in July, in front of so large an audience that two Gordon Highlanders were drafted in to support the police. The charge was altered from murder to culpable homicide because of the degree of provocation that Smith had endured, and the jury took just fourteen minutes to find him guilty of that. Lord McLaren sentenced him to penal servitude for life.

'Thank you, my Lord,' Smith replied. He accepted the sentence without expression. Life in prison was probably better than life under the scourge of the bothy bullies.

Murder of a drover

Although the highways and byways of nineteenth-century Scotland were not yet polluted by hundreds of thousands of snarling motor cars, they were busy with other traffic. As well as the farmers' carts that carried produce to market, there was always a steady stream of pedestrians walking from one place to another on business or social outings. There were also packmen, travellers, merchants and cattle drovers.

The drovers had a very responsible job; they were the Scottish equivalent of the cowboys of the American west, except that they had lesser distances to travel and moved by foot. Drovers travelled through some of the roughest terrain in the country, following the drove roads that cut across hundreds of miles of moorland and hills, but it was in the more populated areas that they often faced their greatest threats.

In June 1825, George McKay was one of a group of men taking a drove of cattle south from the Highlands. When they passed the farm of Gart Cannon, near Fintry in Stirlingshire, a small group of farm servants gathered to watch them pass. Such a sight provided entertainment in the bleak world of endless toil that was the lot of nineteenth-century farm labourers. For some reason, one of the labourers kicked out at a passing cow with his heavy boot.

Donald McKay, another of the drovers, took instant revenge by attacking the labourer and knocking him to the ground, but more labourers came along, joined by a number of women. The foreman sent one of them, James Dobbie, to drive the straying cattle off the grass around the farm house, but three of the drovers rushed at him. He tried to defend himself but they knocked him down with their heavy sticks and started to thump him as he lay bleeding on the ground.

As the drovers flailed away, a gaggle of women charged out of the farm house, all fire and fury, and threw a volley of stones at both the cattle and the drovers. John Dobbie ran to help his brother James but the drovers knocked him down as well. John helped James to his feet and they ran away, with the fleet-footed drovers close behind. The drovers were yelling in Gaelic and waving their sticks, as the Dobbie brothers turned around, tore stones from the ground and started to throw them. John Dobbie lifted a particularly large stone and it crashed against the head of George McKay, who dropped at once: dead.

John Dobbie was charged with murder but when the Lord Advocate heard that the stone was thrown in self-defence he advised the jury to find him not guilty. Dobbie walked free.

Scottish rural life was no idyll; the men and women were kindly and hard-working, but nobody knew when murder could arise from the hot temper of a trivial dispute.

18
Of Thieves and Muggers

In common with every other nation, Scotland was plagued by thieves. There was nothing that could not be stolen, from horses and cattle to the contents of a gentleman's pocket but perhaps the most common targets were private houses and shops...

Methods of burglary

Burglars did not always enter their target property directly. They often broke into a property above, which was less well secured, and came down through the ceiling. Such a case occurred in early March 1835, when thieves tried to rob George White's jeweller's shop at 178 Trongate in Glasgow.

They used false or skeleton keys to enter John Keith's bookshop next door, mounted the stairs and broke into the warehouse, which extended above White's shop. To get into the warehouse, they cut out an entire panel of the door. As they passed John Keith's desk, they broke the lock and stole £5 as a keepsake before moving on to the real object of the night.

Using an auger, they bored holes in the floor and removed a section of lath and plaster so they could drop down into the jewellery shop. Unfortunately for their hopes, the sound of falling plaster woke the night watchman in the shop; he jumped up and grabbed a pistol, but the thieves heard him and ran for their lives and liberty.

They were so panic-stricken that they left all their equipment behind, which could serve as a fine example of the tools of the burglar's trade. There was a lantern that could be shaded to direct only a tiny beam of light so it would attract no attention, a chisel, a large gimlet (a hand tool used to drill small holes), an auger for drilling larger holes, a crowbar and a rope ladder. The ladder was apparently a splendid piece of work, brand new, with mahogany steps to ensure easy and safe access. There were also two large bags, which were designed to fasten around the chest of the thief. The stolen goods would be secreted in these, and if they were then concealed under a greatcoat, nobody would know that the thief was carrying anything. It was much safer than holding a bag that might attract the attention of a passing policeman.

Cutting a hole in the ceiling was a mode of burglary much favoured by the Scottish urban thief. That method was used in February 1857 when thieves clambered onto the roof of Mrs Lennie's optician's and jeweller's shop in Princes Street, Edinburgh. They were fortunate that the roof had a balcony with a parapet that hid them from the street below, so they had privacy in which to work. They bored a number of holes in a rough rectangle, pushed out the section of the plaster ceiling that had been weakened, and dropped a rope ladder down to the shop. They stole around £1,000 worth of rings and other jewellery.

The use of rope ladders was also common throughout the period. In another Edinburgh theft at a flesher's (or butcher's) shop in Nicolson Street in 1856, the thieves again broke into the flat above, cut through the floor and dropped by rope ladder. On this occasion the thieves were unlucky as, the butcher, a man named Rennie, returned unexpectedly. The would-be robbers fled before they had time to steal anything; they left their ladder behind.

Others thieves were less sophisticated. In January 1837, Mary Ann Murphy, David Skinner and Mary Johnston appeared at the High Court charged with breaking into a spirit dealer's in the Grassmarket, Edinburgh. Murphy was an old hand at the game and had forced off a window shutter with a poker and broken three panes of glass. Murphy and Skinner were sent to jail for eighteen months and Johnston for a year.

In yet another case at a house in Edinburgh's Castle Street in 1838, the thieves entered through a window at the back of the house. They stole £50 in notes and a variety of silverware but were disturbed and left all their equipment behind. The police secured a huge bunch of various keys, including skeleton keys, a hand vice and a file, as well as the rope ladder, complete with hoops that could attach it to walls or ceiling joists.

Generally, the better secured the property, the more ingenious the method by which the thief gained access.

Husband and wife team

William Marshall was a man satisfied with life. On Saturday, 11 May 1839, he looked around his business in New Buildings, North Bridge in Edinburgh and was content they were as secure as any jewellery shop could be. There were only two apartments: the front shop, where his business was performed, and a small back warehouse, where the stock was stored. An open archway connected the two rooms. The window was secured with a locked shutter and when he closed the door at half past eight that night he locked that firmly behind him.

However, early on the morning of Monday, 13 May, there was a hard knock at the door of Marshall's house. When he answered it, a policeman told him that his shop had been robbed. Marshall threw on his clothes and hurried through the quiet streets to the shop. The thief had circumvented all his precautions by cutting a neat hole in the ceiling of his warehouse and dropping a rope ladder the fifteen feet or so to the floor. The ladder was cleverly constructed, with wooden treads. He noticed that the treads were painted on one side and bare wood on the other, as though the wood had once been part of a piece of furniture.

When Marshall checked his stock, there were over fifty watches missing, twenty-nine of them gold, and dozens of silver spoons. These were easily portable items for which there was a ready demand.

The police had been well aware that the flat above the shop was empty, and a few days earlier the beat officer had noticed that the entry door was open. He had told Marshall, but there was no real worry, as there were workmen in and out of the flat all the time, renovating the property for the next tenant. Now, as Marshall counted the cost of the theft, he wished he had paid more attention to the police's warning.

Alexander Colquhoun, a criminal officer (a detective), examined the flat above Marshall's shop. He worked out that the thief had broken in, removed the hearthstone from the room directly above Marshall's storehouse, cut the hole and fastened the rope ladder to one of the joists above and to the floorboards below. The knots of the ladder were interesting, and a policeman and ex-sailor named Patrick Campbell believed they had been fastened by a seaman.

The thief had climbed down the ladder, robbed the shop and returned the same way. He had left the debris from his work in the flat, together with a small saw, two chisels and the stump of a candle, which presumably gave him sufficient light to work by. He had also left a false or skeleton key that fitted the lock and opened the door as efficiently as the proper key. Colquhoun tried the ladder out and it held his weight. He also noticed a piece of puce-coloured cloth wrapped around the handle of the false key.

Colquhoun interviewed the men who were working in the flat. Alexander Thornton was employed in building up partition walls, and said the door facing the stairway was always bolted in place for security. He also said that he had once found the door to the flat open but had not thought much about it: there was nothing inside to steal and he had not considered that anybody would attempt boring through the ceiling to rob the shop below. However, the morning after the robbery he had noticed marks on the door, as if somebody had inserted pipe clay inside the lock in order to make an impression to create a false or skeleton key.

There was also work being carried out in the second-floor flat, where a tailor had his home and workplace. Thornton said that some of the workmen passed him from time to time and one had shown great interest in his flat; he had come in about a dozen times to poke around, but he never spoke. When this man had lingered in the flat, Thornton had chased him away, saying it was half past ten and time he was at his own work. The man looked prosperous, and was well dressed in a green coat with a velvet collar, light trousers and a black hat.

George Ross also worked in the flat above Marshall's shop. He was a cabinetmaker and had seen a woman hanging around the flat a couple of times. He described her as wearing a red shawl over her black gown, with a black bonnet on her head; she was a very respectably dressed woman and had spoken pleasantly to Ross: 'You are busy,' she had said. Ross thought she was viewing the house with the intention of leasing it when all the work was completed. The woman had asked a fellow cabinetmaker named George Elder if the flat was to let.

As usual, the police circulated a description of the stolen items to all the local pawnshops and informed the police of every major city of the burglary. This was a routine procedure, as thieves needed to swap their loot for hard cash, and pawn shops were the most common establishments for resetting stolen goods. The police had one major advantage, for watches all had a unique identification number engraved on the back. Honest brokers could find this number, check with their list of stolen watches and report to the police. Dishonest brokers could file the number off and engrave another one. On this occasion the system worked perfectly, but from an unexpected location.

Henry Bolton was an established watchmaker and watch repairer in Oldhall Street in Liverpool. At the end of July 1839, a man came in with a collection of watch bars – a watch bar was the strip of metal that attached to the watch and often carried the owner's name on it. The man asked Bolton to engrave his name on the bars and fit them to the watches. He gave his name as Edward Harris of Dublin, and said he would return at four that afternoon. It was then half past two. Bolton set to work, but discovered that a previous owner had already had his name engraved on the bars, but they had been clumsily filed off. Honest men were unlikely to do such a thing, so Bolton suspected that the watches had been stolen: he notified the police.

When he inspected the watch plates more closely, Bolton also saw that the watch manufacturer had engraved the watch number on the underside, which was a very unusual precaution. Whoever had filed off the name and number on the top side had not thought to look underneath. Bolton checked the numbers with the list of stolen watches with which the police supplied him, and found they matched watches taken from Marshall's shop.

The police did not immediately arrest Edward Harris. Instead they ordered a constable to watch the shop from a distance. Constables John Toole, Ainsworth and Lloyd watched Harris enter the shop about half past four, but did not pick him up at that time.

When Harris came into the shop to collect his watch bars, Bolton said that they were not ready yet and asked him to return at about seven. Harris did so, and Bolton signalled to Toole that he was the suspect. As Toole watched, a young woman joined Harris. Toole followed them until they entered a pub; he remained outside for over an hour as the couple refreshed themselves. They were so long that

Toole wondered if they had left by another door but eventually the couple emerged and Toole followed them again.

They walked a fair distance and entered a lodging house in Regent Street kept by a woman named Mrs Buddle. Again Toole waited outside for a while before he decided to fetch help. However, as he was finding a colleague, Harris and the woman left Mrs Buddle's house. Both constables had to wait another half-hour until the couple returned, when Toole promptly arrested them. Toole searched the suspects and the house, and found sixteen watch plates with the numbers still engraved, others with names filed off, some silver spoons and a number of pawn tickets. The woman proved very reluctant to help, but eventually she emptied her pockets of six pawn tickets from Liverpool, two from Edinburgh and three from Leith. The police took them to jail.

On the journey to jail, Harris and the woman had been able to drop a bag, but the police found that as well. It held a gold watch with the name 'Marshall' on it. The police sent Harris and his wife back to Edinburgh. They made their usual inquiries and discovered that Harris was a false name. The man was named Charles Dewar. He was around sixty years old and a native of Edinburgh. His father had built Dewar Place near Haymarket in that city. Dewar had been a midshipman in the Royal Navy, but had transferred to the Merchant Navy, sailing as first and second mate out of Leith without giving any cause for complaint. His maritime experience would have given him the skill with knots. His father was a relatively wealthy man and Dewar succeeded to his fortune; life should have been sweet.

However, Dewar was a man of lavish tastes and spent all his inheritance on wine, women and high living. He married a much younger woman named Sophie, and while he was at the gambling tables or carousing in the pubs, she was trying to support them by working long hours at low-paid employment. Life was hard for her.

The police visited the Dewars' house in Park Street. They found that two shelves had been ripped out of the closets; the other shelves were painted the same colour as the treads of the rope ladder. The rope from the sash windows had also been cut away, but what remained matched the colour of the rope from the ladder. It seemed pretty obvious that the rope ladder had been made from materials in the house in Park Street.

Colquhoun questioned David Baird, the factor of the Park Street house. Baird said that Mrs Dewar had leased the house in May 1838. She took out the lease in her husband's name, which she gave as Robert Dewar, and she said he was a shipmaster. Mrs Dewar seldom allowed Baird back into the house to check its condition but he knew there was no furniture and the Dewars lived in poverty. That changed around the middle of May 1839, when their appearance suddenly altered, as if they had come into some money.

The case came to trial in January 1840. Dewar pleaded not guilty, but as the evidence against him mounted up he changed his plea to guilty and was sentenced to fourteen years' transportation. Sophie was found not guilty and released. She smiled to her husband as she left the court and was lost to history.

Robbery in Dumfries

In late November 1872, thieves broke into the shop of Halliday and Thomson, ironmongers and jewellers of High Street, Dumfries, and stole jewellery valued at around £1,000. They got access from a narrow lane named the Pass Colley, which ran behind the business. The shop backed onto a warehouse, the yard of which formed one wall of the Pass Colley. The thieves clambered over the access door between the yard and the lane, and hurried across the yard, but there was a locked and bolted wooden door to get past next. The thieves hacked a hole in this, slipped through a knowing hand and drew back the bolt. That got them into the warehouse, but there was yet another locked door between them and the shop.

The owners of the firm had taken more precautions with this door and covered it with iron plates, so there was no chance of cutting through a panel. However, there was a weakness. The frame of the door, into which the bolt slotted, was of wood, and the burglars sawed through this, pushed open the door and entered the shop.

It is possible that the thieves knew exactly what they were doing; their timing was perfect. The partnership of Halliday and Thomson was about to dissolve and they were in the middle of a sale, with everything they had laid out in the shop. The thieves had all the time in the world to select exactly what they wished and vanish into the night.

Crime spree in Forfar

In the summer of 1870, Forfar and the surrounding area seemed to be under siege. There was hardly a night without news of a break-in or a robbery. Three of the principal businesses, the East Port Savings Association, the West Port Grocery and Baking Association, and the Little Causeway Society were targeted, and in each case the burglar used the same technique. He bored holes in the door with an auger, pushed out a square of wood, thrust through his hand and drew back the bolt. The thief also hit the houses of military officers, Charles Talo's Hotel in Brechin and the Aldbar Railway Station. He had broken into Talo's by the same technique as he had used with the businesses.

At the same time, a known thief named William Wallace just happened to have moved to Forfar. The police suspected he was involved but naturally every time they looked for him, he had vanished. Constables McGibbon and Stewart knew that Wallace was clever, so they decided to be a bit cunning themselves. They found a position on rising ground from which they could survey the town and the surrounding area, opened up a telescope and settled down to search for their quarry. Eventually they saw him sneaking into a bothy at Craignathro Farm. When they hurried down, he was hiding inside the bothy; he saw them coming and tried to hold the door closed against them. The police forced their way in and snapped handcuffs around his wrists. Wallace ended up with ten years' penal servitude.

Coming through the window

Professional thieves were highly skilled, with a variety of methods and tools for breaking into other people's property. They were adept at cutting through wood – either the locks or bolts in doors, or the bolts that held shutters together. They were also skilled at working with glass.

On the night of 3 December 1870, David Dakers of Easthaven, between Dundee and Arbroath, checked the doors and windows of his house were locked and at about half past ten he went to bed. After a while he awoke and heard a scratching noise, but he thought it was probably just rats and closed his eyes again. When he woke in the morning, he found that somebody had scraped the plaster from around the window and removed the entire window frame to get access to the house. The intruder had lifted a money drawer from the room in which Dakers had been sleeping and escaped with just £2.

Around the same time a thief broke into a bootmaker's shop in Carnoustie by the much simpler technique of smashing the window, thrusting his hand through the hole and unfastening the window.

Sometimes the sophistication of the tools used by burglars was surprising. In one haul in London in August 1897 the police captured a great number of tools for boring into and breaking open safes, but of very fine quality steel. However, there was one implement made of top quality steel and worked by an electric battery which was carried in a leather shoulder bag. The battery also powered a bull's eye light that directed a thin beam onto the target. That showed a very professional attitude to the gentle art of burglary.

Steel-nerved thief

Some thefts were a matter of pure nerve. On Tuesday, 8 May 1838, a man described as a gentleman, smoothly spoken and dressed in a brown surtout (frock coat) and striped brown trousers entered the shop of Grierson the jeweller in Edinburgh's Leith Street. He was dapper; about five-foot-three-inches tall and dark-haired, with a foreign accent.

The dapper man smiled at the young assistant and asked to be shown a selection of gold watches that were on display in the window. He chose four watches and two chains, and asked the assistant to pack them in a box that he had conveniently brought with him. When the items were safely packed, the gentleman asked for sealing wax, which the assistant found in the back shop. Once the box was secure, the gentleman asked that it should be sent to 88 Great King Street, which sounded like a very respectable address in the New Town. The watches would be paid for on receipt.

Rather than send the assistant, Grierson took the box himself. Unfortunately, there was no such place as number 88 on Great King Street and he returned to the shop annoyed that he had been the victim of a pointless hoax. He opened the box to put the watches back on display, only to find that the box contained some small stones. When the assistant had been searching for sealing wax, the suave gentleman had switched the box containing the watches for an identical box holding the worthless stones.

Two months later a man named Lyon Bernhard was arrested in London and charged with the theft. He was brought to Edinburgh and the High Court sentenced him to seven years' transportation.

Iron-nerved and cheeky thieves

Spirit shops were often the target for robbery. On the night of 5 October 1817 an expert robbed such a place only a few long strides from the watch house at Calton Hill. The soldiers on duty at the Calton Jail had a permanent guard at the watch house.

The thieves knew exactly what they were doing. First they stole the street lamp from outside the building. With light so conveniently provided, they picked the lock of the front door, bored a hole in the wood and pushed open an iron bolt. The door gave access to a long, dark corridor that led to a set of stairs and another locked door, which they opened by sawing out the lock. The spirit shop was next.

They stole a large quantity of spirits, as well as around £50 in cash and notes, left the lamp behind and tidily shut the outer door behind them as they departed. The sentries on duty at the watch house neither heard nor saw a thing.

Other thieves were less lucky and got arrested just for looking suspicious. This happened to a man named John Williamson, whom the Edinburgh police picked up in April 1837. They had been watching him for some time and took him to the police office to be searched. Their instincts proved correct, as he was a known thief who also lived under the names of John Allison, George Thomson and John Thomson. When they searched him, they found a large bunch of skeleton keys and a matching pair of files. The police tried the keys and found they effectively opened a selection of locks, so they kept this man with many names in custody until they decided what best to do with him.

Other thieves were nothing but cheeky. On 14 September 1820, two thieves entered a common stair in Giles Street, Leith, and crept to the topmost landing. They had watched the occupants leave the building, so they knew the house was empty. Using a skeleton key, they got into the house and robbed it of all the money, as well as all the clothes. Unfortunately, there was too much to carry, so one of the thieves stripped himself naked, left his old tattered and soiled clothes behind, dressed in the house owner's best and slipped away. They were never caught.

Shades of *A Christmas Carol*

Many people will be familiar with the scene in Dickens' *A Christmas Carol* where Scrooge's bedding was stripped and taken to the pawnbroker. In April 1823 this exact thing happened in Edinburgh. A woman arrived at the broker's shop with a selection of bedclothes and small articles of clothing. The broker took the items and issued a receipt, but he was suspicious of the woman so notified the police. It turned out that the woman was a maidservant and when her mistress had died, she had stripped the bed on which the corpse lay, then stripped the body of anything that might be sold and took the lot to the broker. She was given sixty days for her trouble.

Next are the contrasting careers of two criminals: one a long-time professional thief, the other a bungling amateur.

The career of Scotch Jimmy

In common with every other nation, Victorian Scotland had her share of professional criminals. Most were shadowy figures who hid behind a veil of aliases, emerging only when they were unsuccessful and the police dragged them to court. James Muirhead was one such. The full details of his criminal career will probably never be known, but a few highlights have been recorded, when the glare of publicity fell on him and he was exposed.

Muirhead may have been born in Edinburgh around 1848. At five-foot-five-inches tall, with a fresh complexion and brown hair, he was a successful man in his profession, working at the top end of the scale, rather than simple theft or shoplifting. Indeed, Muirhead made enough money from his work to look and act like a gentleman. He often dressed in a frock coat and top hat, travelled by cab or coach, and spoke French like a native. He seemed to have a talent for languages and accents, for he was able to switch from Edinburgh Scots to Doric, from a Highland brogue to purest Cockney. He was a chameleon in other ways as well, for when he was not polishing his top hat, his Edinburgh life centred round gamblers of the lowest type.

Muirhead's early career is a matter of conjecture, but he was certainly active in Belfast in the 1870s. In November 1878 he was arrested in that city for a number of swindles in pawnbrokers' shops and was sentenced to penal servitude for five years. However, no sooner had he come out than he was believed to have returned to his old career.

On a Saturday night in September 1885, there was a jewel robbery in the sale room of a jewel merchant in St Enoch Lane in Glasgow. The robbers got away with a huge haul that was worth over £5,000. Muirhead was one of the chief suspects and the police from Caithness to Kent began to search for him. The London police were particularly active, as Muirhead was already well known there. For months, there was no success; for all their network of informers, their modern telegraph system and highly trained officers, the combined forces of the British police drew a blank. They believed that Muirhead had left the country for either Europe or the United States.

It was not until April 1886 that Chief Inspector Langridge of Bow Street in London arrested Muirhead. He did not come quietly; it took a number of police to restrain him. Muirhead was brought north from London to Glasgow to be charged with the robbery, although there was a rival claim from Ireland, where he was also wanted for passing forged bills.

Despite all the best efforts of the police, Muirhead escaped both these charges and moved south again, but he had no intention of abiding by the law. He operated fairly extensively in London and at the Middlesex Quarter Sessions in April 1888 he was convicted of stealing furniture from Wilson Barrett, who was one of the best known actors of the period. Barrett had his own company and attracted huge audiences to his plays such as *The Silver King* and *The Sign of the Cross*. He had lived at the Priory, North Bank, London (a house George Eliot had called home) but when his wife died, Barrett moved to a new house in Hampstead.

Although Barrett no longer lived at The Priory, the house was not empty, for his daughter lived there with a female servant and a St Bernard dog. About the middle of November 1887, someone Barrett described as a 'shabby-genteel person with a sandy moustache and a sandy complexion' came to the door and told the servant he had come for Barrett's letters. At that time Barrett's mail was still being delivered to The Priory. The shabby-genteel man knew the name of the maidservant and of Barry the dog. He advised the maid to 'look sharp or the guv'nor would be wild as he was a-waiting for them'.

That was the first of a number of visits in which the genteel man with the Cockney accent carried away Barrett's private correspondence. After a while the genteel man brought a true gentleman with an American accent to look over the house with a view to leasing. The two checked every room and disappeared. The following day Barrett was in the process of moving house, so his furniture was packed when the genteel man reappeared in a cart, persuaded the legitimate removals men to help him pack some of the most valuable items onto his cart and trotted away. The genteel man was Muirhead but the identity of the other remained a mystery.

Barrett called this exploit 'one of the most impudent robberies that was ever conceived'.

Muirhead ended up inside for another five years, but the experience did not quell his criminal tendencies. In 1893, he had hardly regained his freedom when the Edinburgh police pounced on him for fraud. It seems that he had assumed the persona of the caterer for the officers' mess at the Jock's Lodge barracks and visited a number of shops in the New Town, ordering on the army's credit. He liked to take a cab to the front door of the shop, select the finest food and wine for the officers, and have his selections carried to the cab before he drove away.

That little series of escapades earned him another three years' penal servitude, followed by a further five years with the police closely supervising him. Perhaps the police did not supervise closely enough, for not long after his release from Peterhead in the summer of 1895 Muirhead was again in trouble.

In December of that year, somebody used a false key to open the outer door of the Edinburgh Co-operative Stores. The burglar, or burglars, then faced a wooden inner door. They broke through one of the lower panels and crawled into the office, where there was a half-ton steel safe. They moved the safe away from the wall to give themselves more room, then used a five-foot-long jemmy and a selection of wedges to break in. Only a very skilful professional could have done that. Muirhead was one of the suspects, but he seems to have slipped away from the law on that occasion.

Muirhead was also suspected of being involved in a robbery at the loan office of William Scott, pawnbrokers at Bain Square in Dundee, that year. Once again, the robbers were professionals. They used the time-honoured Scottish method and broke into a flat above the office, bored holes in the floor, kicked out a square large enough to clamber through and lowered a rope to the floor below. There were three safes in the office, two full of jewellery handed in by customers and the third with the business books of the firm. The burglars had bored holes through the casing of the safes but had not got inside. When the shop workers arrived the next day, they found the floor littered with safe-breaking equipment, including jemmies, boring braces and levers, as well as a chunk of lead. The lead was used to deaden the sound of hammers clanging on the iron safe. The police believed that somebody had disturbed the burglars in the middle of their work, so they had fled the scene. Muirhead was again suspected but never convicted.

On 17 March 1896, there was a robbery at the Eglinton Street branch of the post office in Glasgow, and again Muirhead was suspected of being involved. The robbers stole £21 in cash and £70 in stamps, plus postal and money orders worth around £376. Muirhead – now better known by his London nickname of 'Scotch Jimmy' – was immediately suspected. The police thought he had worked with a twenty-six-year-old Edinburgh man named Thomas Reid, who was another convict out on licence. The Glasgow police sent descriptions of both men around the country and tried to trace their movements.

Reid and Muirhead were tracked to London and then to Monte Carlo, where Reid had altered his name to Reeve. From there, Reid and Muirhead had slipped back to Greenock. Both men were in the area in the middle of May 1896, when there was another significant robbery that the police believed Reid and Muirhead were involved in. This time the target had been the co-operative store on Main Street in Bridgeton, in the East End of Glasgow. The entry was typically robust: the thieves cut a hole in the back wall of the shop and crawled in. The co-op had a small safe, which the thieves manoeuvred onto a two-wheeled barrow and moved to an area that allowed them space. Then they set to work, levering the door right off its hinges and stealing the £77 that was inside.

Inspector Gordon of the Eastern Police Office recognised the *modus operandi* as being that of Reid and began the usual round of inquiries. He checked to see if there were any known associates of Reid in the city, and was encouraged when a man named Miller was fined for drunkenness in Bridgeton. As Miller knew Reid well, Gordon set Detective Johnstone and a constable to watch his house on Newhall Street in case Reid came to call. When a telegraph boy came to the house, Johnstone intercepted the message.

The telegraph asked Miller to 'send him the key of his bag'. It had been posted in Liverpool and had been sent by 'T. Anderson, Southport'. Anderson was a known alias of Reid. Gordon had a false key sent to Southport, and when the mysterious Anderson collected it, the police arrested him. It was Thomas Reid. For good measure, the police also grabbed Miller and a third man named James Reilly, who lived with him.

In the meantime the hunt for Muirhead continued. The police knew that the stolen postal orders were useless until they were officially stamped, so when a stamping machine was stolen from a post office in London's Blackfriars Road they put two and two together and looked for a likely culprit.

The first suspect was a forty-four-year-old diamond merchant from Peckham in London, named George Roberts. His name was not known to the police, but Roberts was caught with a £1 postal order that had been stolen from Eglinton Street. When Roberts presented the order at a post office in Battersea, the counter clerk was immediately suspicious. He checked the number and said he would have to hold Roberts there until the police arrived.

Roberts did not wait to argue his case but simply walked out of the post office and into a waiting car. He went in one door and straight out the other onto the road, but the clerk had followed him out. As soon as Roberts emerged onto the road, the clerk grabbed him and shouted for the police. He was in more danger than he realised, for when the police searched Roberts they found he was carrying a loaded revolver. They knew him better as James Muirhead. As he was a ticket-of-leave convict and had not reported to the appropriate authorities, Muirhead was charged with that offence as well. At that time he was forty-four, short, with receding light brown hair and blue eyes. If he was not in enough trouble in Glasgow, the Edinburgh police still wanted to question him about the Co-operative safe robbery, where £187 had been stolen.

Before Muirhead was sent to Glasgow to be questioned, Inspector Marshall of Scotland Yard asked that he be detained longer in London so he could be investigated about a murder in Muswell Hill. However, there was insufficient evidence to hold him and he was sent north.

Around the time of Muirhead's arrest, a general dealer of Old Kent Road, twenty-six-year-old James Girdle, was also arrested for trying to steal a stamping machine. While buying a postal order, he had distracted William Wakerley, the clerk, for a second by pointing behind him and saying, 'Is that a mouse or a rat?' and grabbed the date-stamp machine. After he left, Wakerley called the police, who found a large number of postal orders at Girdle's flat, all stolen from Eglinton Street in Glasgow. They also found the missing post office stamping machine.

At the court in Glasgow, Muirhead was sentenced to seven years' penal servitude. He had pleaded guilty in the hope of a lesser sentence, but Lord McLaren did not agree. There was despair on Scotch Jimmy's face as he was led below; that was the last time Muirhead appeared in front of a judge, at least under his own name. The third man connected with the robbery, Thomas Rice Reid, was given a seven-year sentence.

Other criminals had shorter and more unlucky careers.

The thin thief

Sometimes thieves just had no luck at all. That was the case for David Bertie, a Dundee cattle feeder who turned his hand to burglary. He did not operate in his home city but moved upcountry to Forfar, where he may have believed pickings would be easier.

Bertie began his career of crime on Tuesday, 23 May 1877, when he targeted the Manor House, a substantial stone-built property in which he anticipated prosperous pickings. Bertie watched the house first, checking the windows, lit and unlit, and then he approached, but the householder, Thomas Craik, had seen him sneaking through the dark and prepared to defend his property.

Bertie sidled up to an unlit window. There was a small row of iron spikes on the outside ledge, but he believed he was sufficiently agile to circumvent that minor barrier. He noted that the window was locked but tested it anyway. As he had hoped, it was shut but not properly locked. He bent down, put both hands under the lower casement and pushed upward. The window creaked a little, but not sufficiently loudly to alarm the inhabitants of the Manor House. Bertie slid his hands inside the house, and yelled in sudden pain as Craik gave him a hearty smash over the knuckles with a heavy walking stick.

Bertie withdrew suddenly back out of the window, swore as his trousers caught on the spikes, wrestled free and tried to run, but Craik chased him across the garden, waving his stick. Although Craik was in his dressing gown, he caught Bertie as he reached Castle Street, and held him fast. Bertie was a small, very slender man with a pathetic look on his thin face and an unfashionable pair of checked trousers, now with a tear in the seat. Craik held him tight and looked up the street. As always there was no policeman when one was needed, and he had no desire to walk the streets of Forfar dressed in his night things. He let Bertie go and returned to the Manor House.

Probably cursing and definitely nursing his bruised knuckles, Bertie tried his luck elsewhere. He walked to the Lowden household at Laurel Bank. This was another solid and substantial residence in a large garden with potentially excellent pickings. Bertie looked for an entrance, chose a very small but unlocked window and squeezed his way inside. Bertie was obviously as clumsy as he was unlucky, for the servants heard him clattering his way through the rooms and raised the alarm. Lowden strode downstairs to search for the intruder, but Bertie had already taken fright and escaped back through the window.

Perhaps Bertie thought 'third time lucky', for he did not give up in disgust but tried another house. This time he tried the manse of the Reverend Cumming of the West Free Church, but once again he was discovered and fled for his freedom.

Three attempts at burglary in such a quiet little town as Forfar were a bit too much and the police were soon on the trail of the burglar. They visited all the houses that Bertie had attempted to rob, and found a small fragment of checked cloth he had left on the window spikes at Manor House. Police from beyond Forfar were also searching for the bungling burglar. Constable Birse of Kirriemuir was also in town. He listened to the description of a small man with torn checked trousers. Purely by coincidence, as soon as he arrived in Kirriemuir, Birse saw a man who exactly matched the description. Naturally, he scooped the suspect up and contacted the Forfar police.

And that was the end of David Bertie's brief career as a thief.

There was plenty more crime in Scotland.

19
Prison and Punishment

When criminals were caught, they faced an escalating system of punishments. There were fines or short spells in prison, followed by longer spells, if the criminal continued on his or her path. However, many criminals did not surrender tamely and sought to escape from jail. Not all were successful.

Escape from Glasgow Jail

On 1 September 1800, Thomas Millward and Peter Wright broke out of Glasgow jail. They had been held together in a cell in the upper level, but broke the iron grille on the window, ran along the slate roof and dropped a rope the three storeys to the ground. Wright was first down and vanished into the streets of Glasgow. However, when Millward tried to follow, the rope did not hold his weight and he was badly injured in the fall. He got up and staggered away, but was found two days later in the Old Vennel. He was too weak to resist and was carried back to prison. There were many other attempts to get out of jail free.

Escape by blanket

In the early nineteenth century, prisons were not as well designed as they became later, and the prisoners seemed a very desperate bunch. One Sunday evening in the autumn of 1825 a guard named Alexander McColl and two turnkeys came to put the seventeen prisoners into their cells but instead found a revolt.

The prisoners knocked the guards down and wrestled them for the keys. Charles Watson, the guard who held the keys, fought back but when a prisoner bit his hand to the bone he dropped them, and the convict scooped them up. The prisoners threw the guards inside the cell and were searching for the correct keys when McColl fought his way free, grabbed hold of the bars on the cell window and bellowed 'Murder!' at the top of his voice.

The criminal cells were close to the debtors' section, and the turnkeys there heard McColl's roar. The convicts succeeded in locking up the turnkeys but McColl was a tough man and struggled free three times to raise the alarm. The keys could help the prisoners move around within the building – they would lock and unlock the cells – but they were useless for anything else. The door to the exterior was locked from the outside. The prisoners knew that, so instead of battering at a locked door, they swarmed into the chapel, which was the only apartment with a decent-sized window.

It was quite a drop from the chapel window to the ground, so the prisoners used the time-honoured method of tying their blankets together and clambering down, one at a time. Unfortunately for them, McColl's shouts had alerted the governor, Mr Watson, who armed himself with a blunderbuss and waited at the bottom of the blankets. He shouted that he would shoot the first man who made it to the ground, and the prisoners reversed their direction of travel.

While he stood sentinel in the courtyard, Watson sent one of the debtors' turnkeys to the police office to request assistance. On the breathless run to the police office, the turnkey met John Smith, one of the Commissioners of Police, and blurted out his story. Smith was an adaptable man and hurried to a nearby coffee shop, where he knew a number of gentlemen gathered at that time of evening. He quickly told them what was happening, and half a dozen smartly dressed gentlemen followed him to the prison, keen to do their bit.

In the meantime the turnkey had reached the police office and roused the police. Mr Hardie, the superintendent, issued cutlasses to every available man and marched them over to the jail to contain the trouble. The onset of so many determined and well armed men took all the fight from the prisoners and they filed meekly into the cells to be locked up for the night. Hardie was not finished yet, and recruited a dozen cavalrymen who patrolled the outside of the jail for the remainder of the night.

Glasgow saw a further attempted mass escape later in the century.

Crimea in Glasgow

The Crimean War is nearly forgotten in Scotland now, but at the time it was a major event that dominated people's thinking. It was fought between 1854 and 1856, and was Britain's first Continental war since Waterloo. The Charge of the Light Brigade and the Thin Red Line occurred during the Battle of Balaclava in this conflict, but the fighting also seems to have influenced Glasgow's criminal element.

On Tuesday, 29 April 1856, the South Prison in Glasgow was the scene of another attempted escape. At about half past three a turnkey named Nicol McIntyre was bringing in a prisoner who had just been convicted at the police court. It was part of McIntyre's daily routine and after seventeen years' working in the prison he thought nothing of it until a group of seven prisoners rushed out and attacked him. They grabbed his keys, threw him into a cell and locked him in.

A nineteen-year-old youth named Daniel McMillan led the attack.

Despite his youth, he was a hardened criminal. A few years previously he had been sentenced to twenty-one years' transportation. He had returned long before his time, so his future was nothing but grim; he had no reason to be quiet. Another of the men was Charles Edwards, who had also returned from transportation and within three weeks had robbed an elderly man of his watch. Lord Deas had ordered him sent back to Australia for a further twenty-one years. Thomas Black and John Duncan were also in the thick of things and both were facing long spells in exile.

With McIntyre out of the way, the prisoners ran into the southern court of the prison, where they were challenged by a second turnkey, a man named Samuel McLauchlan. He was also taken by surprise as the prisoners surrounded him, grabbed the massive key he carried and began to batter him senseless with it. McLauchlan fought back and, despite the bloody wounds on his head, took hold of the key and held on as the prisoners milled around him, shouting furiously and landing the occasional kick for good measure.

The noise attracted the attention of one of the female turnkeys and she yelled and ran for help. Leaving McLauchlan lying in his own blood, the prisoners ran to the northern court, but as all the outer gates were locked they were still trapped inside the prison. Knowing there was no escape, they became desperate and searched for weapons, determined not to give up tamely. They picked up lumps of coal, a broom staff, a gas bracket, half bricks and whatever they could find; Daniel McMillan hefted a poker and waved it around, defying anybody to come near him.

There was a narrow passageway that joined the north and south courts together, a place that seemed a natural stronghold for the wild young men. They closed the gate at both ends and declared they would 'hold it like true Britons against all the Russians could do'. Criminals and bad men they may have been, but they were still prepared to act like patriots.

By that time the prison authorities had sent for help and a strong body of police marched into the prison, came to attention and awaited orders. The prisoners made the most of the opportunity and pelted the police with a hail of stones and bricks but at last the police charged, broke down the locked gate and met the prisoners in a frenzied scuffle in the confined passageway. With nothing to look forward to but misery, the prisoners fought a desperate but hopeless fight, and men on both sides were injured before the police emerged as victors. Apart from McIntyre, who had a broken finger, none of the police or turnkeys was seriously hurt.

Glasgow was not alone in experiencing prison trouble.

A grave for men alive

Old Edinburgh had two prisons – or three, if the Canongate Tolbooth could be included. The first was the castle, where royal and political prisoners were held, as well as prisoners of war. The second was the City Tolbooth, which squatted, dark and unlovely, to the north-west of St Giles' Church, slap in the centre of the city. At one time the disembodied heads of those executed for political crimes were displayed on top of the north gable of the tolbooth, but by the nineteenth century such sights were only a distant memory. There was still the occasional public hanging or whipping, but the headsman's axe was no longer in use in Edinburgh.

Anybody entering the tolbooth would immediately see a sign on the wall, with the cheerful words:

> A prison is a house of care,
> A place where none can thrive,
> A touchstone true to try a friend,
> A grave for men alive.

Sometimes a place of right,
Sometimes a place of wrong,
Sometimes a place for jades and thieves,
And honest men among.

The tolbooth was a grim building but as a jail it was less than successful, particularly when it held men of influence. Most escaped or were allowed to escape. The entrance was in a turret beside St Giles', through a massive door guarded by a red-coated guard with musket or Lochaber axe. There was a main chamber, known as the hall, where the prisoners gathered during the day, usually in some merriment despite their confinement. One of the Town Guard was always present. On Sundays the hall acted as a chapel, and it was equipped with a pulpit.

A turnpike or circular stair led to the cells, although they were known as apartments. One cell was of iron. The floor above the hall had a single room for felons, with a long bar on the floor. The condemned were chained here until they emerged to face the hangman. There was also a box of plate iron that legend claimed had been used to hold a notorious jail breaker. It was known as 'the cage'. On the next floor up was another similar room.

Outside the building to the west was the platform for executions. In 1817 this grim old tolbooth was destroyed, with the stones used for the sewers of Fettes Row. The arched doorway, door and lock were appropriated by Walter Scott in his house at Abbotsford in the Borders. In its place rose the Calton Jail, now also gone.

Edinburgh's smallest jail, the Canongate Tolbooth, still stands, but it could be as porous as the others. On 19 October 1819, a Major Campbell escaped from the Canongate Tolbooth without any difficulty and disappeared for a few days. However, the police had their informers and learned that rather than merge into the labyrinth of the Old Town, Campbell had moved to the much more elegant George Street, where he found lodgings at number eleven.

A sheriff officer named Aitkin, backed by the police, knocked on the door and demanded that he give himself up, but Campbell was not inclined to co-operate. He knocked a hole in the ceiling of his room, scrambled onto the roof of the house and sat there in defiance. As they had no inclination to run around on the slates far above the street, the police were at a loss, until Aitkin called up a couple of chimney sweeps.

Used to heights and as nimble as seamen, the sweeps hounded Campbell back into the arms of the law and he was once more placed in jail, but this time securely shackled to the floor.

Alternatives to jail

The nineteenth century saw huge changes in the punishment and reformation of criminals. In the opening decades of the century, convicted prisoners were liable to a whole raft of punishments, including being sent to join the Royal Navy. For example, in November 1806, John Dewar was sent to Edinburgh Bridewell for stealing wood from different wood yards around the city, but he asked if he could volunteer for the navy instead. A lenient judge agreed.

There was also the treadmill, which was similar to a large hamster wheel around which the convicts walked for hour after hour. In August 1823, Sir John Hippisley wrote to the Secretary of the Home Department, saying that the treadmill was 'injurious to the health and often to the life' of prisoners. Other punishments were more brutal.

Flogging a rapist

In June 1825 a travelling Irishman named James Hensey took a fancy to a young lady, who most definitely rejected him. Hensey did not take her 'no' for an answer and continued to pursue her company, one way or the other. He followed her as she continued her daily routine and as she walked past the farm of Bush near Langholm, he pounced on her and subjected her to a nasty sexual assault before running away. The girl fought back as hard as she could and told her parents, who informed the police.

The girl bravely gave evidence to the Dumfries Circuit Court and at the end of April 1826, James Hensey was found guilty of assault with intent to ravish. He was sentenced to be whipped through the streets of Dumfries, followed by fourteen years' transportation. Just after noon on Wednesday, 26 April, he was taken out of the jail, stripped of his shirt and tied by the waist to the back of a low cart. He looked at the crowd that had gathered, then tilted forward his broad hat so the expression on his face could not be seen. It was obvious he was not a happy man as he placed his hands on the back of the cart.

Hensey was a short man, and his clothes were battered with wear, so he cut a sad figure as a police officer led the cart on its slow trundle through the streets. A number of constables acted as escort to keep back the fascinated spectators as the punishment began. The many women in the crowd perhaps watched with some degree of satisfaction. The man chosen to wield the whip was broad and strong; he wore a long grey coat and his face was disguised behind a covering of black paint, with a broad red stripe down the centre and a hat pulled well down, in case he should be recognised by Hensey's friends or relations. He hefted a whip of nine tails, each one knotted for effectiveness, and he landed a painful twenty hard strokes on Hensey there and then.

The crowd gasped at the force of each blow and Hensey writhed and yelled as his pale skin was marked and cut. Despite the nature of Hensey's crime, the crowd began to feel sympathy for him and demanded that the flogger be less severe. Maybe aware that he had to live in Dumfries and his life could be made difficult, the man used a lighter touch as he inflicted the remaining forty strokes in two different places in the town.

Once the cart had completed its circuit, Hensey was returned to the care of a surgeon in the jail. He still had to undergo the long years of his transportation, but he was said to say he would rather have been hanged than endure the humiliation of a public flogging.

The most final punishment was death. On the eve of Queen Victoria's succession to the throne, there were still a number of crimes that carried the death penalty. These included high treason and murder; attempting to murder by poison; attempting to murder by stabbing or cutting; rape or unnatural offences (homosexual sex or sex with animals); piracy, if there was also an attempt to murder; burglary – which was housebreaking between nine at night and six in the morning, and accompanied by violence; fire-raising, if the building was occupied; casting away any ship if the life of anybody on board was endangered; and using false lights in an attempt to wreck a vessel.

Overall, however, many more criminals would be imprisoned, and the authorities took steps to ensure that their time in jail would be memorable and hopefully rehabilitating, while the experience would not teach them further criminal behaviour by association. In January 1838, Frederick Hill, Inspector of Prisons, recommended that the silent system be introduced to Calton Jail. He also thought that work such as oakum picking should be given to the prisoners and that they should keep half their earnings, which were to be paid when they were released. There was to be a schoolmaster and a library of books 'as are likely to foster a taste for reading' but no newspapers unless the governor approved. Visits to convicted prisoners were only to be allowed on the governor's express permission and only for five minutes, while prisoners awaiting trial were allowed only one visitor a week. Visitors who the governor thought were of 'bad character' were banned.

Tormenting the mind

Another idea that Scottish prisons used was the 'separate' system, where prisoners were not allowed to talk to each other. They wore masks so their faces were never seen and even in church or at work they had individual cubicles so they were never able to communicate with anybody except the guards. This system was used in Perth Penitentiary, for children as well as adults. However, in 1848 Captain Kincaid, the Inspector of Prisons, recommended that it had a bad effect on the mental and physical health of young boys. The other systems at that time were intended to demoralise the inmates rather than reform them. That year there was a recommendation that young offenders should not be placed in prison with mature men but housed in special reformatories for youths between the ages of eight and eighteen. The offender would be taught a trade and subjected to 'moderate discipline'. After a few years, the boys would be shipped off to Australia as exiles. They were to be pardoned on arrival in Australia, on the condition that they did not return to Great Britain until their original sentence was completed.

The nineteenth century was not a good time to be caught breaking the law. The system was designed to break the prisoner's mind as well as his or her body, and ultimately remove him or her from society.

20
Assaults

Next to drunkenness and theft, assault was probably the crime that was most likely to affect law-abiding people in Scotland. There were many reasons for assault, from a drunken brawl to a precursor to robbery. This chapter will look at some examples of the latter.

Scottish robbers had various methods of attack in the nineteenth century. Perhaps the most common was by using a woman to decoy the victim into a dark and lonely place, either up a close or even inside a house, and then for a man or men to attack the victim and pummel him helpless as the woman rifled his pockets of anything valuable. However, there were other methods.

Robbing a pay clerk

At the end of May 1879, Arthur Wilkinson was returning to work. He was a pay clerk of the ink manufacturer A.B. Fleming and Company of Caroline Park in Edinburgh and had picked up the firm's wages from a bank in Leith. Wilkinson was so engrossed in hurrying along the road that he did not notice the two men who walked toward him.

At the last moment one called out his name: 'Arthur!' Wilkinson looked up and the man threw a handful of white pepper in his face, while the second punched him to the ground. The pain was instant and Wilkinson rolled on the pavement, nearly blind and quite helpless, as they grabbed the leather bag that contained the wages – £200, which was a huge amount of money.

Wilkinson struggled to his feet and tried to chase them but they had too much of a lead. When they jumped a fence and raced off toward Edinburgh, two railwaymen gave chase. They must have been fit, for they managed to catch one of them, a young apprentice coppersmith grandly named as James Grant McIntosh Rodger. As sometimes happened, Rodger immediately offered to give up his haul in return for his freedom.

The railwaymen agreed and found the missing wages thrust into a hole in the ground within a small copse. The police used their network of informants to find out who Rodger's associate might be and arrested a plumber named Frank Williamson two days later.

That was a unique use of pepper; there were other methods and sometimes people found that travelling companions could be predators or saints.

Steamboat robbery

Travelling was often a hazardous occupation, with thieves waiting in railway stations and carriages. There were also thieves on the steamboats that crossed and criss-crossed the Clyde, Forth and Tay. In January 1875, Irene Dewar of Dunfermline heard of some urgent family business in Peterborough, so she gathered together all the money she had and headed south. She was in the packed saloon cabin of the North British Railway ferry between Burntisland and Granton when a group of young men bustled against her and walked away. Only a few moments later she checked her travelling bag to find it was gaping open. Her purse, with £2 7s – all the money she had with her – had been stolen. Naturally she was upset, but a number of passengers compensated for Mrs Dewar's loss, raising the money for her. The thief was not found.

Sometimes a would-be robber discovered he had caught a tiger by the tail.

Surprise for a footpad

In the late evening of 29 December 1819, Robert Ogle was walking with his dog along Bonnington Road between Newhaven and Edinburgh. At that time this was a semi-rural area. There were no street lights; it was deserted and often lonely, but that night there was a group of four young men walking in the same direction. As Ogle passed a nursery, the group behind him split up, with two hurrying on toward Edinburgh and the other two lagging behind.

The leading two men overtook Ogle and then stopped while the two at the rear rushed up behind him. No fool, Ogle knew that there was trouble ahead. The most broad shouldered and muscular of the men pointed to Ogle's dog.

'That's my dog!' he roared. 'You stole my dog.'

Without bothering to argue the point, Ogle pulled a pistol from his pocket and thrust the muzzle onto the nose of the muscular thug.

'I am afraid you are mistaken, sir, that dog belongs to me.'

When Ogle pressed the muzzle of the gun a little harder, the thug backed off. 'I beg your pardon,' he said. 'I see I must be mistaken. That dog is certainly yours after all.'

He turned and ran for his life, with his companions following him. Ogle put his pistol away and continued to Edinburgh.

Some other attempted assaults were equally unsuccessful.

Attack in Moray

On 10 July 1809, Charles Morison, the Cromdale schoolmaster, was walking along the road above Ballindalloch when a large man slipped out of the trees and came beside him. For a few moments, the two men looked at each other. The stranger was quite distinctive, with a white bonnet pulled low over his head and a heavy greatcoat left open to show his red waistcoat above a bright tartan kilt. At five foot eight he was about the same height as the schoolmaster, but more muscular, and much more dangerous when he produced a large knife.

When the kilted man demanded his money, Morison had to make a quick decision. He had no weapon except a walking stick, but he had no intention of handing over anything. Schoolmasters had to work hard for the little they earned. Grabbing hold of the top of his stick, he shouted that it was a sword stick, and pretended to twist it open to reveal a concealed blade. The threat was enough; the kilted man turned and ran toward Aberlour. Morison continued on his way.

Other attacks were much uglier.

Attack in Perthshire

Very early on the morning of Saturday, 24 May 1896, twenty-year-old Jessie Telfer was driving her milk cart between Perth and Crieff. She knew the road well, having driven it many times since she took on her position as a servant at Cloag by Methven, so she was feeling quite relaxed as she approached the fourth milestone on the road west of Perth. She had just passed the farmhouse of East Powside when her horse became skittish and she sawed at the reins.

She had her horse under control and moving at a slow walk when a tall, broad man in a long waterproof cloak and a knickerbocker suit dashed across the road and grabbed hold of her horse. Jessie asked him quite sharply to get away, but he snatched hold of her and pulled her from her seat. Jessie struggled, but she was taken by surprise. Her attacker was very strong, and in moments he had dragged her to the wood at the side of the road.

Although she tried to fight back, the man slapped her hard across the face and clamped a hard hand over her mouth.

'If you scream,' he said in a hard voice, 'I'll strangle you.'

With Jessie too terrified to make a noise, he pulled her into the shelter of a dry-stane dyke and raped her.

The man fled, and a few moments later a young boy noticed the unattended milk cart in the middle of the road. He hurried over to help, just as Jessie emerged from the wood, dazed, upset and with her face covered in blood. The boy helped her back onto the milk cart and took her into Perth.

The police immediately began a search for the man in the knicker-bocker suit. They made no progress until 27 May, when a Perth police sergeant read a report of the assault in a newspaper and spotted a man who answered the description of the rapist. The sergeant challenged the man, who immediately jumped up and fled.

The police made their usual inquiries and discovered the man was named Archibald Anderson. He was twenty-four years old, agile and tanned. Anderson had an interesting history. He was originally from Leven in Fife, and was a saddler to trade, although the police knew him better as a poacher. At one time he had been a miner and an odd-job man, and he had a conviction for assault with intent on another woman. Not long before, Anderson had joined the Royal Highlanders in Aberdeen, but lasted only a couple of weeks before he deserted.

The police sent a circular describing Archibald all around the country, warned the army that he may try to enlist again under a different name, and told cycle hirers to be on the lookout for him. They also said that he might be found in the company of other poachers.

Unfortunately, there was more than one man in Scotland named Archibald Anderson, and when the press announced the story, a totally innocent man was targeted. He was a Dundee man and had been in the police force, but when his name was published a detective and a constable began to track him. He wrote to the local Dundee newspaper to protest his innocence, but luckily the police made an arrest before the Dundee Anderson was pulled in.

On 29 May, Constable Mackie, the beat constable at Cluniebridge, saw a man he thought was suspiciously like the suspect and shouted for him to stop. The man took to his heels, with Mackie following. The chase lasted over an hour, with the suspect leaping over fences and dodging between trees before he eventually escaped.

However, Mackie was not inclined to give up. He telegraphed the police in Perth and Cupar, and Inspector Macfarlane from Perth took charge of the hunt. Macfarlane called up all the available police, so there was a thin blue line of constables, plus a number of civilian volunteers, surrounding the hills between Auchtermuchty and Newburgh. They formed a hedge of watchers, with the local game-keepers and farmers within the hills alerted to watch for the fugitive. It was the Pitcairlie gamekeeper, a man named Strathearn, who next sighted the suspect. The man was passing Lochmill Farm about a mile south of Newburgh and heading toward Auchtermuchty. Strathearn told the nearest policeman, who in turn alerted Inspector Macfarlane.

Macfarlane ordered two constables to head toward the suspect from Auchtermuchty and two more to head southward from Newburgh; the suspect should have been caught between them. The constables from Auchtermuchty saw him first, and the suspect turned at once and ran into a field. The police followed, charging over the open field, clambering over the slithering coping stones of a dry-stane dyke, leaping fences and blowing their whistles. For a while the suspect seemed to be getting away but unfortunately for him, there was another pair of policemen waiting for him.

Constable MacPherson of Perth made the arrest. He was relieved to see that they had got the correct man: it was Archibald Anderson.

A huge number of people waited at Newburgh to see Anderson and were disappointed when Inspector Macfarlane quickly bundled him on the evening train to Perth. Anderson appeared at Perth Circuit Court in June and was sentenced to ten years' penal servitude.

Assaults were quick and sordid but there were many other offences in the criminal's calendar.

21
A Medley of Crime

Crime could be sordid, sad or just brutal. This chapter gives a few examples of some of the most unsavoury of Scottish crimes of the nineteenth century.

Stealing a child

Child stealing or plagium was not a common crime even in the nineteenth century, but it did happen then and is still known today. Helen Wade was one of the few people convicted of plagium. In April 1877, she was in Main Street of Camlachie in Glasgow when she saw a three-year-old girl named Catherine Hamilton playing in the street.

As was often the case during that period, Catherine's mother, Elizabeth, was at her work in a mill and the child was left alone for long periods in the day. Wade casually snatched her up and carried her away. She caught the train to Liverpool, but naturally Elizabeth Hamilton alerted the police, who asked if anybody had seen anything.

A woman carrying a struggling child attracted attention and a Glasgow policeman followed the trail to Liverpool, where he found and arrested Wade and collected Catherine, tearful but otherwise not much the worse for her experience. Wade said that she had lost two of her own children and Catherine had 'taken an affection to her'. It is entirely possible that Wade needed psychological help but instead she was sentenced to be transported for seven years.

Other youngsters had a more protracted ordeal to survive.

Cruelty in Keith

Although there is a perception that the people of the Victorian age were harder to their children than is common today, there was also a strong streak of humanity that recognised the boundaries between firmness and cruelty. When they heard of cruelty to children, ordinary people had a tendency to react, sometimes strongly. Such a scenario occurred in May 1876.

Sergeant Alexander McBeth was not normally very busy in the small Moray town of Keith. There was the usual crop of petty crimes, such as drunken shouting at the weekends, some minor pilfering and the odd dispute that led to a black eye and strong language, but serious crime was rare. On Monday, 22 May 1878, an ironmonger named William Ross approached Sergeant McBeth with the news that Mrs Laing – the wife of William Laing, flesher and cattle dealer – was treating her servant girl abominably. Ross had been doing some work at the house and he had seen the little girl drifting about in a terrible state. Ross told Sergeant McBeth that the girl would not live another two days. McBeth noted the complaint but did nothing about it.

About seven in the morning of 25 May the servant girl sneaked out of the house and tapped on the door of a neighbour, Jane Stewart. The girl was terribly emaciated and absolutely filthy, and begged a crust of bread. At first Stewart thought the girl was 'wrong in her mind', as she was 'so dirty and pitiful like' but when she tried to smile, Mrs Stewart recognised who she was. Her name was Amelia Fraser and she was sixteen years old. She seemed terrified and when Mrs Stewart gave her 'a piece' she put it in her skirt and swayed a little, saying: 'If I be caught, what a whipping I'll get.'

'They would not strike you, would they?' Mrs Stewart asked.

'The whole of them strike me,' the girl replied, 'but she is the worst.' She showed Mrs Stewart the back of her head, where there was a deep cut where, she claimed, Mrs Laing had hit her with one of Mr Laing's boots. Mrs Stewart noted her swollen and battered hands and her generally filthy appearance.

By now, kind-hearted Mrs Stewart was in tears. James, her husband, came to see what was the matter and when he saw the state that Amelia was in, he informed the police.

This time Sergeant McBeth acted. Accompanied by Mr James Macdonald, the Inspector of Poor, he knocked on the door of Laing's house, heard an angry female voice and pushed his way in to see the servant. Mrs Laing was there, and Amelia was on her knees cleaning fire irons. McBeth told Mrs Laing that they had been informed that the girl had been 'ill-used' and they had come to see for themselves.

Mrs Laing knelt beside the servant. 'Oh, Amelia', she said, 'how could that have been said about you?'

McBeth and Macdonald bundled Amelia away from the Laings', despite Mrs Laing's protests: 'For God's sake, don't take her out of the house in such a mess as that.'

After seeing the chief constable, McBeth took Amelia into Helen Stewart's lodging house in Mid Street, where Stewart washed her and the local police surgeon, Dr Turner, made a thorough examination. Amelia had been in the Laings' house for the past six months. Helen Stewart said that Amelia's fingers were like claws and she could not wash herself.

Turner found her starved, filthy, crawling with vermin and covered in bruises and half-healed wounds. Dr Turner had to shave the hair from her head to rid her scalp of lice; her stockings had rotted to her legs and the material was embedded in the sores and chilblains that covered her feet. Mrs Jane Stewart came to visit her after a day or so and said she had 'never seen anybody in such a state in my life'.

When she was questioned, Amelia said she had entered the Laings' service at Martinmas 1875 and that at first she had been treated well, but that had gradually changed. Rather than treating her with kindness, Laing had locked her in a box bed and kicked her awake in the mornings. Amelia had not washed for about a month and for the past three weeks had eaten nothing but dry bread, rotten vegetables and raw meat that the Laings threw out. She claimed she had been less well fed than the fowls and the pigs. She had slept in the stable for the past month and had been locked in the house and was unable to leave. Other people in the town commented on Amelia's appearance and how she had been neat and tidy when she had first arrived at the Laings' house but had deteriorated and was often seen crying and distraught. Elsie McGregor, who was a servant in the house next door, had heard Mrs Laing calling her a 'damned bitch and a dirty devil'. Amelia also claimed that Mrs Laing had struck her on the face with a whip and on the back with a poker.

Naturally, in a small and tight-knit community such as Keith, the news spread quickly and the good people were indignant at this cruelty in their midst. At six o'clock on the Saturday afternoon, the town crier walked the streets and called the populace to a meeting on the Markey Leys at nine o'clock that evening. About 1,000 people gathered, which must have been a huge percentage of the local population, and they were angry. Somebody had brought an effigy of Mrs Laing, which was kicked about and then burned. With their feelings aroused, the mob surged to the Laings' house. They massed at the door, yelling and shouting abuse, but there was no attack until Mr Laing came to the front door and, by accident or design, he barged into an elderly man named Petrie.

Neil Robertson, the Chief Constable, Sergeant McBeth and a constable tried to keep order, but that minor incident inflamed the situation and the mob began to throw stones. Within a few moments, all the windows on the front of the house were shattered but the Laings had retreated to the rear. Some of the more respectable people now tried, but failed, to quieten the mob. They remained until about one in the morning and then gradually dispersed, having made their feelings known. In the meantime, Amelia's father John Fraser came from the farm at Dulsie Bridge in Nairnshire, where he was grieve. He took Amelia home; her ordeal was over.

The crowd gathered at the Laings' house again on the Monday but there were no windows left to smash, so they merely made threatening noises. After the previous violence the police had been reinforced, so sixty special constables waited on the fringe. The body of grim-faced men armed with long batons may have helped keep the situation in hand. The police arrested the Laings and took them to Banff Prison, with a howling mob baying at their heels all the way from Banff railway station to the jail.

It was six months before Amelia Fraser recovered the weight and health she had lost, but then she, or her father, pushed for compensation from William Laing. He resisted, saying the acts had been committed by his wife when he was not present. The case dragged on until 1878, when the Laings appeared at the Court of Session. There were many witnesses who said they saw Amelia looking thin and badly used, and Amelia herself said her hands were so sore she could not eat and she was very overworked. Mrs Elizabeth Laing gave her version of events. She said that Amelia was fed sufficient and never complained about not having enough to eat. Nor was she overworked, but she was dirty. Mrs Laing claimed she was dishonest, dirty and lazy, and that she chose to sleep in the stable.

Despite the evidence of the police and the inspector of the poor, the case went against Amelia and for Mrs Laing, who walked free.

Immorality

Sometimes Scottish courts faced terrible people across the bar, but were unable to prosecute them because of a lack of witnesses. Such a case occurred in August 1834, when James and Sarah Balfour were taken to the police court in Edinburgh. It is uncertain whether the forename of either was correct, and it is uncertain exactly what their relationship was. They may have been father and daughter, siblings or even husband and wife. It is known that the female Balfour was only fifteen years old. At that time, the age of consent was twelve.

The pair ran a brothel. While James Balfour attended to its business, Sarah scoured the streets for young girls. They would trust her, as she was not much older than they were, and she would bring them to the house, where at first they were fed and given small gifts. When trust was established, the girls would return, whereupon James Balfour would hold them prisoner for a period of time so his clients could use them as sex objects.

That system worked for a while, but when Sarah kidnapped one poor girl from school and James held her overnight, things turned sour. The girl escaped. She complained to the police and the Balfours were arrested. Unfortunately, there was no witness and no evidence except the child's own words, so the Balfours were released.

The thought of what might have happened to these children chills the blood.

The Glenluce horror

Although the popular image of Victorian crime is that of Jack the Ripper stalking his victims through the stinking slums of London, some of the worst crimes were committed in the quietest parts of the countryside. One of the most brutal murders of the late nineteenth century, and one that was never solved, was in Glenluce, about ten miles from Stranraer in the far south-west. It was like a tale from a horror story.

At two in the morning of Tuesday, 1 June 1880, the villagers of Glenluce were woken by the frantic screams of sixteen-year-old Mary Anderson. She came banging on their doors, desperate for help and crying that there had been a murder. As she woke her neighbours, they rushed to her house and found a terrible scene. Anderson lived in a two-storey whitewashed public house near the centre of the village and only a stone's throw from the police station. There was a byre immediately to the rear and then access to open countryside.

James Milligan, the owner of the house, was on his bedroom floor, hacked to death and covered in blood. There was a burned blanket over his body and the murderer had opened up his skull with an axe. Milligan was over seventy years old and had lived in the village for decades without exchanging a cross word with anybody. His housekeeper, Grace McCredy, lay in the stone-flagged passage that divided the building between the residential and the commercial parts of the house. McCredy was mutilated but still alive, if only just.

McCredy was around sixty-five years old and a native of Glenluce. She was dressed in her night clothes. It was weeks before she was able to speak clearly, but when she became lucid the police heard her story. It did not help much. She had been in bed when she heard the attack and when she rose somebody had hit her. She had five separate wounds on her head, plus defensive injuries on her hands and arms, where she had tried to fend off the blows. The ground around her swam with blood and McCredy's bloody fingerprints were on the bedroom doorposts, which she must have grabbed during the assault.

After breaking into the furniture to search for loot, the murderer had removed his boots, possibly to keep silence, for the marks of stockinged feet were seen amidst the blood. The intruder had also tried to murder young Mary, but the blow of his axe had thumped into the pillow and she slipped away. When the killer was busy with McCredy, the girl hid under her bed.

Not content with mere murder and assault, the intruder had added fire-raising to his crimes when he set Milligan's bedroom and McCredy's bed alight, possibly attempting to hide his night's work. At that time young Mary had been hiding under the bed but had endured the heat and smoke until she heard the intruder leave the house by the back door. Only then did she run for help.

The people of Glenluce set to work to put out the fires in the house, hurling pails of water onto the flames. At first they had little success, and the flames and smoke seemed to take control of the house. Men and women toiled with splashing buckets, but it was a losing battle, partly because the dense smoke denied them proper access to the seat of the flames. They thought that paraffin or something similar had been poured onto the pillows before the murderer set them alight. It was not until one clever person thought to open the back window and throw buckets of water inside Milligan's bedroom that the flames were gradually subdued.

The inhabitants of Glenluce knew that no local could have done such a thing, so they immediately suspected it was one of the many tramps who frequented the countryside. Two of this breed had come up from Stranraer to the village on Saturday and remained over the weekend. One of the wanderers had been spotted in Kirkcowan, nine miles away, on the Monday night.

When the police investigated, they suspected that the murderer had hidden in some quiet corner of the house or the pub during the day, but had emerged at night to rob and murder. It was much later that the police realised that the window had been forced. They also found a felt hat in the house – size six, which was indicative of a man with a small head.

The intruder had gone through Milligan's pockets and had stolen keys and his gold watch; he had also smashed open a large chest. He had taken over £100 in notes, plus silver, debenture loans and railways shares whose value could have run into the thousands of pounds in a room upstairs. Milligan had been a wealthy man, and the murderer must have known exactly what he was doing. The police believed that the murder had been merely a prelude to robbery.

The police discovered a bloody axe in the house; they found out that there had been an axe stolen from a joiner a few miles outside the village. Apart from the small hat, the police got their first real clue when a local woman named Graham told them that she had seen a powerfully built man standing on the road. He had noticed her watching out of her window and stared back without fear.

McCredy was taken to a neighbour's house, where she lay semi-conscious and deranged for days. There were fears that she might also have died. The police turned their attention to the only eyewitness that they had.

Mary Anderson was around five foot five, a cheery-looking, dark-haired girl who was a capable worker and had never given anybody any trouble. After the murder, she moved back in with her mother and the rest of her family in a one-roomed, smoky cottage in Kirkstyle Brae. When the police interviewed her there, she said that she was sleeping in the kitchen and was wakened by Grace McCredy shouting: 'Oh the villain! He has murdered Mr Milligan!'

Mary had sat up and shouted out, 'What do you mean by that, Grace?' but immediately she spoke, 'a clear thing struck the pillow'.

She saw somebody pull McCredy out of bed and tried to help but she was too scared to move. As the intruder dragged McCredy into the passage, Mary was terrified and slid out of the bed. She could not run, so she squeezed into the fifteen-inch-high space under the bed: there was nowhere else. She saw the shadowy figure of a man come back into the kitchen, carrying an axe. She saw him drop the axe three times, with the weapon clattering on the stone floor. Mary described the intruder as a short man, well built and young, wearing a dark coat and trousers and a round felt hat, but no boots. The intruder broke open a wall press, rifled it, piled pillows together and set them alight. He robbed all the drawers in the room, set fire to the bed and left for Milligan's room.

Even though the bed above her was ablaze, Mary lay still, probably stifling her coughs. She watched as the intruder used a stick to pull pillows toward Milligan, and then he returned once more to the kitchen. He added more fuel to Milligan's smouldering bed. As the clock struck two, Mary heard a cart pass the house. The intruder did not hurry, but ignored McCredy's moans that she had been murdered. Mary saw the man lift his boots, give McCredy a last heavy thump and disappear from her view. She heard the click as the back door closed.

Immediately the intruder left, Mary emerged from under the bed and tried to extinguish the flames, but without any success. Instead she pulled on her petticoat and ran to McCredy, but she was unable to help her, so she opened the front door to clear the smoke and hurried, sobbing, to the police station. The constable on duty came as far as the front door but refused to enter the house until a doctor came. He sent Mary to waken Dr McCormack. The police listened to Mary's story, but it did not help their investigations a great deal. They examined the local area and realised that at that time of the early morning the intruder could easily have sprinted to the wood at Balkail and beyond. He had many square miles of open countryside in which to vanish.

On the Tuesday night the police widened their net and arrested four people in Newton Stewart: two itinerant pedlars and their women. They were taken back to Glenluce but the police did not find sufficient evidence to hold them. Instead the pedlars were sent to Stranraer, where they were charged with a separate count of theft and given twenty-one days. The police also pursued three men 'of a suspicious appearance' who caught the ferry *Tuscar* from Stranraer to Glasgow. They disembarked at Greenock and vanished.

The thief who broke into the joiner's shop had used the same methods to force the lock of Milligan's house, so the police suspected one man had done both. The authorities offered a reward of £100 for information leading to the discovery of the murderer.

For a while, it was open season on tramps throughout south-west Scotland. Another tramp was arrested in Stranraer, closely questioned, found innocent of the murder but given fourteen days for begging and *pour encourager les autres*. This tramp owned some joinery tools, which apparently made him a legitimate target. His wife did a runner but the police caught her at Portpatrick. She also had a good alibi and was released. There were other tramps arrested at Portpatrick but without evidence. They were also set free.

After a few days, the police learned that a spring cart had been seen driving away from Glenluce and somebody had seen a man washing his trousers in a burn at Carronbridge, near Thornhill. The man had a female friend who wore a very distinctive bonnet. The police throughout the south-west asked people if they had seen a woman with that particular design of bonnet. They followed the bonnet through the small villages of Leadburn, Abington and Douglas, where they found her. The woman was perfectly innocent, as was her husband.

As the days passed and the police made no arrests, the people of Glenluce became more nervous. Many of them bought revolvers and waited for the return of the murderer. Some remained awake all night, in case he should choose to rob their house. More secure locks were placed on the doors.

When the police were tired of arresting stray tramps, they turned their attention to men who owned carts and who might have been in Glenluce on the night of the murder. Their searches proved pointless, and then McCredy recovered enough to make a statement. She turned everything upside down when she said she thought that her attacker had been a woman.

Armed with this new information, the police began their hunt again, but to no avail. The murderer was never caught. There was one question unanswered: what was Mary's part in all this? Her story lacks some credibility – the axe thudding on her pillow; hiding under a burning bed – and nobody else actually witnessed the attack. Mrs McCredy said she had been attacked by a woman; perhaps the police could have searched closer to home to find another suspect.

Other acts of horror were even more obscure

Reign of Terror in Ross

Even as late as the 1820s, parts of the Highlands were deemed as remote as any region of the British Empire. So much so that crimes committed there were often concealed by remoteness and bad communications. The roads to areas of the north-west were poor at best; the people spoke only Gaelic and closed ranks against outsiders. Information that leaked out was sparse and often inaccurate, laced with rumour and speculation. Crimes could be committed with impunity unless there was a figure of authority willing to press for information – and the local population were inclined to co-operate. If they were not, then the Gaelic mist could conceal the truth.

The situation in Wester Ross was particularly bad. Much of the Highlands had been demoralised by forced evictions and the slow erosion of the Gaelic culture, but this area had also seen a major legal wrangle over ownership of the Dundonnell lands around Loch Broom, so even the landowners were at each others' throats. It seems to have been this dispute that led to a shocking sequence of events that, even if half true, mirrored the excesses that were the norm in rural Ireland.

Unfortunately, much of the documental evidence upon which historians depend is lacking, and only hearsay, rumour and unsubstantiated newspaper reports give any detail. If only a fraction of what they claim is correct, the situation in Wester Ross approached anarchy.

One particularly brutal crime occurred at a farm named Bracklagh at Little Straths near Gairloch, where two horses were apparently flayed alive. There were tales of cattle being mutilated, of tails and ears being cropped, of sheepfolds being opened so the animals strayed and were lost in the night. Worse were the night-time attacks on Dundonnell House with muskets, when a reputed force of at least ten men fired shots. The story goes that the people of Dundonell returned fire and the assailants withdrew into the shadow of the dark.

In August 1826, some unknown person or people sneaked through the night and set fire to the barn first and then the farmhouse of Gorstanour. The occupant, John McKenzie, the ground officer at Dundonnell, ran out of the house with buckets and roused the farm servants. As McKenzie and his men tried to douse the flames, a number of people on the surrounding hills fired muskets at them; thankfully nobody was hit. That same month, Dundonnell's barns and outhouses, full of stored grain and winter fuel, were set alight and guns fired into the servants' homes.

There were other attacks on Dundonnell in this bitter dispute over land: the mill was fired and the millstones smashed, so the miller fled the area in fear of his life. Shots were fired at the house, and the inhabitants, two old ladies, were terrified.

The local authorities were very quiet when all this excitement occurred, but they did make one arrest. Roderick MacLean, better known as Rory Shallager, or Rory the Deerstalker, was taken to jail. However, he was not charged, and after three weeks he seems to have been set free again.

On 12 December 1826, the gunmen were back. They hid on the hill slopes in the dark of night and fired into the house of a worker named David Fraser. The crack of the musket echoed among the hills, but the shots were wild; nobody was hurt. In March 1827, Gorstanour Farm was set alight again, and in the humid, midge-ridden dim of an August evening, some quiet men drove the cattle of Roderick Mackenzie of

Kildonan into a bog. A number of the animals drowned. Soon afterward, men with sticks and dogs drove a flock of Murdo Beaton's sheep over the edge of a cliff; they were dashed to pieces on the bottom.

The campaign of terror and attrition against the Dundonnell estate continued. Another Dundonnell tenant, Donald Farquhar, had a cow maimed. In January 1828, Murdo Beaton was again targeted, as dark figures crept up at night and hurled fist-sized rocks through his cottage window. One hit his pregnant wife as she lay in bed. That same month somebody smashed the windows of Dundonnell House and cut down about thirty ornamental trees on the front lawn.

According to newspaper reports, the Procurator Fiscal was informed of all these events and crimes but did nothing. Witnesses tried to find him but he was strangely absent when they arrived. Without the Fiscal's petition, the sheriff could not act and so the perpetrators of the alleged crimes were neither hunted nor punished. Local people guessed that the perpetrators came from a neighbouring estate, but there were no arrests and no court cases. A veil of rumour shades the facts of these events, so all that is known is that there was trouble in Wester Ross around the estate of Dundonnell and nobody was brought to justice. Other horrors were all too real.

Horror in Shetland

Some crimes are vicious, some are evil, some are ludicrous, but many are just soul-wrenchingly tragic. Among the latter is the murder of a child or children by their parents, and sadly that was a scenario that was all too common in the nineteenth century. Perhaps it was stress due to lack of financial support in the days before the Welfare State; perhaps it was work-related depression, and often it could have been the social stigma of bearing an illegitimate child, but there was barely a week went by without some parent, usually the mother, killing her child.

However, the killing spree that occurred in Lerwick on 25 March 1858 surpassed most for sheer horror and utter tragedy. At that time, Lerwick was a comparatively small place, with one single main street from which darted a number of lanes that led either to the sea that was the lifeblood of Shetland, or towards the slope behind the houses. The town lived for the sea, so there was the scent of salt water and the melancholic cry of gulls in every house. Everybody knew their neighbours, so the death of one person affected all.

The Williamsons lived in a three-storey stone-built house, with its gable end to the main street and its entrance in Fox Lane. It was solid and respectable, with no hint of the tragedy that was to occur behind its doors. In 1858, there were a number of people living in this solid house. Peter Williamson was forty-four years old and head of the household. He was a native Shetlander, born in Burraland in the peninsula of Northmavine in 1814. As was common in the period, Williamson juggled a number of jobs. He was a general merchant, dealing with a multitude of goods and chattels, importing them into Shetland via the harbour and distributing them to many outlets throughout the island archipelago. He also ran a small farm, and acted as an agent for the whaling ships that called into Lerwick for supplies and to top up their crews with the skilled local seamen.

Peter Williamson had a wife of whom he seemed fond. There was no history of domestic discord. Agnes was thirty-eight and attractive. Between them they had produced sixteen-year-old William, fourteen-year-old John, twelve-year-old Agnes, Gilbert, who was about ten, and four-year-old Peter. Finally, the household had a servant, who lived in the kitchen on the ground floor of the house. Gilbert was with a relative on the night of Wednesday, 24 March 1858, the day the Williamsons' world fell apart.

There was no indication that tragedy was imminent. Williamson spent the Wednesday in his office-cum-shop opposite his house. In the evening he had a conversation with two business friends, but rather than discuss trade, Williamson spoke of Burke and Hare, Calcraft the hangman and the lives of famous murderers. Williamson's friends were surprised at this type of talk, especially as he seemed very knowledgeable about the lives and careers of some of the worst criminals of the century. Even stranger, he discussed the most effective way of murdering somebody, with the idea that a blow on the head with a hammer would be quick and simple. He ended with a laugh and turned down an invitation to join his friends for a closing drink. They all parted friends.

Williamson closed up the shop and crossed Commercial Street to go home to his family. There was a doctor in the house attending to little Agnes, who was ill and had been moved to her parents' room for the sake of comfort. A man of regular habits, at eleven in the evening Williamson told the maidservant to lock up and go to bed. He stayed up a little longer.

Nobody knows exactly what happened next, but the police tried to piece together a rough sequence of events. They came to the conclusion that he got out of bed at about six in the morning and started a murder spree that shocked Lerwick. Williamson first checked that the maidservant was sleeping, and then returned upstairs to his own bedroom. He hefted a heavy meat cleaver, an open razor and a knife, looked down at his sleeping, sweet-tempered wife and began his morning's work.

Williamson lifted the cleaver, took aim and landed a mighty blow on Agnes' head. She woke with a terrible start, stared at him and tried to escape, but he struck again and again until she was helpless. She was still alive and perhaps still conscious when Williamson put down the cleaver and slashed her throat with his razor. The medicine the doctor had prescribed must have put little Agnes into a deep sleep, for she had not stirred during the murder of her mother. Williamson cracked her head and slit her throat in exactly the same manner as he had murdered his wife.

With the females of his family disposed of, Williamson trundled upstairs to deal with the three sons who slept there. They had heard the sounds of slaughter from the room below and tried desperately to escape the blood-smeared madman who had once been their loving father. Williamson caught them one by one. William was first. His head and throat were sliced open but at sixteen he was strong and active enough to slide free and run for his life. Young Peter had no chance; he was killed in his bed. John, aged fourteen, tried to hide beneath the covers of his bed. His father grabbed him and the cleaver and razor finished him off as well.

There was one final act in this bloody Lerwick drama. Williamson lay down on his back on the floor of the bedroom, leaned against the leg of a chair and sliced his own throat so deeply that he cut to the bone.

In the meantime William had run to his mother, to find her dead in her own bed, so he ran to the maidservant for sanctuary. As soon as the maid saw his bloodied and battered face and throat, she began to scream in high-pitched horror. A band of workmen outside heard the noise and ran for the local policeman. However, before the police arrived, a group of local men pushed into the house to investigate the noise. Not surprisingly, they were shocked by the carnage. Mrs Williamson was still living, but only just. She died as the men crowded into her room. Except for the badly hurt William, all the children were already dead. Only the maid had escaped the massacre.

The people of Lerwick could not think of a motive for Williamson's actions. He had always been thought of as a decent, respectable man with a good marriage and a close family. But now a few remembered, or thought they remembered, that he had been a bit short of late, a bit quick-tempered, less talkative than usual. They searched for an incident that could have changed him and remembered the loss of one of his close friends. Then they remembered his recent conversation about Calcraft and Burke and Hare.

With the death of Williamson, the police had little chance of discovering a motive for the crime. Local speculation offered nothing on which to hang a reason, but there were dark tales of a distant ancestor named Williamson who had emigrated to London decades earlier and who had butchered two families. He had been sentenced to hang but had committed suicide before the sentence was carried out. Perhaps there was a faulty gene somewhere in Williamson's DNA – or maybe there was no connection at all.

That was Shetland's only mass murder in recent centuries, and it unsettled the people of Lerwick. The Williamson house remained empty for a while, as nobody wished to live there, and eventually it became the Custom House. On a happier note, young William Williamson recovered from his wounds.

Epilogue

Scotland has changed a lot since the heady, rumbustious days of the nineteenth century. Thirty-ton trucks and powerful buses have replaced mail coaches with their horses and long brass horns; there are no more gangs of railway navigators roaring into nervous small towns, no more cattle drovers on the unfrequented byways, and it is many years since body-snatchers waited for a dark night to unearth a fresh corpse. It is unlikely that pirates now land on Hebridean beaches to bury their silver, there are no coaches rattling across the pre-dawn dark of Fife to bring two duellists to their destiny, and British Army regiments no longer riot *en masse* in the streets of Scottish towns.

Some things, however, are unchanged. Banks have to constantly update their security to counter increasingly sophisticated threats from thieves; husbands, wives and partners argue, fight and sometimes murder each other; children are still abused; thieves steal from the vulnerable; and muggers infest the night-time streets. Only a thin blue line of police, backed by security cameras and a great deal of unseen work, stand between the decent, law-abiding woman or man and the predators who await their opportunity for plunder. In that, Scotland is no different from any other nation.

Select Bibliography

Books

Barrie, David (2008), *Police in the Age of Improvement: Police Development and the Civic Tradition in Scotland, 1775–1865*, Devon: Willan Publishing.

Briggs, Asa (1963, 1968), *Victorian Cities*, London: Penguin.

Burt, Edmund (1754, 1998), *Burt's Letters from the North of Scotland*, Edinburgh: Birlinn.

Cameron, David Kerr (1978), *The Ballad and the Plough*, London: Victor Gollancz.

Cameron, Joy (1983), *Prisons and Punishment in Scotland from the Middle Ages to the Present*, Edinburgh: Canongate.

Chesney, Kellow (1970), *The Victorian Underworld*, London: Maurice Temple Smith Ltd.

Cochrane, Lord (1888, 1983), *Circuit Journeys*, Edinburgh: David Douglas; Hawick: Byway Books.

Cochrane, Lord (1856), *Memorials of his Time*, Edinburgh.

Devine, T. M. (1994), *Clanship to Crofters' War: The Social*

Transformation of the Scottish Highlands, Manchester and New York: Manchester University Press.

Donnelly, Daniel and Scott, Kenneth (editors) (2005), *Policing Scotland*, Devon: Willan Publishing.

Dundee Council Minute Books, (various years) Dundee City Archives.

The Dundee Directory

Fenton, Alexander (1987), *Country Life in Scotland: Our Rural Past*, Edinburgh: John Donald.

Fraser, Derek (1979), *Power and Authority in the Victorian City*, Oxford: Basil Blackwell.

Godfrey, Barry and Lawrence, Paul (2005), *Crime and Justice 1750–1950*, Devon: Willan Publishing.

Grant, I.F. (1961, 1995), *Highland Folk Ways*, Edinburgh: Birlinn.

Grimble, Ian (1980), *Clans and Chiefs*, London: Blond & Briggs.

Haldane, A.R.B. (1997), *The Drove Roads of Scotland*, Edinburgh: Birlinn.

Hamilton, Judy (2006), *Scottish Murders*, New Lanark: Geddes & Grosset.

Hughes, Robert (1987), *The Fatal Shore*, London: Vintage.

Hunter, James (2000), *The Making of the Crofting Community*, Edinburgh: Birlinn.

Jones, David (1982), *Crime, Protest, Community and Police in Nineteenth Century Britain*, London: Routledge & Kegan Paul.

Knepper, Paul (2007), *Criminology and Social Policy*, London: Sage Publications.

Knight, Alanna (2007), *Burke and Hare*, Kew: The National Archives.

Livingstone, Sheila (2000), *Confess and be Hanged: Scottish Crime and Punishment Through the Ages*, Edinburgh: Birlinn.

MacKenzie, Osgood Hanbury (1995), *A Hundred Years in the Highlands*, Edinburgh: Birlinn.

McLaren, Duncan (1858), *The Rise and Progress of Whisky Drinking in Scotland and the Working of the Public Houses (Scotland) Act*, commonly called the Forbes McKenzie Act, Glasgow; Edinburgh: Scottish Temperance League.

Minto, Charles Sinclair (1970), *Victorian and Edwardian Scotland*, London: Batsford.

Murray, Patrick Joseph (1857), *Not so bad as they seem: The transportation, ticket-of-leave, and penal servitude questions*, Glasgow: Knowsley Pamphlet Collection.

Murray, W. H. (1973), *The Islands of Western Scotland: the Inner and Outer Hebrides*, London: Eyre Methuen.

Rafter, Nicole (2009), *Origins of Criminology: A Reader*, Abingdon: Routledge.

Smith, Gavin D. (2002), *The Secret Still: Scotland's Clandestine Whisky Makers*, Edinburgh: Birlinn.

Smout, T.C. (1969), *A History of the Scottish People 1560–1830*, London: Collins.

Smout, T.C. (1987), *A Century of the Scottish People 1830–1950*, London: Collins.

Tobias, John Jacob (1972), *Nineteenth-Century Crime Prevention and Punishment*, Newton Abbot: David and Charles.

Whitmore, Richard (1978), *Victorian and Edwardian Crime and Punishment*, London: Batsford.

Whittington-Egan, Molly (2001), *The Stockbridge Baby-farmer and other Scottish Murder Stories*, Glasgow: Neil Wilson Publishing.

Wordsworth, Dorothy (1997), *Recollections of a Tour Made in Scotland*, New Haven and London: Yale University Press.

Newspapers and periodicals

Aberdeen Journal
Caledonian Mercury
Dundee Courier and Argus
Dundee, Perth and Cupar Advertiser